Perspectives on Racism and the Human Services Sector

A Case for Change

Edited by Carl E. James

Today's social services agencies are faced with the challenge of responding to the diverse needs and expectations of a growing multicultural population. This volume examines race and racism in Canada from historical and contemporary perspectives and explores the extent to which these factors operate within social services systems related to immigration, settlement, the justice system, health, and education. The contributors, including practitioners, educators, and policy makers, argue for specific changes in current approaches to service delivery and provide practical suggestions for services that make it possible for various communities to be served more effectively. The collection also proposes an anti-racism approach to service provision to produce a system that is beneficial to all Canadians, particularly Aboriginals and racial and ethnic minorities.

CARL E. JAMES is a professor in the Faculty of Education at York University. He is author of several books, including *Seeing Ourselves: Exploring Race, Ethnicity, and Culture*, and co-editor, with A. Shadd, of *Talking About Difference: Encounters in Culture, Language, and Identities*.

Perspectives on Racism and the Human Services Sector:

A Case for Change

edited by
Carl E. James

UNIVERSITY OF TORONTO PRESS
Toronto Buffalo London

© University of Toronto Press Incorporated 1996
Toronto Buffalo London
Printed in Canada

ISBN 0-8020-2954-X (cloth)
ISBN 0-8020-7779-X (paper)

Printed on acid-free paper

Canadian Cataloguing in Publication Data

Main entry under title:

Perspectives on racism and the human services
sector : a case for change

Includes bibliographical references.
ISBN 0-8020-2954-X (bound)   ISBN 0-8020-7779-X (pbk.)

1. Racism – Canada.   2. Human services – Canada.
3. Minorities – Services for – Canada.
I. James, Carl, 1952–   .

HV3176.P47 1995   305.8'00971   C95-932017-2

This book has been published with the help of a grant from the United Way
of Greater Toronto.

University of Toronto Press acknowledges the financial assistance to its
publishing program of the Canada Council and the Ontario Arts Council.

Contents

Foreword

This book fills a gap in college and university curricula for future human services providers. Until now there have been few systematic attempts to address racism in the actual provision of these services. Accepting the challenge for change is not easy, because often the inherent racism of the policies and practices of service agencies are invisible. They generally reflect the perspective of mainstream Canadians and the belief that agencies' accountability is to the bureaucrats of various levels of government. The result is the maintenance of an unsatisfactory status quo.

This book courageously takes up the challenge and generates many valuable insights for the transformation of the status quo. It fulfils multiple tasks admirably. One of these tasks is that of providing analyses of the racism inherent in the immigration system, including settlement services; the justice system and human-rights law; the education of social service students; and the delivery of health and social services. Another task is that of raising awareness of the outdated values and myths that still prevail in the human service sector and that sap the ability of the practitioners responding to the needs of minority groups. Yet another task is that of enhancing a common understanding of what it means for Canada to be a multicultural and multiracial society. This book shares the conceptualization and the vocabulary of anti-racism activists, thereby enhancing a critique of prevailing myths and values that have proved to hinder effective delivery of services. In additional, it contains ample suggestions regarding improving curriculum in professional schools associated with this sector.

It is useful to learn of the distinctions inherent in the languages and assumptions associated with various approaches to service delivery (those discussed include the assimilationist approach, the 'add-on,' multicultural approach, the integrated approach, and the ethnocultural, community-based approach). Understanding what lies behind certain types of remarks and attitudes is valuable for the educator in all settings in which she/he operates, whether it be in the classroom, in workshops, committee meetings, or panel discussions, or in informal encounters. Such insights contribute to that important step towards re-engineering the human service sector to serve the purpose of better identifying and responding to the needs of racial-minority groups who are often defined by the discriminatory practices of the institutions that impact on their lives.

Accounts of Canada's racist past complement language analyses and value critiques in this book. Textbooks in schools and in institutions of higher learning have yet to recognize this past, and this book is rendering a great service by providing the much-needed materials. It is to its credit that rather than dwelling on this dismal record and let it simply weigh on the spirit, this book contains an equal measure of analyses of the best strategies to build a better future. The effect of systemic discrimination on the policies, programs, procedures, and practices of service agencies have yet to be understood and changed. One of the merits of the book lies in its multidisciplinary analyses of how this can be achieved.

The group that has suffered the most from the hegemony of Europeans in North America is, of course, the Aboriginal peoples. An evolving racist framework set the context of this country's infamous treatment of Aboriginal peoples. This historical negative relationship can be traced to the early fur trade through the later practices dominated by paternalistic measures to 'help' Aboriginal peoples to adapt to the ways of European settlers. Attempts to make amends were sometimes driven by guilt, and were always influenced by the misguided idea that it was best for Aboriginal peoples to be like Europeans. As Canadians, we should all find opportunities to learn from the Aboriginal peoples, from their collective resilience, their capacity for survival, and their ability to hold onto a sense of who they are. We have much to learn from their success in keeping their issues on the nation's agenda for change. The Oka crisis was a dramatic defining moment in the history of Canada.

In this country there have been other defining moments in the patterns of racism for other groups. This point is vividly illustrated in this book by accounts of the enslavement of and systemic discrimination against African Canadians, the immigration and citizenship policies and measures enacted against Chinese Canadians, the measures excluding Jews fleeing from Nazism, the opposition to East Indians attempting to immigrate, and the internment of Japanese Canadians during the Second World War.

Recounting the historical past, though painful, is necessary in order for us to recognize the unequal distribution of resources and the unequal access to decision making concerning these resources. Unless the origin and the perpetuating mechanisms of the existing power structure are understood, it is impossible to approach the difficult task of generating new power relationships.

If change is to occur, we should take cultural differences seriously. We should adopt the view that these differences are not so much the problems of minority groups as the problems of human services providers, who should be expected to provide solutions. Demographics and fiscal reality have generated a 'market-driven social service environment.' In such an environment, when both public and private funders demand that services be relevant, service agencies have no option but to take into consideration the cultural differences of the recipients of their services as well as the historical and present injustices they endure. Steps to generate excellence in service provision are discussed in this book. They include placing the need of the service recipients first; demanding that boards and staff reflect the racial diversity of the population served; and adopting the principle that service users should play a prominent role in shaping the services they receive.

Mere recognition of the factors perpetuating racism in service provision is not enough. Strategic decisions are needed. Should differences be assimilated into the mainstream? Should dealing with racial minorities merely require measures 'added on' to existing approaches? Or should an ethnocultural, community-based model be adopted? And in this day of proliferating rhetoric, how does one tell which organization really 'has its act together' and is making genuine attempts to provide access to mainstream services by removing barriers based on language, race, culture, gender, and class? A careful reading of this book provides insights to these important and inescapable questions. Now that there is a growing recognition of the need to get rid of racist institutional practices, service providers need to know how to act on these realizations.

The many papers in this book provide an extensive coverage of major issues on anti-racism work relating to the human-services delivery system in Canada. They are good starting points for students preparing for careers in social work, health care, law, human rights, and public administration. This book will provide an excellent text in these disciplines.

GLENDA SIMMS

Acknowledgments

Anti-racism work is difficult and challenging for practitioners, particularly as we engage in actions to bring about organizational change to ensure unrestricted access to services and equitable participation within institutions. Change is necessary to eliminate the structural barriers to equity, but attempts to bring about the needed changes are often met with resistance. Addressing this resistance requires leadership, dedication, solidarity, collaboration, and goodwill on the part of managers, service providers, and members of our communities.

All the contributors to this volume have demonstrated this leadership and commitment to engage in processes that will lead to organizational change through social, political, and organizational action. I feel privileged to have collaborated with them on this valuable project. I thank all of them for their cooperation in, and commitment to, making this book a reality. I wish to acknowledge the particular contribution of Arnold Minors, an anti-racism practitioner who is dedicated to ensuring that anti-racism pedagogy is understood and practised. For this reason he worked to keep this project going. In doing so, Arnold provided a model for what it means to engage in anti-racism work. He encouraged us to be bold in our thinking and confident in our commitment to equity and justice. I am sincerely grateful to Arnold – a friend and colleague – for encouraging me to undertake this editing task.

While I take responsibility for the book as it is now conceptualized and presented, it is important to mention the efforts of the staff and volunteers of the United Way of Greater Toronto, who developed the project as a follow-up to their 1991 publication: *Action, Access, Diversity! A Guide to Anti-racist/Multicultural Organizational Change for Social Service Agencies*. In particular, I wish to acknowledge the efforts of Jennifer Walcott, who recognized the need for this kind of resource for service providers and initiated this project. We thank her. Special thanks are due also to Paula Neves, who coordinated the initial stages of this project. She gave generously of her time and energy by recruiting contributors and providing critical and insightful advice on the early drafts of the manuscript. I wish to acknowledge as well the financial contribution of the United Way of Greater Toronto, the efforts of Susan Pigott in the publication process, and the comments offered by the members of the project's first Editorial Board, who reviewed and commented on early drafts of the manuscript.

I am grateful to Elma Thomas and Mary Clabassi for their computer, typing, and general assistance. Their patience and support were important to the completion of the work. My appreciation also goes to Maxine McKenzie for her editorial comments and assistance. Thanks to the people at the University of Toronto Press for their support and counsel, particularly to Press editor Virgil Duff and copy-editor John St James. The critical comments and suggestions provided by the Press's reviewers and by members of the editorial committee were valuable for strengthening the manuscript.

Finally, I must express special appreciation to Kai for his constant support.

Contributors

Carl E. James teaches in the Faculty of Education at York University. He works in the areas of anti-racism education, culture, youth, and urban education. His experience as a youth and community-development worker and educator has put him in touch with youth locally, nationally, and internationally. James holds a Ph.D. in sociology and is the author of several books and articles, including *Seeing Ourselves: Exploring Race, Ethnicity and Culture* (1995); *Making It: Black Youth, Racism and Career Aspiration in a Big City* (1993); *Talking About Difference: Encounters in Culture, Language and Identity* (1994, co-editor); and *Educating for a Change* (1991, co-author).

Valerie Bedassigae-Pheasant is a member of the Whitefish River First Nation, Manitoulin Island. Her mother is from Wikwemikong and her father's people are from Wisconsin. Their lineage is Potawatomi/Odawa. Bedassigae-Pheasant specializes in Native education, and has worked in the local (First Nation), provincial, and federal school systems. Currently working on her Ph.D., she also conducts anti-racism workshops and seminars in the community.

Mark L. Berlin holds a B.A. (University of Toronto), L.L.B. (University of Ottawa), and M.Phil. (Cambridge University). He has been Senior Policy Advisor for Human Rights and Acting Director of Race Relations for the former Department of the Secretary of State. He has taught at Algonquin College and Carleton University and in the Faculty of Law at the University of Ottawa. He also teaches courses for the bar admissions program of the Law Society of Upper Canada. Berlin is currently

Senior Counsel, Criminal Law Policy, in the Department of Justice, Ottawa.

Dawit Beyene, Carrie Butcher, Betty Joe, and Ted Richmond at the time of writing all worked at the Ontario Council of Agencies Serving Immigrants (OCASI), the provincial association of more than 130 community-based immigrant service organizations serving about half a million immigrants and refugees across Ontario.

Cleta Brown, B.A., L.L.B., L.L.M., a crown counsel in the province of British Columbia is a graduate of Dalhousie University, the University of Victoria, and the London School of Economics. She is the former general counsel to the Ombudsman's office of British Columbia. Brown is an active volunteer with the legal office of the British Columbia branch of Harambee Centres, Canada, and sits on the board of the Canadian Women's Foundation.

Hon. Rosemary Brown, P.C., L.L.D.(hons), M.S.W., B.A., the Chief Commissioner of the Ontario Human Rights Commission, was the first black woman to be elected to public office in Canada. A graduate of McGill University and the University of British Columbia, she was a social worker and counsellor before to seeking political office. Brown is a member of the Privy Council and the Security Intelligence Review Committee, and sits on the boards of Queen's University and MATCH International Centre. She is the author of *Being Brown: A Very Public Life*, her autobiography, and a speaker on human rights, anti-racism, and feminist issues.

Carol Pigler Christensen, M.S.W., D.Ed., is a professor and former director of the University of British Columbia School of Social Work. Before joining the faculty at UBC, Christensen initiated Cross-Cultural Studies as an area of study in the Faculty of Education and the School of Social Work at McGill University. She was a lecturer in Copenhagen, Denmark, where she developed and taught courses in family therapy. Her long-standing interests and major professional activities are in the areas of cross-cultural and anti-racism education, model building, and research. She has published extensively, and conducts workshops and seminars locally, nationally, and internationally in these areas. Christensen is program director of the Multicultural Family Centre, designed to train students to work more effectively with immigrant and refugee populations.

Sabra Desai, M.S.W., is a certified social worker (C.S.W.), and a human-rights, anti-racist, feminist educator and consultant, working in the field of equity, organizational change, and community activism. Desai is currently completing a Ph.D. in community psychology and teaches in the School of Social and Community Services as well as the Business and Industry Services Centre at Humber College of Applied Arts and Technology, Toronto.

Adrian Johnson is the Principal of ASSOCIUM. He is a consultant who assists organizations to address issues of effectiveness and to deal with organizational stress resulting from change, particularly in a context of social justice. His client list includes organizations from the public, private, and volunteer sectors. Johnson is an active member of the Urban Alliance on the Race Relations. He is the past chair of the Alliance for Employment Equity: served on the steering committee of the National Employment Equity Network; has been a member of the Volunteer and Community Development Committee of the United Way of Greater Toronto; and chaired its Anti-Racism Organizational Development Sub-Committee.

Akwatu Khenti holds B.A. and M.A. degrees from the University of Toronto. A political scientist specializing in development studies, he has worked as a community-development worker for the Jamaican Canadian Association, and as executive director and consultant to a number of Caribbean and African associations. Khenti has worked with the North York Board of Education, where he wrote units on African Canadian history for use in middle schools. He is a founding member of the African Relief Committee (AFRIC), an NGO that supports elementary schools in Africa, and currently works as human-rights coordinator with the Inter-Church Coalition on Africa. Khenti's work has taken him throughout Canada and many parts of East Africa. He also lectures on Black history and culture.

David Matas, M.A., B.A.(Juris), B.C.L., is a lawyer in private practice specializing in refugee, immigration, and human-rights law. He has lectured in constitutional law at McGill University and, more recently, in international law, civil liberties, and immigration and refugee law at the University of Manitoba. Matas has worked/volunteered with a number of task forces and organizations, including the Task Force on Immigration Practices and Procedures (1980–1), the League for Human Rights, Bnai B'rith Canada, the Canadian Council for Refugees, and Canada–South Africa

Cooperation. He is the author of *Canadian Immigration Law* (1986) and *The Sanctuary Trial* (1989), and co-author of *Closing the Doors: The Failure of Refugee Protection* (1989).

Arnold Minors is coordinating associate of Arnold Minors and Associates (AM&A), a firm that provides organizational-effectiveness consulting services to public and not-for-profit sector organizations. Its work is based on the belief that equity is a key contibutor to the effectiveness of organizations. Minors has been a member of the boards of Oolagen (a children's mental-health centre); Chinese Information and Community Services; Ontario Association for Family Mediation; and the Board of Health for the City of Toronto. He is a member of the Metropolitan Toronto Police Services Board. He holds a B.Sc. in chemistry and mathematics from McGill University and an M.B.A. in organization development and labour law from Queen's University.

Karen R. Mock, Ph.D., is the national director of the League for Human Rights of B'nai Brith Canada, a national agency dedicated to combating racism and bigotry. A registered psychologist, she specializes in human development, interpersonal communication, multiculturalism, and race relations, and lectures, conducts research, seminars, and workshops, as well as publishing in these areas. Before joining the League, Mock worked as a consultant and, for twenty years, in teacher education at the University of Toronto, Ryerson Polytechnical University, and York University. Currently, she oversees research on hate groups and anti-Semitism in Canada, intercultural and interfaith dialogue, and related issues in education and the criminal-justice system. Mock is the past president of the Ontario Multicultural Association, a former member of the board of the Urban Alliance on Race Relations, and past chair of the Canadian Multiculturalism Advisory Committee.

Corinne Mount Pleasant-Jetté is a member of the Tuscarora First Nation. She is currently an assistant professor in the Faculty of Engineering and Computer Science at Concordia University in Montréal, and also holds the position of Advisor to the Dean – Communications and Equity Affairs. With over twenty years' experience in the field of education, Jetté has also been active as a consultant and writer on issues related to human rights and Aboriginal affairs. She is the past president of Montréal's Centre for Research Action on Race Relations, has chaired the External Advisory Committee on Employment Equity to the President of the Treasury

Board of Canada, and has contributed discussion papers to the Royal Commission on Aboriginal Peoples. In recognition of her work in the field of public education on human-rights issues, Jetté was named a member of the Order of Canada in January 1993.

Charles Novogrodsky is an education and organization-development consultant in ethno-racial and gender equity and human rights. He has worked in the equity field for almost twenty years, developing educational programs for school, community, and organizational use. Novogrodsky has delivered numerous equity courses and workshops for managers, supervisors, workers, volunteers, and trainers, and is the author of several articles, books, and training manuals, including (as co-author) *Combatting Racism in the Workplace: A Course for Workers*. He has designed training programs for police and has been a feature speaker at conferences, including the Employment Equity Congress of the Institute for International Research. Mr Novogrodsky is principal, Charles Novogrodsky and Associates.

Joanne St. Lewis is a law professor and former director of the Education Equity Program in the Faculty of Law, Common Law Section, at the University of Ottawa. A bilingual lawyer, St. Lewis has extensive experience in the area of human rights. She has held positions with the Ontario Human Rights Commission and the Ontario Race Relations Directorate. She is also former executive director of the Women's Legal Education and Action Fund (LEAF). From 1985–7 she was Special Assistant on Government Affairs to the Grand Chief of the Crees of Quebec and was involved in the negotiations of the 1986 La Grande Agreement.

Glenda P. Simms was appointed president of the Canadian Advisory Council on the Status of Women (CACSW) in December 1989. Dr Simms is an educator, orator, and social change agent. She has had a long-standing involvement with women, racial minorities, Aboriginal peoples, public housing, and community issues. A founding member of the National Organization of Immigrant and Visible Minority Women of Canada, she served as president of the Congress of Black Women of Canada. During the course of her career, Dr Simms has advised federal and provincial governments on employment equity, development education, Native education, and women's issues.

Cynthia Stephenson holds an M.A. in French language and literature from the University of Toronto. She has over four years' experience with employment equity within the public sector, and is currently manager of Employment Equity Consulting Service, Ontario Region, Human Resources Development Canada. Stephenson has worked as director of Equity Advisory Services, Employment Equity Branch, at the national headquarters.

Kass Sunderji has been working in the area of anti-racism, human rights, and employment equity for the past ten years. He has held positions of manager and senior program officer with the Federal Department of Canadian Heritage. As an equity consultant, Sunderji was part of the team that developed the Policing in a Multicultural Society (RIMS) course.

Carol Tator has spent twenty years working in the fields of multiculturalism, anti-racism, organizational development, and employment equity. As both the president and acting executive director of the Urban Alliance and Race Relations for several years, she worked directly with racial-minority organizations, communities, and individuals. As a private consultant, Tator has assisted government agencies in conducting organizational and employment-systems reviews and worked with numerous educational and human service organizations in developing and implementing policies, programs, and practices designed to improve racial and ethnocultural access and participation in their organizations. She is the co-author of *The Colour of Democracy: Racism in Canadian Society* (1994) and teaches in the Department of Anthropology at York University.

PERSPECTIVES ON RACISM AND THE HUMAN
SERVICES SECTOR: A CASE FOR CHANGE

Introduction:

Proposing an Anti-Racism
Framework for Change

In an economically, ethnically, and racially stratified society like ours, individuals' inability to gain access to, and receive, services that address their particular needs and expectations is not merely a result of their failure to take advantage of available services. Rather, it is in part a consequence of the structural barriers that are inherent in society. Within this context, human service agencies are expected to provide services that are responsive and sensitive to the diverse needs and expectations of their clients/participants. For today's human service practitioners this is a formidable challenge.

So, how are agencies addressing these challenges? What structures must be in place in order to respond effectively to the diverse needs and expectations of a changing population, and of racial minorities in particular? What leadership are agencies providing to ensure equitable access to service, job, and volunteer opportunities?

With the understanding that human service practitioners are at the forefront of providing leadership, addressing inequalities, and confronting change, this collection of readings provides a theoretical context, support, and direction to practitioners in order to assist in the construction of a shared understanding of the issues and expectations that will enable all involved to serve our changing communities effectively. In this context, when we think of change, we think of the significant increase in the racial-minority population. It is estimated that by the year 2001, the racial-minority population of Canada will be about 18 per cent, while in some urban centres like Toronto, Vancouver, Montreal, and Calgary this segment of the population will range from 20 to 40 per cent (Samuel 1992).[1] With this increase, issues around race and racism must be taken into account as human service agencies seek to address the structural barriers and tensions that these two factors pose for racial and ethnic minorities. In exploring the issues here, we are guided by four objectives:

- to provide a framework for the analysis of race and racism;
- to examine the historical and contemporary contexts of racism in Canada;
- to examine systemic racism in human service delivery; and
- to provide models to guide and support organizational change.

These objectives are premised on the notion that those involved in human service delivery must respect differences, provide equitable services, and advocate for social justice and human rights. Hence, we must understand how the structure operates to advantage some citizens and disadvantage others. Race and racism are part of this structure and help to determine the nature of individuals' participation in agencies, as well as their access to services and the type of services that are provided.

FROM A MULTICULTURAL TO AN ANTI-RACISM APPROACH TO SERVICES

While many agencies have attempted to respond to the multicultural reality of our population by using a multicultural approach to the provision of services, there is growing evidence, as discussed by many of the contributors in this collection, that the multicultural approach is limited in that it fails to address directly structural barriers, and racism in particular. We propose an anti-racism approach. In the following, we lay out some of the basic premises, practices, and implications of these two approaches.

Multiculturalism

Premises
- Society is democratic and egalitarian; therefore, citizens have freedom of choice – freedom to access and participate in whatever service they wish.
- Prejudice, ethnocentrism, anti-Semitism, and racism are a result of ignorance – a lack of contact and awareness of people of 'other cultures.'

- Culture is a set of information and observable practices (e.g., dress/'costume,' art, dance, religious practices) that can easily be communicated. Culture and cultural groups are static and monolithic.
- Absence of direct contact with groups suggests an absence of preconceived notions about the group; thus, no prejudice is held about the group. The idea is: 'I don't know enough about those people to have any biases about them.'

Practices
- Providing everyone with the 'same treatment' is seen to be proving equal treatment, irrespective of race, ethnicity, gender, class, sexual orientation or dis/ability.
- Majority-group norms and behaviour, both personally and professionally, are seen as 'neutral' and 'value-free.'
- There is a reliance on making contact – i.e., participating in 'cultural celebrations' and activities – with different racial and ethnic groups as a way of heightening awareness and thus eliminating biases and prejudices.
- There is a focus on 'tolerating' rather than 'valuing' or 'accepting' differences.

Implications
- There is a failure to recognize social stratification and the resulting differential starting points for members of society based on ethnicity, race, gender, class, dis/ability, and sexual orientation.
- There is a failure to recognize the relationship between choice and access and the role of social structure in creating and denying access and choice.
- Identifying minority groups primarily in terms of ethnic or racial culture negates the subcultural variations within the groups and the complex set of values, interactions, and norms that are inherent in all cultural groups.
- With the assumption that professionals are objective or neutral, individuals, particularly dominant-ethnic-group and middle-class members of society, tend to ignore the extent to which their 'cultural lenses' inform interpretations and conclusions about other group members.
- Insofar as the culture of the dominant group is seen as the 'norm,' then awareness and sensitivity cannot be built without first recognizing the hegemony of the values, traditions, symbols, and governance of that group and its relationship to minority groups.

- There is a tacit acceptance of the idea that individuals' failure to 'make it' in society is due to their inability to successfully become bicultural (inability to adapt) and/or to the choices they make.

Anti-Racism

Premises

- Society is stratified; there is unequal distribution of power and by resources. Access to power and opportunities are influenced by race, ethnicity, class, gender, sexual orientation, dis/ability and other corresponding factors.
- While race is acknowledged as a social construct, it is regarded as central to any analysis. The emphasis is on the dominant and minority-group relations in terms of power differences.
- Racism is seen as an ideology that is rooted in the socio-economic and political histories of colonialism and oppression. It is woven into the fabric of society.
- Culture is not static, it is dynamic; and its expression is related to the distribution of power based on race, ethnicity, class, gender, sexual orientation, abilities, and so on.
- Cultural differences between dominant ethno-racial groups are not the issue or problem. Rather, the ideology that forms and sustains racism is the problem.
- The experiences of oppressed groups are critical to the analysis of how inequality and racism produce differential social situations.
- There is a recognition that the actions of the dominant group towards minority groups shape daily life as well as the perceptions of their positions and their potential in society.
- Society's institutions must reflect the diverse needs and aspirations of racial and ethnic minority groups in their missions, policies, practices, and services.
- Institutions and individuals are not neutral. There is a set of norms and values by which they operate.
- Individual empowerment through social action is the key to change.

Practices

- There are ongoing analyses of individuals' experiences in relation to power and of the degree of representation of groups within all the institutions in society.
- Power relations are challenged; and there is advocacy around equal

access to power and participation in the society, as well as the recognition of voice.

- Analyses of social systems is ongoing. There is a recognition that cultures and subcultures within social systems will change and evolve in response to the challenges to existing systems.
- Human services practitioners and institutions recognize the norms and values by which they operate, and they assess the extent to which these norms and values influence the relationships between agency, staff, and community.
- Community-action programs are designed to challenge internalized stereotyped images and construct more viable images.
- Groups that have been disadvantaged/oppressed are particularly identified for support with programs dealing with employment equity, access, affirmative action, and so on.
- There is a focus on individual and group needs and aspirations, which are in turn analysed and addressed primarily in relation to their experiences with the dominant ethnic group.

Implications
- This approach makes conscious deep-rooted ideologies, attitudes, and stereotyped images about 'other,' that is, racial and ethnic-minority, groups.
- Cultural practices are not pathologized, but are explored in order to provide a context for understanding the needs and behaviours of individuals.
- Through collective action, minority-group members will be able to challenge the status quo, influence change, and receive the benefits that are due to them.
- It is recognized that receiving information about minority groups does not result necessarily in increased tolerance or acceptance. In fact, it can result in intolerance and decreased acceptance, particularly when groups are presented as exotic with 'foreign' culture. Hence, with the understanding that individuals' location in relation to class, race, sexuality, and so on does affect how information is received and interpreted, critical self-reflection and interrogation are necessary in order to understand, and make the most productive use of, information.
- There is the belief that institutions or organizations should change, can change, even wish to change, and sooner or later will be ready for change.

The difference between the multicultural and anti-racism approaches to the provision of services can be found in the acknowledgment of and emphases on power as a factor that influences the life chances and social and economic situation of racial-minority citizens. Both approaches seek to address the cultural differences to be found among the people who work within, and seek the services of, human service organizations. But while the multicultural approach focuses primarily on cultural differences, in some cases constructing difference as 'foreign' – that which is brought from another country and is 'tolerated' – the anti-racism approach recognizes that racial-minority groups' cultures are constructed within our stratified society. Hence, the culture of minority groups results from their position in society relative to the dominant ethno-racial group. The lived experiences of minority-group members are understood within the context of the dominant culture.

Anti-racism sees institutions and individuals as dynamic; there is constant change, thus analysis must be ongoing. Services must provide clients and participants with the tools to engage in critical analyses so that they understand their situation. From such analyses will come social action which will bring about the necessary economic, social, cultural, and political changes that will benefit all concerned. In essence, the anti-racism perspective provides a framework for the critical examination of issues of racism, sexism, classism, anti-Semitism, and heterosexism that are inherent in our society and seeks to bring about social change through collective analysis and action.

ORGANIZATION OF THIS COLLECTION

The chapters are organized around four themes. In Part One, 'Perspectives on Race and Canadian Society,' James provides a perspective in which to conceptualize the issues of race, culture, and identity. He states that by paying attention to the definitions and meanings of terms we use we acquire a conceptual framework for analysing and understanding our own behaviours and locations, and those of others. James provides definitions of the terms and argues that, in order to provide effective services to racial minority clients/participants, human service providers must pay attention to the ways in which the dominant culture in Canada structures the experiences of everyone. James's discussion is followed by a comment by Jetté on the experiences of Aboriginal peoples.

Jetté's comments provide a context for us to understand the historical roots of Canada and how our respective locations and social positions in the society are an outgrowth of our historical relations with Aboriginal peoples. Jetté points out that exclusion and silence have been a fact of life for Aboriginal peoples since the arrival of 'that misguided Italian who thought he had discovered India.' Since these first encounters Europeans have attempted to acculturate and assimilate Aboriginal peoples. Further, according to Jetté: 'While some might opt for the more charitable explanation that no malice was intended, there is little doubt that such imposition of foreign ideals and values has been nothing short of catastrophic for the remaining survivors.'

Part Two, 'Racism in Canada,' presents articles that dispel the myth that racism does not exist in Canada. The authors all demonstrate that racism is an inherent aspect of Canada's development throughout the years, both in historical and contemporary times. Brown and Brown in their commentary reflect on the inescapable truth that racism is not something that occurs only in the United States; it is part of our reality. Khenti puts racism in Canada into a global and historical context, and Bedassigae-Pheasant, with particular reference to education, discusses how the European colonizers oppressed Aboriginal people. Matas discusses how racism and discrimination have been part of our immigration policies, and St. Lewis examines how racism operates generally within the judicial system.

In his article 'The Relationship between Racism and Antisemitism' (1992), Michael Banton noted that 'both racism and antisemitism relate to hateful experiences,' which were responsible for the 'uncontestable discrimination' against Jews that prevented them from immigrating to Canada during the mid-1900s (see also Matas). Anti-Semitism, like racism, was part of the mechanism that the Canadian government used to control the flow of immigrants and influence intergroup relationships. Therefore, as Mock discusses, insofar as anti-racism attempts to address the inequalities in our society related to the social construction of individuals on the basis of race and/or ethnicity, then it is appropriate that we examine the connections between racism and Semitism in this collection. The section concludes with comments from Sunderji in which he reflects on the issue of voice. He argues that racial minorities have no voice in determining the literary or artistic expression of Canadian culture. As a result, they remain marginal – unable to participate equally in the cultural and social institutions that shape their lives.

Part Three reports on 'Racism and the Human Service Sector.' Assuming that human service agencies and practitioners serve some of society's most vulnerable members, Brown and Brown comment that there must be changes in programs and practices if the clients/participants are to receive adequate services. Christensen concurs and goes on to discuss the need for appropriate education of social service workers. This is a significant discussion, since as major socializing agents educational institutions are charged with the responsibility of preparing citizens to live and work within our culturally diverse communities. Therefore, if prospective human service workers do not gain an understanding of the anti-racism paradigm so that they develop the knowledge and skills necessary to work effectively with racial and ethnic minorities, then the changes that are needed to address the issues of inadequate and insensitive services to minorities will not materialize. As Christensen argues, this particular training needs to take place in the social-work educational process, since practitioners do not get it in any other areas of the education system. Tator, in the chapter that follows, also emphasizes the need for training and provides models that practitioners might use in service delivery. The staff of the Ontario Council of Agencies Serving Immigrants (OCASI) provide insights into their roles and the issues with which they have to contend as they work with new members of our society. They argue strongly that, to address the needs of newer citizens, an anti-racism approach is the most relevant and appropriate.

As has already been pointed out, the anti-racism framework indicates that providing services to individuals must assist them to get a critical understanding of their situation in order to engage in action that will bring about change. Part Four, 'Implementing Change,' therefore provides frameworks and models to guide and support the implementation of organizational change. Sunderji introduces the section by commenting on the fact that equitable access to social services is a right and not a privilege. Novogrodsky, in 'The Anti-Racist Cast of Mind,' discusses the challenges to anti-racism work, important ingredients of effective advocacy, and the mind-set that is required for doing this work. Minors, in the chapter 'From Uni-versity to Poly-versity: Organizations in Transition to Anti-Racism,' outlines a six-stage model to help organizations assess the extent to which they are culturally sensitive and inclusive in their provision of services. In 'Towards an Equitable, Efficient, and Effective Human Service System,' Johnson discusses the roles of the various constituencies in the organizational change process. He outlines the current dilemmas and the radical shifts in thinking that must occur if we are to meet the daunting social, cultural, economic, and political challenges ahead.

In implementing change it is necessary to be familiar with policies that might facilitate the process. For this reason, the articles by Berlin and Stephenson provide brief but practical overviews of human-rights and employment-equity legislation respectively. Jetté concludes the section by reminding us of the need for change. She leave us with a challenge that Aboriginal peoples, who have been silent over the years, will not remain silent much longer – 'their voices of protest will grow stronger in days to come.' Could this be the same for other racial minorities?

In her Afterword, 'Common Issues, Common Understandings,' Desai reinforces the themes of the contributors: that there is a need for social service agencies – administrators and practitioners alike – to do things differently in order to have a more effective and equitable social service system that will ensure a more healthy society. She emphasizes the need for understanding and recognition of the interconnections between the individual, ideological, institutional, and political climates. Desai points out that in undertaking change, organizations must have a vision that must be systematic and comprehensive.

This collection is by no means a complete treatment of all the issues, strategies, and constraints affecting the implementation of anti-racism changes in the human service sector. Neither can we say that all of the contributors wrote convincingly from an anti-racism perspective. If we consider that multiculturalism and anti-racism are situated on a continuum, with individuals at different points on that continuum, then we can accept the variations among the collection. Nevertheless, it is fair to suggest that, given their respective locations, each contributor has brought some knowledge and understanding of the issues that are useful to service providers as we negotiate and implement changes within our agencies in order to better serve our communities.

We are very aware that individuals differ both in their analyses and interpretations of the issues, and consequently in how they write about the issues. We do not all share the same location and experiences, and sometimes, even when we do, we interpret things differently. This is evident in the languages of the contributors. The reader will notice inconsistencies in the use of terms such as 'racial minorities,' 'visible minorities,' 'people of colour,' and 'racialized communities.' We did not attempt to make the terminologies uniform, for we believe that they reflect both the writers' particular political perspectives and the particular meanings they wish to convey about the factors or issues they are discussing. Furthermore, the use of terms is always problematic, and usually difficult to streamline. This tension in the use of language is also evident in our attempts to write in ways that are accessible to everyone.

For this reason, we present writings that represent different genres. Specifically, the collection includes not only academic writing, but also commentaries by racial-minority Canadians who speak the language of experience.

Finally, it is impossible for us to expect that we can address in one book the complexity of the issues that need to be addressed. Consequently, what this collection can best offer is a framework and some insights that will further the debate and point towards some possible actions that might address agencies' and workers' needs. We have presented the anti-racism framework as one that will enhance our efforts to make services more effective. None the less, given the nature of anti-racism work, it is inevitable that there will be differences among readers, community representatives, human service practitioners, educators, trainers, community workers, police officers, politicians, and others. There will be differences in what is understood about anti-racism work, how it is understood, the stages at which people are located, and what needs to be explored. We might agree about what has taken place and must take place, but disagree on how much change or what kind of changes must be implemented. The field of anti-racism is a dynamic one; we cannot avoid the debate that will take place. However, what we can hope is that the debate will lead to changes that satisfy the needs and expectations of *all* Canadians, particularly racial and ethnic minorities.

NOTE

1 Specifically, Samuel estimates that the racial-minority population will in Toronto increase from 35.1% in 1996 to 44.6% in 2001; in Vancouver, from 30.8% in 1996 to 39.3% in 2001; in Edmonton and Calgary, from 20% each in 1996 to 25% in 2001; and in Montreal, from 15% in 1996 to 19.9% in 2001.

PART ONE

Perspectives on Racism and Canadian Society

Chapter 1

Race, Culture, and Identity[*]

Carl E. James

Since the 1960s, considerable attention has been paid to the Canadian cultural mosaic so that there can be greater intercultural understanding. Despite this attention, we still find ourselves grappling with the multicultural nature of our society and with issues of awareness, sensitivity, appreciation, and acceptance.

As we attempt to understand the multicultural and multiracial nature of our society, we find that there is much ambiguity and confusion about the terms culture, ethnicity, race, multiculturalism, prejudice, ethnocentrism, and racism, to name a few. Yet these terms provide frameworks for the way we view ourselves and interact with others. If we are to become effective human service workers or public servants – teachers, counsellors, police officers, political representatives – it is imperative that we understand what the terms mean. For this reason, in this chapter, we provide definitions for the terms. By paying attention to the definition and meaning of the terms we use, we acquire a conceptual framework for thinking, using, and discussing them. As Jackson and Meadows point out: 'Individuals' definitions or conceptual frameworks ... may either hinder or facilitate an understanding of the behaviours and experiences that occur in their lives and the lives of others. Often a change in the conceptual framework can open a whole new realm of understanding of these behaviours and experiences' (1991: 72).

This chapter examines the traditional way in which we have conceptualized the issues and discusses a viewpoint and approach that, is often

---

[*] This article is adapted from *Seeing Ourselves: Exploring Race, Ethnicity, and Culture* (Toronto: Thompson Educational Publishing 1995).

overlooked. Central to this viewpoint is that as Canadians, we have a core set of values and expectations that we all adhere to. It is this adherence to a set of cultural practices within a society or nation that provides individuals with 'a commonality' – that is, adherence to a dominant culture. This dominant culture influences their lives, structures their values, engineers their views of the world, and patterns their responses to experiences. It also determines the structure and nature of the subcultures (for instance, those based on ethnicity and race) that exist within the society. In other words, as Beverly Jones stated it: 'Every society has a dominant culture. Institutions are formed around the assumptions of this dominant culture. But because the dominant culture doesn't have to look outside itself, it remains largely unconscious of its own assumptions and characteristics. The subordinate culture, by contrast, must interact with the dominant culture to survive. By necessity, the sub-culture becomes bicultural, while the dominant culture is observed but not observant' (see Poplin 1992: A23).

This chapter begins by discussing the culture that is identified as 'Canadian' and proceeds to examine how, in a stratified, multi-ethnic, multiracial society such as Canada, the dominant or majority ethnic group determines the major elements of that culture. In the sections that follow, I discuss how ethnic and racial subcultures are developed and expressed in Canada and examine the mechanisms such as ethnocentrism, prejudice, racism, stereotyping, and discrimination that help to produce and maintain the culture and subculture. Building on the theme of commonality – that there is a dominant culture to which all Canadians adhere – I discuss the inevitable acculturation process of immigrant, ethnic, and racial minority-group members and how it affects individuals and communities and the development of individual cultural identity. The chapter concludes by suggesting that human service workers should acknowledge that there is a dominant culture that directly influences, and consequently will help to explain, along with subcultures, the behaviour patterns and issues of racial and ethnic minorities.

CULTURE AND CANADIAN SOCIETY

We are all familiar with the statement, 'We are multicultural; there isn't a Canadian culture.' This inability to acknowledge that we all share, contribute to, and participate in 'a Canadian culture' reflects the general lack of cultural self-awareness on the part of some Canadians – a deficiency that often leads to insensitivity to, and intolerance of, those who are 'different.' Although we have difficulty acknowledging and defining a Canadian culture, we talk frequently of a Canadian society. Sociologist Michael Carroll defines society as 'any fairly large group of people who (1) share a common culture, (2) think of themselves as having inherited a common set of historical traditions, (3) engage in a relatively large amount of mutual interaction, and (4) see themselves as being associated with a particular geographic area' (1990: 23).

If we acknowledge that we live in the society of Canada, then we must also acknowledge the implicit and explicit set of practices and values to which everyone within the geographic boundary of Canada adheres – a culture. What then is culture?

Simply defined, culture is the sum total of ways of living. It is a dynamic and complex set of values, beliefs, norms, patterns of thinking, styles of communication, linguistic expressions, and ways of seeing and interacting with the world shared by a group of people in a particular physical and human environment (Hoopes and Pusch 1981: 3). According to Adler, 'no one is culture free' and 'though all human beings are born, reproduce, and die, it is culture which dictates the meaning of sexuality, the ceremonies of birth, the transitions of life, and the rituals of death' (1977: 27).

Within all cultures exist subcultures. A *subculture* may be defined as 'a group of people within a larger sociopolitical structure who share cultural (and often linguistic or dialectical) characteristics which are distinctive enough to distinguish it from others within the same culture' (Hoopes and Pusch 1981: 3). In this chapter the subcultures to which we will refer are those of ethnic and racial minority groups. These subcultures are also dynamic and represent a combination of the cultures of origin as well as those values, customs, and patterns of thinking these groups have cultivated as a result of their position in the dominant society. These subcultures are a reflection of the groups' minority status and an expression of their acceptance and accommodation in a given society.

Members of minority subcultures are likely to be bicultural or multicultural, combining elements of the dominant culture and of the subcultures to which they belong in order to ensure survival and participation in the dominant society. In this way, individuals not only carry culture, but also create culture. So there is a dynamic reciprocal relationship between the dominant culture, subcultures, and the *culture* of the individual. Therefore, it is inevitable that Canadian culture, like cultures everywhere, will always be changing, since individuals change as they acquire new information through interactions with new technologies, and with people and media from other countries. Therefore, cultures are not static, they are always in a state of transformation; in other words, *culture is dynamic*.

It is inappropriate to conclude that, because Canada is made up of several ethnic cultural groups, there is no central set of cultural codes to which all Canadians, regardless of race and ethnicity, adhere. The following sections will attempt to discuss the question of culture.

THE EVOLUTION OF A CULTURE IN CANADA

Canada is inhabited by peoples of different ethnicities, languages, religions, and races. Yet often, when we identify 'who is Canadian' or talk of 'mainstream Canadians,' we think mainly of the English, and to a lesser extent French people, despite the fact that Aboriginal peoples populated this region long before the French and English arrived. Part of the reason for this tendency relates to the fact that the English and French established institutions such as governments, courts, schools, and religions on European models, while at the same time erasing institutions that had been long established by the First Nations. Institutions are crucial in maintaining a culture. They are carriers of culture. And insofar as the French and (primarily) English established institutions that represented their concept of a functioning, democratic society, they were in effect ensuring the survival of their cultures.

While Canadian institutions were modelled on those of Europe, they still evolved quite differently from those of the colonial powers. This could not have been otherwise; the distances were too great, the circumstances too different. Canadian institutions also evolved differently from those of the United States and Mexico. While Canada shares the North American continent with both nations, we experienced and processed the major events and developments of the last two hundred years differently.

The institutionalization of two official languages gave further legitimacy to the English, and to a lesser extent the French, dominance. The resulting duality of institutions, and the frame of mind it has fostered, has influenced the way in which all cultural groups are treated. This duality also has created some space for the preservation of certain cultural practices that is not found in the United States. (This is not to say that immigrant groups are more successful at maintaining cultural integrity in Canada than in the United States.)

The policy of multiculturalism within a bilingual framework, introduced in 1971, recognized the cultural pluralism in Canada. With a significant percentage of the population claiming an ethnic origin other than French and English, it seemed appropriate that we should move from a bicultural to a multicultural framework as a way of governing our diverse population. The multicultural policy reaffirmed that Canada is not an 'assimilationist' nation and recognized, theoretically at least, that all 'ethnic groups contributed and should continue to contribute to Canadian society and culture by retention of their ancestral culture and tradition' (Burnet 1981: 29).

Despite the philosophy of multiculturalism, however, the English, and to a lesser extent the French, have continued to play a central role in defining Canadian society and culture. For the most part, minority groups and immigrants have had to change elements of their behaviour (based on their subculture) in order to gain access to institutions and take advantage of the opportunities in society. While they may maintain some aspect of their ancestral culture, by and large their cultural practices reflect the parameters placed upon them by laws, values, and codes of behaviour developed and institutionalized by the English and French.

MINORITY-MAJORITY GROUP CULTURES

Many Canadians want to believe that there is no differentiation between ethnic and racial groups in our society. Such a belief is a denial of the social stratification that makes some groups more privileged than others. In examining culture it is important to pay attention to the majority-minority situation. Doing so alerts us to the influence and power that various ethnic and racial groups have in the formation of the national culture and to the ways in which this culture accommodates and promotes social interaction and participation in the society. Literally, 'majority' means greater than and/or in larger number, while 'minority' means less than and/or in smaller number. But sociologically the words have broader meanings.

Majority group refers to the dominant group in society that controls the economic, political, and social participation of other members of society. Members of the majority group usually occupy élite or privileged positions. Power within society, rather than absolute numbers, often guides the use of the term 'majority.' For example, while women outnumber men in Canada, they lack the power base of men. As Adler points out: 'The cultural identity of a society is defined by its majority group, and this group is usually quite distinguishable from the minority sub-group with whom they share the physical environment and the territory they inhabit' (1977: 26).

Minority groups, by contrast, are usually 'defined by the majority power elite on the basis of perceived physical, cultural, economic and/ or behavioural characteristics' (Kinloch 1974: 150). Minority-group members are subordinate to the dominant group in society and often receive different or negative treatment. According to Smith: 'We use race and ethnicity to define one's power status within the society. Each multi-ethnic/multiracial society develops a social distance scale between and among the various ethnic and racial groups. Such a social distance scale is usually anchored in the mainstream society's cultural value and feelings about the minority group. Those groups against which majority members have strong sanctions are those that they perceive as being the most unlike them, and therefore, the group for which they feel the greatest amount of social distance' (1991: 70). In Canada, the majority racial group is white; correspondingly, the majority or dominant ethnic group is English or Anglo-Celtic. The remaining racial and ethnic groups can be classified as minorities.

Inevitably, social position will influence the kinds of subcultural patterns adopted by majority and minority ethnic and racial groups. While the majority group enjoys the privileges of its status in society and gains access to all the social, economic, and political institutions without compromising its cultural identity or having to overcome barriers related to race or ethnicity, minority groups usually experience exploitation and oppression (Smith 1990: 70). Minority-group members are very aware of the dominant cultural ideals. They grow up in an 'environment that is inescapably bicultural,' one where knowledge of their own culture and that of the dominant group is often necessary for survival (Hoopes 1981: 22).

Insofar as our society comprises people of various racial and ethnic minority groups, it is reasonable to expect that elements from the subcultures of these groups will be evident in the Canadian culture. But the degree to which these minority racial and ethnic groups' subcultures are reflected in Canadian culture depends on the economic power and size of the respective ethnic groups, their history and length of time in Canada, their commitment towards maintaining their ancestral culture, and existing constraints that limit their cultural expressions. Nevertheless, because groups do not operate in isolation, elements of these minority groups' subculture will become incorporated into the Canadian culture over time. Such incorporation will only take place, however, if the elements assimilated are not in conflict with the dominant majority ethnic-group culture that forms the basis of the Canadian culture.

ETHNIC-GROUP MEMBERSHIP AND CANADIAN CULTURE

We often hear the terms (and may have used them ourselves) 'ethnic population,' 'ethnic person,' 'ethnic food,' or 'ethnic music.' In some cases, 'ethnic' is used to refer to such groups as the Italians, Portuguese, and Ukrainians. In other cases, 'ethnic' is used interchangeably with 'race' and 'immigrant' to socially define or locate people. At times, it connotes a negative stereotype.

Canadians commonly believe that ethnicity is based on how people choose to identify themselves and is presumably of no concern to society. But in reality, ethnicity is not simply a matter of individual choice. It is a matter of ancestry, membership, and belonging, and members of society play a role in helping each of us define our ethnicity.

Ethnic group may be defined as a reference group of people who share a common ancestry and history, who may or may not have identifiable physical or cultural characteristics, and who, through the process of interacting with each other and establishing boundaries with others, identify themselves as being members of that group (Smith 1991: 181). Ethnic-group members often, but not always, speak a common language. They are identified as a distinct group by a common set of values, symbols, and histories (ibid.: 182). Often religious affiliation is also part of ethnic identity. This identity is maintained over generations not only by new immigrants, but also by group members who develop or maintain interest in their ancestral group and subculture.

All Canadians belong to one or several ethnic groups, be they English, French, Italian, Korean, Japanese, Ukrainian, African, or other. To say you are Canadian is to identify your nationality or citizenship – not your ethnicity. Individuals with several ethnic identities are 'free' to identify with all of them. However, they often identify with the one that formed the basis of their socialization at home or with their peers, the one that seems most acceptable to the dominant group in society or the one by which others identify them.

Ethnicity is not readily apparent to many English Canadians who have been in Canada for generations. For example, as one person noted: 'To me, ethnicity was something that belonged to people that differed from the so-called average White Canadian – differing perhaps because of language, accent or skin colour. Thus, I believed ethnicity was something noticeable or visible. I believe my ignorance regarding my ethnicity is because I belong to the majority in Canada. Because the majority of Canadians are White, English speaking, descendants of Britain, I have only thought of myself as a Canadian. In essence, I didn't realize I had ethnicity because I did not differ from the stereotypical image of an average Canadian' (see James 1995: 39–40). This lack of self-awareness often leads to the questionable categorization of certain groups as 'ethnic' and others as 'Canadian.' Since all Canadians have an ethnicity and hence belong to ethnic groups, it follows that apart from majority-group members, all other Canadians live by their ethnic subcultures and the dominant culture. This is not unlike what happens in other ethnoculturally diverse countries such as Belgium, Switzerland, Tanzania, Kenya, Trinidad, Jamaica, and the United States.

That all Canadians, regardless of ethnic origin and official-language skill, live by Canadian culture is evident in our daily contacts. For example, a Chinese woman who has resided in Canada for fifty years and who speaks very little English would still be living her life through the Canadian laws, value system, and so on. It is true that she will be doing so by means of her ethnic subculture, which has changed over time, 'mixed in.' The Chinese that she speaks will certainly be different from that spoken in China or Hong Kong. Similarly, her eating and social habits will have changed somewhat because of the Canadian social and environmental context. While the rest of us might claim that this person is Chinese, noting her competence in English or French, her area of residence, or her family practices, she in fact has many cultural elements in common with us. Her Chinese language will have become a 'Canadian version' insofar as it has developed and been practised outside of China or Hong Kong. And if she visits China or Hong Kong she will note a difference in accent and in words and expressions used.

Recently, a colleague of Portuguese descent told me that her mother, who speaks very little English and has been in Canada for nearly twenty years, returned to Portugal after a six-year absence. During her visit, differences in language, food preparation, and other day-to-day activities made her feel like an immigrant in her country of birth. Thus, ethnic-group membership and second-language proficiency do not impede individuals from adapting and adhering to common cultural elements within Canada.

Acculturation

Acculturation and assimilation are part of the socialization process of all immigrants and of ethnic and racial minority-group members. These are processes of adjusting to, and / or adopting the values, norms, and habits of, the host or majority group of the society. *Acculturation* is a process that minority groups and immigrants go through in response to overt or systemic pressures from the dominant group(s) to adopt, conform with, or adjust to majority values, customs, behaviours, and psychological characteristics (Sodowsky, Lai, and Plake, 1991: 195). *Assimilation* is one aspect of acculturation. But while acculturation means that individuals incorporate cultural elements of the dominant ethnic group of society, assimilation means that considerable elements of their ethnic or racial subcultures are relinquished in order for them to 'fit in.'   Assimilation is inevitable, since the power of the (host) majority will be too much for any immigrant or minority group to resist, and therefore the group will assimilate into the majority.

As racial and ethnic minority-group members or immigrants interact with majority-group members, particularly in the major public, educational, social, cultural, and recreational institutions where the majority group's norms and values dominate, some degree of acculturation is inevitable. This is even more likely to occur as minority groups recognize that success or upward social mobility depends on the inculcation of the majority group's values and thus on being able to operate within the larger society.

Many factors affect the rate of acculturation, including the relative number of the groups involved in the contact situation, the rate of entrance of minority groups, where they settle, the extent to which they are isolated or segregated, the age and sex composition of the groups, the influence of individuals either in opposing or encouraging assimilation, and the crises experienced (Berry 1958: 240).

Minority and immigrant organizations also play a significant role in the acculturation process. For example, many provide citizenship and second-language classes to enable members to have greater access to employment and educational opportunities. Others disseminate information about Canadian laws, policies, events, and so on affecting the lives of community members. For many people, particularly those who do not speak English, 'ethnocultural' organizations also provide a means of connecting with others and contributing in a meaningful way to life in their communities.

The process of acculturation is not necessarily a self-imposed pressure to change or adjust to a new and dominant culture. Often, members of the host or dominant group may direct pressure at minorities and immigrants. While it may be true that many ethnic groups have maintained their ancestral cultures to varying degrees, it is important to note that all reside in Canada and that in order to participate fully in Canadian life must conform to certain major institutions of society; for example, the law. Furthermore, every group encounters educational institutions, the major socializing force outside of the family. Like other Canadians, minority-group members and immigrants learn the elements of culture through education. The textbooks used and the language spoken in schools inform everyone of the cultural norms of our society and so we learn the behaviours that are expected of us. Through interaction with educational and other institutions, minority-group members are likely to become acculturated.

Finally, as has already been noted, culture, and by extension subculture, are dynamic and are influenced by the social and physical contexts in which they exist. For example, the cultural practices, customs, and so on of the African or Scottish or Italian ethnic subcultures in Canada differ from those found in countries where they are the national culture.

Essentially, there is a central Canadian culture in which all Canadians participate regardless of race, ethnicity, religion, and other core identities. The variations that exist do not take away from the fact that we all ultimately adhere to, and participate in, similar activities and must be able to understand and predict each other's behaviour and expectations. This is what makes a society. What has evolved in Canada, therefore, is a mixture of values, beliefs, and traditions that together produce our unique Canadian culture. Through family, school, work, peers, and other agents of socialization, we learn the expectations, rules, values, and norms required to function effectively in our society.

RACE AND CULTURE

There is often a lexicon problem with the word race. 'Race' is often confused with 'ethnicity,' 'immigrant,' and 'culture,' and the terms are frequently used interchangeably. Our attempt here is not to debate the merits of identifying people by race, but to assert that there is a subculture based on the *arbitrary* classification of human beings who share hereditary physical characteristics.

According to psychologist James Jones, race refers to 'a group of people who share biological features that come to signify group membership and the social meaning such membership has in the society at large. Race becomes the basis for expectation regarding social roles, performance levels, values, and norms and mores of group and nongroup members and in-group members alike' (1991: 9). Skin colour (red, yellow, black, brown, white) is often the basis upon which status allocation and group membership take place (see Harris 1993).

In what some social scientists call 'colour caste societies,' colour becomes the defining factor of individuals and whole groups of people. It denies some racial groups and individuals the full expression of who they are by classifying them as a 'colour' rather than as individuals with a complex set of skills, interests, and identities. For groups of people, colour becomes a homogenizing factor. For instance, commenting in the *Globe and Mail* on the potential appointment of the first Black person to the Supreme Court, University of Toronto law professor Lorraine Weinrib observed: 'The appointment of a Black person to the court might be perceived as a move that was politically sparked because of the colour question or the race question in Canada. We tend to label people as one thing and nothing else – as a woman, or a visible minority, or a Black, even though people have much more complex identities' (Fine 1992: A7).

Race is significant as long as groups are identified and acquire status according to selected physical traits. When we refer to race we mean not only the biological category but, more significantly, *the social meanings that society has attached to it*, and the ways in which individuals and groups have internalized these meanings and acted upon them. It is the behaviour patterns that individuals develop as a consequence of these social meanings that we refer to as their *subculture based on race*. This description indicates that individuals' behaviours are determined socially and psychologically, rather than biologically.

ATTITUDES, IDEOLOGY, AND ACTION

Cultures and subcultures have mechanisms that ensure survival, stability, and a hierarchial structure. Mechanisms such as ethnocentrism, prejudice, and racism are often sustained by stereotyping and discrimination.

Ethnocentrism is defined as the tendency to see things from the point of view of your own culture and to see your own culture as being somehow better than others. It can also mean assuming that what is true of your culture is also true of others (Carroll 1990: 22).

Prejudice is derived from the Latin noun *praejudicium* meaning a precedent or a prejudgment 'insofar as preconceived opinions have been assumed to be true before having been put to the test. [It] is based on invalid negative attitude' (Driedger 1989: 350). Prejudice may express a favourable or unfavourable feeling towards a person or thing before or not based on, actual experience. But what is significant to our discussion is the use of 'prejudice' in reference to ethnic and/or other minority groups to express a negative attitude. Perhaps the most succinct definition comes from Hoopes and Pusch, who describe prejudice as 'hostile and unreasonable feelings, opinions or attitudes based on fear, mistrust, ignorance, mis-information – or a combination thereof – and directed against a racial, religious, national or other cultural group' (1981: 4).

Racism may be viewed as an ideology or attitude held of 'people of another race, which is based on the belief that races are distinct and can be regarded as "superior" or "inferior"' (Yeboah 1988: 14). It is an uncritical acceptance of a negative social definition of a group identified by physical features such as skin colour. People justify their racist attitudes and perceptions by associating perceived differences between groups with the presence (or absence) of certain biological characteristics and social abilities.

While racism is similar to ethnocentrism and prejudice in that it combines the preference for a given group of people with contempt for another, it is critically different in one aspect: power. As Dobbins and Skillings explain: 'Racism includes access to enough power to enforce one's racial prejudices. In this sense, although people of colour can be on the receiving end of racist acts in this society and frequently hold prejudices about members of the dominant group, as a group they lack power to enforce or act on these prejudices. For this reason, it is said that people of colour do not act in racist ways unless they are acting as agents for the dominant power structure' (1991: 41). Racism in multiracial societies such as Canada relates to 'the manner in which the politics of a White power base influence society in the economic, educational, legal, and artistic structures of the culture. It has very little to do with real differences' (ibid.: 42). And as Neufeld (1992) explains, 'seeing racism as something common to all racial groups does not take into account the effects of unequal power.'

Racism exists in different forms: individual, institutional, and structural (see figure 1). *Individual racism* is the negative attitude that individuals hold of others. It is like an ideology – a set of ideas and related beliefs held by a person who may or may not act upon them. Individuals, particularly those from the dominant racial group, are primarily the ones with the social, economic, and political power to benefit from this attitude. *Institutional racism* exists where established rules and policies reflect and produce differential treatment of various groups within organizations or institutions. According to Dobbins and Skillings, these regulations 'are used to maintain social control and status quo in favour of the dominant group' (1991: 42). Institutional racism is directly related to individual racism, as individuals are the ones who develop and implement the policies and rules, and they understand that they must adhere to the regulated norms, role relationships, and sanctions that comprise the 'order of things.' Institutional racism is also related to societal (or structural) racism in that it 'promotes and sustains the existing inequalities that are present in our social system' (Anderson and Frideres 1981: 208).

Structural (or societal) racism refers to inequalities, rooted in the way the society operates, that exclude substantial numbers of people of particular racial groups from significantly accessing and participating in major social institutions (Hughes and Kallen 1974: 106). Some people refer to societal racism as systemic or cultural racism. Whatever the term, the idea is that racism is rooted in the structure or fabric of society. Since racism is so rooted in the everyday operation of society, it has an impact on everyone, and the fact that it is expressed in very subtle forms produces devastating results. Institutional and systemic racism are particularly important when examining racism and discrimination in Canada. As a consequence of these forms of racism, minority-group members are denied access to the education, occupational, and political opportunities and social services that are necessary for full participation in the society.

Figure 1 illustrates the dimensions of racism and discrimination. It shows that individual racism (attitude and ideology) and discrimination (the action) operate within or are derived from the institutions and system (structure or society) within which individuals live.

Evidence of racism can be observed in many institutions in our country. For instance, while in 1986 approximately 7 per cent of the Canadian population consisted of racial minorities, this percentage was not reflected in our federal-parliament or provincial-legislature representations. This is not unlike what happens in many professions and workplaces. Also, the lack of minority-group representation in the main literary and historical resources (that is, textbooks, national and regional holidays) of our society reflects the lack of importance we give to the contributions of minorities, both as a group and as individuals, in the building of the Canadian society. To have courses and texts that do not incorporate the historical and literary contributions of non-British Canadians is to set them apart, hence creating unequal access to learning for

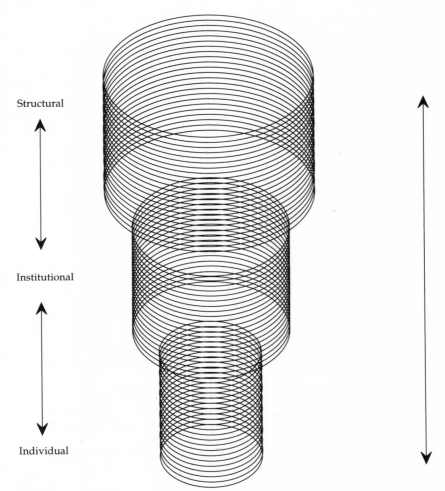

FIGURE 1 (Source: C.E. James, *Exploring Race, Ethnicity and Culture* [Toronto: Thompson Educational Publishing 1995], 140)

ethnic and racial minority-group students. Geneva Gay refers to this as 'intellectual discrimination and educational inequity' (1990: 231).

The acceptance of such a situation by large numbers of Canadians indicates the level to which racism is an inherent part of our culture. The fact that political, economic, and social institutions and standard history texts do not reflect or acknowledge the contributions of the country's many ethnic and racial groups reinforces racism. This situation further underlines the functional nature of the concept of race that is used to maintain psychological control of one designated group over others and to help define and limit non-dominant groups.

This situation is also evident in the practice of stereotyping, a mechanism that, as pointed out earlier, helps to sustain the attitudes of ethnocentrism, prejudice, and racism. *Stereotyping* is defined as a tendency to overgeneralize about, and categorize, individuals based solely on preconceived notions about their racial, ethnic, or religious group affiliation. This tendency is often accompanied by a strong belief in the 'correctness' or 'truth' of the stereotype and a disregard for fact or for new or other information.

Discrimination is the unequal treatment of people or groups through the granting or denying of certain rights. It can be defined as 'applied prejudice in which negative social definitions are translated into action and political policy, the subordination of minorities and deprivation of their political, social and economic rights' (Kinloch 1974: 54). Discrimination is evident in differential treatment. For example, research has shown that racial and ethnic minority groups in Canada achieve lower levels of education, are likely to experience higher unemployment and underemployment, and have greater difficulty in obtaining jobs than members of the dominant group (Anderson and Frideres 1981; Head 1975; Henry and Ginzberg 1985; James 1990, 1993). Researchers attribute these findings to discrimination practised by teachers and employers as a result of societal, institutional, and/or individual racism.

Discrimination is also inherent in the educational and employment system as a result of the many forms of racism. Henry and Ginzberg (1985) note that racial discriminatory acts are not isolated to a 'handful of bigots.' There are barriers existing in our society that deny certain categories of people access to the full benefits of the society. Through discrimination, certain groups are able to maintain their position of privilege, largely at the expense of other groups who are deliberately or inadvertently excluded from full and equal participation in society.

INDIVIDUAL CULTURAL IDENTITY

No discussion of culture can be complete without looking at how culture operates at the individual level. This section attempts to explore the construction of culture and its expression at the personal level. The term cultural identity can be used in two different ways. According to Adler, it can be employed as a reference to the collective self-awareness that a given group embodies and reflects. It can also refer to the 'identity of the individual in relation to his or her culture' (Adler 1977: 26). It is the latter concept that is of interest to us here. We wish to understand the dimensions of cultural identity, since it is 'a functioning aspect of individual personality and a fundamental symbol of a person's existence' (ibid.).

Before proceeding, it should be pointed out that while we are referring to cultural identity as influenced by race and ethnicity, the following figure shows that individuals have multiple identities. Their identities are not exclusively influenced by one demographic characteristic rather than another. It is important to take this fact into account when exploring the cultural identities of individuals. Surely, context will make a difference in the cultural identity that operates at a particular time. Figure 2 illustrates the various factors that contribute to an individual's cultural identity.

It shows that characteristics such as sex, race, ethnicity, age, sexual orientation, and ability, together with social factors such as education, immigrant and citizenship status, and political affiliation, are likely to influence a person's attitude, perception, personality, and motivation. Socializing agents such as the family, teachers, peers, mentors, coaches, social workers, 'significant others,' and the society in which the individual lives play a role in the ways in which these factors find expression and influence individuals. Altogether, these interrelated factors play a role in the socialization process, in the culture which is transmitted and developed by the individual, and ultimately the behaviour of the individual.

Take racial, ethnic minorities or immigrants, for instance. Living in Canada means that their ideas, values, and aspirations will be a product of the Canadian culture and, at the same time, of the subculture of the ethnic and/or racial group to which they belong. As a result, minorities and immigrants are bicultural and are acutely aware of the assimilation or acculturation process that they must undergo in order to enjoy the benefits Canada has to offer. The cultural identity of individuals, and in this case minorities, is not based simply on the choices they make, but also on the social forces within society that operate to influence their lives.

In 'Beyond Cultural Identity' Adler elaborates on the relationship between identity and culture by saying that 'psychological, psychosocial, and psycho-philosophical realities of an individual are knit together by the culture which operates through sanctions and rewards, totems and

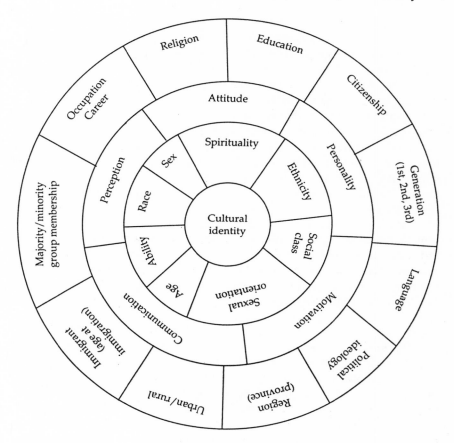

Starting from the inner circle:
1 Individual's personal cultural identity determines lifestyle and behaviour.
2 Personal factors (social), mostly ascribed. (Spirituality, sometimes referred to as religion, is constructed as integral to ethnic identification or affiliation.)
3 Psychological factors: some are based on innate sources; all interact with the personal and social factors.
4 Social factors shared by group members: many are social institutions through which socialization takes place, culture is transmitted, or behaviour is determined.

FIGURE 2 Factors contributing to individual cultural identity
(Source: C.E. James, *Seeing Ourselves: Exploring Race, Ethnicity and Culture* [Toronto: Thompson Educational Publishing 1995], 24)

taboos, prohibitions and myths. The unity and integration of society, nature, and the cosmos is reflected in the total image of the self and in the day-to-day awareness andconsciousness of the individual. This synthesis is modulated by the larger dynamics of the culture itself. In the concept of cultural identity, then, we see a synthesis of the operant culture reflected by the deepest images held by the individual' (1977: 28).

Majority-group perceptions of minority groups – particularly of those who are 'visibly different' – have an impact not only on the interpersonal relations but also on the self-identity of minority-group members. Immigrants and racial minorities often feel they cannot escape the image that the majority group has of them. As Korean Canadian Sun-Kyung Yi writes in her essay 'An Immigrant's Split Personality': 'It's difficult to have a sense of belonging and acceptance when you are regarded as "one of them"' (1993: 407). Smith argues that the internalization of negative or stereotypical images and expectations is often an indication of the extent to which minorities are 'aware of the dominant cultural ideals but prevented from emulating them, and are apt to fuse the negative images held up to them by the dominant majority' (1991: 183). Finally, as Smith argues further:

A large part of the minority child's ethnic identity development entails dealing with this sense of initial rejection of one's ethnic group. The ethnic self moves from an early stage of unawareness and lack of differentiation to one of ethnic awareness, ethnic self-identification, and increasingly ethnic differentiation on the basis of contact situations. Whereas the ethnic identity development of the majority group individual is continually validated and reinforced in a positive manner by both his membership group and by the structure of the society's institutions, such is not the case for many ethnic minorities. Positive reinforcement frees the majority individual to focus on aspects of his or her life other than ethnicity. (ibid.)

CONCLUSION AND IMPLICATIONS FOR HUMAN SERVICE WORKERS

Perhaps the most important issue that has been addressed in this discussion is how as Canadians we can better understand our cultural mosaic and develop an awareness of, sensitivity to, appreciation, and acceptance of each other so that we can better serve our society and respective communities. It is particularly important for human service workers to understand the role and significance of culture and subcultures in the lives of individuals.

We have argued that there is a Canadian culture into which all Canadians are socialized. The ethno-racial group that establishes the cultural framework for the Canadian culture is the majority or dominant group. Given the ethnic and racial diversity of our society, it can be expected that there will be ethnic and racial subcultures within the culture. The subcultural patterns of behaviours displayed by ethnic and racial minority-group members must be viewed within the context of their Canadian existence (as ethnic and/or racial minorities) and not as an import from another society. True, immigrant groups have elements of the culture of the societies from which they immigrate. However, as we have demonstrated, immigrants as well as ethnic and racial minorities of many generations in Canada go through an acculturation process that they recognize is important for their participation in the society.

There are functional benefits in acknowledging the existence of a Canadian culture and its role in the lives of minority-group Canadians. Little is accomplished when the cultural behaviours of racial and ethnic minorities and immigrants are simply attributed to their subcultures. First, such acknowledgment would establish the fact that the Canadian culture is central to everyone's experience insofar as we have a world-view, value system, attitudes, and beliefs developed as a result of our respective social positions as members of Canadian society. This collective experience can be referred to as the cultural identity that 'incorporates the shared premises, values, definitions, and beliefs and the day-to-day, largely unconscious, patterning of activities' (Adler 1981: 26).

Second, there are common traits that Canadians share with one another regardless of subculture, race, or ethnicity. These traits are above and beyond individual and subcultural group differences. For example, it is possible to identify similar values and attitudes among Canadians towards life, death, birth, family, children, and nature.

Third, as Pedersen (1991) makes clear, understanding culture from a broad perspective, in particular the role of, and relationship between, culture and subcultures, alerts us to the complexity in individuals' cultural identity patterns, which may or may not include the obvious indicators of ethnicity, race, or nationality.

Fourth, we must acknowledge that Canadian society as a whole suffers culturally, socially, and economically as a result of the pervasive racism and inequalities that act as barriers to full participation of racial minorities in the workforce and in social services.

Adler (1981) argues that people who live in multicultural, multiracial societies need to be aware of the implications of this diversity and makes the following points.

- Every culture or system has its own internal coherence, integrity, and logic. Every culture is an intertwined system of values and attitudes, beliefs and norms that give meaning and significance to both individual and collective identity.
- All cultural systems contribute to variations on the human experience.
- All persons are, to some extent, culturally bound. Every culture provides the individual with some sense of identity, some regulation of behaviour, and some sense of personal place in the scheme of things. (p.31)

These three points also highlight the functional importance of ethnic and racial subcultures and the need to identify these subcultures as Canadian if we are to inculcate in minority Canadians the feeling of belonging. One important point needs to be added to this list. That is, members of society as a whole must actively work to root out racism, since it serves as a barrier to building a harmonious, egalitarian society.

An anti-racism perspective – a perspective that acknowledges power differentials and works in pursuit of greater equity, must be incorporated into the society's political, economic, and educational practices. To this end, racism must be understood in terms of its relationship to white privilege. And as Neufeld writes: 'That privilege is present not only in individual prejudices, but, even more critically, is enshrined in the very working of society's institutions such as the media, the schools, and government.' Hence, 'given the stakes surrounding the issue of racism, stubborn adherence to comfortable assumptions may well cost more, in the long run, than the effort to expand our way of thinking and responding' (1992: A7).

In economically, ethnically, and racially pluralistic societies, it is imperative that the socializing and service institutions are able to meet the diverse needs and aspirations of all citizens. This will not happen until service providers recognize that awareness and sensitivity cannot be built within a framework where the majority culture is seen as the norm.

Cultural differences between majority and minority groups must not be perceived as problems of minority groups. Rather the problem is the inability of institutions to reflect the needs, expectations, and aspirations of the many racial and ethnic minority groups in their missions, policies, practices, and services. Any movement towards recognition of human potential or recognition of diversity of needs, expectations, and aspirations must be posited on reinventing institutions and services to acknowledge the historically unequal distribution of power and resources and must act conscientiously to address social oppression.

Finally, for those of us who work directly in the human service field, Carter (1991) suggests that to work effectively with people of diverse backgrounds, human service workers need to be self-aware, knowledgeable about the history, experiences, needs, and aspirations of various ethnic and racial groups; Further, workers must be sensitive to the fact that they share some common cultural experiences with members of other ethnic and racial group. As Carter observes: 'It is through the development of a personal-historical-cultural knowledge base that mental health and educational professionals will be able to make visible their cultural filters. Through their visible cultural filters, they will begin to be capable of seeing and understanding with more clarity the cultures of others. When cultural filters or values are visible, effective and meaningful cross-racial and cross-cultural interactions can take place' (1991: 172).

COMMENTS:

Disturbing the Silence: Reflections on Racism and Aboriginal People

Corinne Mount Pleasant-Jetté

I wish to discuss the issue of racism and people of the First Nations of Canada, and the commitment of authorities to respond to the very real problems that continue to face Native communities.

A PERSPECTIVE ON HISTORY

For over four hundred years, the first inhabitants of North America have lived alongside those people who chose to come to the 'New World' and establish for themselves a society primarily based on values of freedom, democracy, and the pursuit of material prosperity. From the first encounters with Europeans, the First Nations peoples of Turtle Island sought to maintain a way of life that was based primarily on respect for all living creatures, on tranquillity, and on the pursuit of social harmony through honour.

While these two sets of fundamental values are not in themselves mutually exclusive, over the more than four centuries of coexistence there have been repeated conflicts between the people of the First Nations and the newcomers to this land – conflicts that have resulted in hostility and misunderstanding which remain to this day.

Much has been written about the historical context in which European explorers, missionaries, and adventurers set out to build new civilizations. But, unfortunately, little written evidence exists to prove with any degree of certainty the extent of the damage that was done to the original inhabitants of North America. Little has been told of the slavery, deprivation, torture, and genocide perpetrated on these aboriginal peoples.

In *A Long and Terrible Shadow: White Values and Native Rights in the Americas 1492–1992*, respected lawyer and Native-rights advocate Thomas R. Berger presents a masterful exposé of the subjugation and disenfranchisement of indigenous peoples throughout North, Central, and South America. His documentation of the real experiences of

Aboriginal peoples through the eyes and words of European missionaries and government emissaries leaves no doubt that the slaughter of hundreds of thousands of people did take place, and was the source of bitter controversy in Europe. In 1992, as the world geared up for the much-celebrated 500th anniversary re-enactment of the voyage of Columbus, Berger's thought-provoking analysis of the imposition of white values on Native societies provided readers with a long-awaited glimpse of history from the other side.

Perhaps one of the most compelling facts to emerge from his remarkable work is that in spite of the unimaginable odds faced by Aboriginal people for more than five hundred years, they have displayed the all-important capacity not only to survive but also to maintain their cultural traditions and emerge as distinct peoples with a tenacious hold on their own identity. Berger's analysis should be required reading for politicians, educators, jurists, and anyone associated with the caring professions.

A number of significant events in the last ten years have motivated Aboriginal people to set the record straight – to right the wrongs of the past, to expose injustice, and to ensure that future history books provide as true a reflection as possible of the way things really were.

AN END TO THE SILENCE

For too many years, there has been all-pervasive silence – silence from our elders, who told us it was not the way of our people to call attention to ourselves; silence from our leaders, who sensed the futility of a public outcry; silence from religious leaders, who taught us to bear our indignity in the name of personal sacrifice; silence from government authorities, who told us it was better not 'to rock the boat.' Silence everywhere – silence ... that is, until now.

Bolstered by recent events, Aboriginal people across this country have reacted by speaking out on a wide range of topics, publicly addressing issues for the first time. Young and old alike have broken the centuries-old silence about the administration of justice, the mismanagement of child-welfare operations, the stark reality of sexual and physical abuse, the desecration of ancestral burial grounds, and the destruction of traditional hunting and fishing areas.

In June of 1990 in the Manitoba legislature, when Elijah Harper stood on principle, grasping only a single eagle feather as his source of inner strength and conviction, thousands of Native people across Canada waited to see if he could fulfil their hopes and single-handedly bring about the failure of the Meech Lake Accord on the federal constitution. They were not disappointed. Elijah Harper epitomized for many the intensity, patience, and perseverance of the hunter. His strength of character brought honour to his people. A moment in time was created that will always be important to Aboriginal people in this country.

Other events in recent years were accompanied by sadness and revulsion, but they too helped crystallize the vision of First Nations peoples. These events were moments in time that have provided Aboriginal people with even more reason to speak out with outrage and righteous indignation. Some of them provoked reaction in local communities, but many others were felt in every Native household across the country.

From our offices and kitchens, we watched in disgust as an infant in a cradleboard was passed through an X-ray security conveyor at an airport in Winnipeg. We heard a jurist from the Northwest Territories say that the rape of a Native woman in the North is somehow less serious than a similar offence against a white woman in the South, simply because a white man in the North sees a Native woman as, in the judge's words, 'just another pair of hips.' We saw the beleaguered face of Donald Marshall, who spent sixteen years in prison for a crime that the provincial government in New Brunswick finally admitted he did not commit. We cried with the family of Native leader J.J. Harper, who was shot to death in Winnipeg by a police officer who suspected he was just another drunken Indian. We felt the anguish of so many families torn apart by the existence of a modern-day brainwashing experiment known as the Residential School system. We were revolted at the continuing saga of sexual and physical abuse that occurred at the hands of our religious educators and 'guardians.' We read with disbelief the staggering statistics on the suicide of Native children.

In fact, we observed in these, and in other moments in time, more and more examples of ignorance and outright discrimination that clearly cast dark shadows over the Canadian horizon. With this level of humiliation and degradation, how could the silence not be broken?

And then came the late summer of 1990.

In what might have unfolded as just another misguided decision by a group of uninformed, foolish local councillors, a decision was taken to develop a seemingly unimportant pine forest into a potentially lucrative golf course. Had the circumstances been different, had the values of mainstream white society not encroached on the traditional cultural values of the Mohawks of Kanesetake, perhaps the whole incident might not have erupted into the powder-keg that will always be known as 'The Oka Crisis.'

Thus, the 'Crisis' became for all First Nations people a significant turning point, one that has profoundly changed the contemporary relationship between the first inhabitants of the land and the descendants of those who came here four hundred years ago. Wherever the next clash of values develops, whether in the logging regions of British Columbia, the river basins of northern Quebec, the forests of Ontario, or the dam sites in Alberta, Native people now have what might be termed a strong 'corporate memory.' They have learned the lessons of Oka.

Within the space of a little over two months in the late summer of 1990, Canadians watched as a police officer was buried, as armoured personnel carriers rumbled through sleepy rural villages in Quebec, as crowds of rowdy citizens shouted mock war cries and burned effigies of their Native neighbours, and as children peeked through curtains at the sight of machine guns trained on their homes. Yes, this critical moment etched itself into the psyches of Aboriginal people everywhere. Even outside Canada, other indigenous peoples saw for the first time a vivid demonstration of how Canada deals with its First Nations people.

Whether young or old; remote, rural, or urban; status, non-status, or Métis; every Native person in Canada was subjected to scenes of some of the most virulently racist activity ever presented on the evening news. Nightly coverage showed in-depth footage of non-Native Quebeckers hurling rocks at innocent people as they ran an expressway gauntlet used to evacuate the sick and elderly from Kahnawake, a Mohawk community outside Montreal. Newspapers covered stories of school officials who refused to allow Native and non-Native children to attend school together. Radio open-line hosts further exacerbated the hatred by inviting racist callers to offer their own solutions to the 'Indian problem.' These graphic examples of blatant racism were particularly harmful to a whole generation of Aboriginal children.

With Oka, the already growing resurgence of politicized First Nations continued to expand. The silence of decades was transformed into outspoken protests from all regions of the country. Canadians learned quickly that First Nations do have articulate, intelligent, and forward-looking leadership.

And what of the teachings of our elders about the benefits of silence? What logic could remain in the supposed sanctity of silence that had been extolled by the nuns and brothers who directed the re-education of generations of our people? Lessons taught and learned through these critical moments have changed the perspective of many people from one of silent observer to that of concerned spokesperson. Obviously, there is no legitimate reason to remain silent anymore.

A TIDE OF COMMON PURPOSE

Canada's Native population is, in itself, multicultural. While some bands or tribes were primarily agricultural, others were nomadic. Still others, especially those located in coastal areas or arctic regions, adopted ways of living directly related to the limitations of their natural environments. Of the 592 registered bands across Canada, most can trace their ancestry to one of six dominant linguistic groups, but specific dialectic patterns produce more than 150 different spoken languages. There are also wide-ranging differences in hair, eye, and skin pigmentation among Aboriginal peoples. Religious practices, ceremonial occasions, traditional dances, and cultural celebrations are widely divergent. The diversity among the eleven Native nations represented in the Province of Quebec alone is no less than that which is presented during the various multicultural festivals held in downtown Toronto every summer. The one common denominator that is fundamental to all Native nations is the unparalleled respect and affinity for Mother Earth. Another common factor is the importance of family relationships.

Anomalies in statistical bases make it very difficult to determine exactly how many Aboriginal people live in urban centres. The only certainty is that growing numbers of Native people are moving away from isolated or rural communities and establishing themselves in medium-sized and large cities. This migration is directly related to socio-economic realities on the reserves, and has been in progress for at least ten years. As well, more and more Aboriginal people are leaving their home communities to pursue education and employment opportunities that simply do not exist at home. Like most newcomers to urban centres, young Aboriginal people are most often drawn to cities with already established Native communities. For some, the transition to urban living is reasonably successful, but a large majority eventually return to their original communities.

It is not unusual, for example, for a seemingly well-established, 'adjusted' Native person to simply tire of city living and return home to a more nurturing and tranquil environment. In recent years, a number of successful entrepreneurs, managers, and professionals have also opted to return to their home communities, where their skills and expertise are in great demand. By choosing to contribute to local Native economies, these individuals are often misjudged by their urban colleagues, who see their departure as 'dropping out.'

A MADE-IN-CANADA VISION OF RACISM

In the uniquely Canadian exercise of searching for our ever-elusive 'Canadian identity,' we are often told how very different our society is from that of the United States. We are told that, unlike the United States, which was forged from a racist westward expansion into Aboriginal lands and a violent revolution against the imperial power, Canada has a non-racist history and a tradition of peaceful coexistence.

This is a myth. The construct of a non-racist Canadian society is a fallacious made-in-Canada vision of some Utopian civilization. History shows us that ours is a society much like every other, that human frailty is the same here as elsewhere, and that racism has existed here and continues to exist. It shouts out from the pages of our history books. It colours the map from sea to sea.

A society that does not admit to its racism is in some ways more difficult to contend with than one where such attitudes are openly and publicly displayed. At the very least, when open dialogue takes place, there is some measure of hope that conflict can be resolved, and that hostility can be tempered by reason. To deny the existence of racism, however, is to encourage its growth and expansion.

Oppression destroys self-esteem; racism destroys trust. Aboriginal people in Canada lack these two vital necessities in their struggle to participate as productive members of Canadian society. And they cannot hope to regain self-esteem and trust without the cooperation of non-Native society. We must retrieve these essential values that supported our ancestors at a time in our history when every aspect of human ingenuity was critical for survival. As the silence of humiliation is broken and is replaced with the call for increased self-esteem and trust, the vicious cycle of self-destruction can be halted.

But where and how can such a process begin?

A TIME FOR CHANGE

Front-line workers and professionals in institutions throughout this country are the gatekeepers who will determine whether positive changes will take place or not. Policy makers and senior administrators will also contribute to the climate for change, but their role is perhaps less instrumental. Carefully worded statements and policy directives may exist within the organization, but the worker-client relationship defines the essence of understanding and respect within any organizational context.

Aboriginal clients who seek the services offered by agencies and institutions must be recognized, understood, and valued as potentially productive, trustworthy, and functional people. While their values reflect a culture and a tradition that are indeed very different from the dominant culture (see chapter 1), such positive treatment will help them to gain self-esteem and trust.

Unquestionably, this process of increased cross-cultural communication will be long and laborious. For every step forward, both the Native client and the non-Native worker may move two steps backward. But the crucial factor is the mutual understanding that may be achieved on even the smallest scale. As social service agencies and institutions review policies and procedures to eliminate any systemic or inadvertent examples of racist attitudes or behaviours, and as more cross-cultural education takes place, there will be improved levels of self-esteem and trust among First Nations clients.

KEYS TO BETTER UNDERSTANDING

With the prospect of further dramatic demographic changes, anyone with an eye to the future knows that enshrined methods of dealing with people must be radically altered if social service agencies and institutions are to offer effective service to Native people. They should follow the lead of their corporate colleagues to learn more about the dimensions of cultural diversity. Just as other sectors of society have found the means to implement such programs in times of down-sizing and budget cuts, a lack of significant resources should not be put forward as a reason to delay this process. Creative ways can be found to venture into the field of cross-cultural studies that do not require vast amounts of time or money. After all, the values and cultural traditions of most Native societies are not the stuff of mystery books and are not shrouded in secrecy.

Perhaps the best place to start is to establish close regular contact with First Nations communities themselves in order to gain insight and practical knowledge into Aboriginal cultural traditions and value systems. Only by stepping beyond the textbook advice of establishing eye contact and shaking hands will human-relations professionals find the answers to the sometimes frustrating questions derived from their previous negative experiences with Aboriginal clients.

Getting useful advice is not difficult. In every Native community – urban, rural, or remote – there are designated leaders or informal counsellors, elders, educators, or members of the local community centre with a keen understanding of the pulse of that community. Though busy, when there is a sincere request for help, they will almost always respond with sound advice or, at the very least, a direct referral to another source of assistance.

The key is trust – trust in the sincerity of the request, trust in any situation that demands confidentiality. The truth is that our people have been subject to intrusion, inspection, and, in some cases, invasion of privacy because they were considered wards of the state. For example, in years past, the infamous 'Indian Agent' was privy to every detail of life in the community. Residents of reserves were required to provide volumes of information simply 'for the record' and had no option but to disclose private information. This historical intrusion into their privacy may also explain the mistrust they feel when non-Natives express idle curiosity or meddling interest in Aboriginal communities. But genuine attempts to communicate with Native community leaders for the benefit of Native clients will be met with cooperation.

The 'shyness' of many Aboriginal people is really a mask that covers their innermost feelings and perceptions. It provides the last, and perhaps most effective, method of retaining those private thoughts and emotions. But as trust is established, the lines of communication with Native communities can be opened and strengthened to reveal the honesty, integrity, and true sense of humour that lie beneath the mask.

Another key to better understanding is the need to recognize the validity, richness, and importance of time-honoured Native beliefs and of what some in the dominant society would term 'superstitions.' When Thomas Berger uncovers the capacity for survival of Native cultural traditions, he makes clear that more than tenacity and physical prowess enabled indigenous peoples to withstand the forces of assimilation and acculturation. The scientific community has already recognized the inherent properties of certain herbal remedies to treat and cure physical ailments, and Western society has only begun to learn that certain Aboriginal rites and rituals are effective in dealing with a number of psychological problems. One need look no further than the nearest Native community to find evidence that healers and spiritual leaders are highly respected for their capacities to help people.

The final key to both the process of increased cross-cultural under-standing and that of coming to terms with racist views of First Nations peoples is the critical need to dispel stereotypes. Myths and misconceptions first created by misguided European missionaries, and later embellished by Hollywood film producers, have left a legacy of stereotypical images that confound efforts to understand our people. When mainstream Canadians recognize the pervasiveness of these stereotypes and set them aside, they will have initiated the healing process.

N'ya Weh.

PART TWO

Racism in Canada

COMMENTS:

Reflections on Racism

Rosemary Brown and Cleta Brown

United Nations statistics reveal that Canada's twenty-seven million people constitute the most culturally and racially diverse nation in the world. As Barbara Ward, the noted British economist has observed, Canada has grown into 'the world's first international nation.' What is even more remarkable is that research also reveals that this nation with its population that speaks more than one hundred different languages has been ranked the nation that ensures its people the best quality of life of any nation in the world. Somehow, for over 125 years Canadians have been able to live in comparative peace with each other and with ourselves – a miracle as nations go.

Such impressive accomplishments are, however, of limited relevance in the context of racism and poverty. Maintaining the peace is becoming more difficult. Tensions between peoples that could be ignored by the majority when the communities of culturally and racially different peoples were small and isolated are becoming a problem as these communities expand beyond formerly unacknowledged and perhaps invisible borders. Geographic and cultural ghettos have become too obvious and too explosive to be denied.

The Canadian experience with racial and cultural diversity has been complicated by, among other things, the fact that the country was not called upon to absorb one race or one culture at a time. Since the 1960s the country has had to respond to a multitude of different races and cultures arriving all at the same time, or at least within such short time spans that it was not possible for it to integrate or become accustomed to any one ethnic group or race before another wave of immigrants, then another, arrived. This immigration pattern would have proved difficult for the most non-racist, tolerant, and racially homogeneous nation in the world. Canada, with its three founding nations, is none of these.

It would be erroneous to base Canada's present racial problems on the fact that perhaps errors in immigration policies were made by the the country's European forefathers. Racism, like sexism and other forms of prejudice, is more complicated and has roots that go deeper than political decisions as to how to increase the population of a country.

Although the many hours and years that have been spent on finding a cure for racism have failed to do so, they have certainly resulted in an array of explanations for its presence in virtually every society in the world. Economists have long held that racism, like sexism, is rooted in the need of economies for cheap labour to be exploited in the pursuit of profit. Indeed, from the point of view of economics, theories around class, gender, and race are interwined, are all part of a whole. They explain that the history of enslavement and dehumanization of any group of people can be traced historically to their value as disposable labour. Such enslavement would turn to active hostility if the labour of the group became perceived as a threat to the existing workforce. And the enslavement of the group ceased only when their labour became unprofitable or the need for it no longer necessary. Even then, however, the prejudice and feeling of superiority towards the group would continue.

Psychologists, by contrast, link racism to the individual's deep-seated fear of 'the different,' especially anyone who is different by virtue of race, economic status, or even such minutiae as smell or dress or form of worship.

Many Canadians have clung to the myth that Canada is not really a racist country. The veracity of this myth is often supported by a self-serving distinction between Canada and the United States in their respective treatment, and the differing circumstances, of the visible-minority communities. The fact that Canada has never been a colonizing state is also sometimes cited.

The United States, it is smugly declared, had legalized segregation, had 'race' riots, and has large disintegrating urban ghettos. Canada, by contrast, has a different past and a different present. Only native reserves are a shared phenomenon. In any event, the United States has unquestionably been more violent and repressive towards its minorities. And so, these differences are relied upon to confirm the truth of the myth that Canada is not a racist nation.

We believe that these historical facts are inadequate, if not irrelevant, to a discussion of racism in Canadian society. Clearly, racism is not delimited by the presence or absence of violence or historical laws. These may confirm its presence, but their absence does not confirm racism's absence.

Racism is part of this country's history. We have been ashamed of this fact and have gone to great lengths to deny its existence, but racism has permeated the relationship between white Anglo-Saxon Canadians and non-white Canadians to a lesser or greater degree throughout Canada's entire 125-year existence. One remembers that the nation, from its inception, has continued to struggle with the problem of its own conjoint founding, with a two-nation reality, and that it has tried unsuccessfully for years to ignore the existence of the First Nations peoples.

Canadian history has provided much clear evidence that belies the non-racist myth. The inhumane treatment of Aboriginal peoples by the laws and governments of Canada and the internment of Japanese Canadians during the Second World War are two glaring examples that demonstrate at least the acquiescience of most Canadians in racist activities.

Present history also provides many instances of non-governmental institutionalized racism. Rarely discussed are the old quota systems employed by many professional schools and institutions with respect to the admission of Jewish students. The racial covenants in sales and purchasing contracts in select housing subdivisions, such as the British Properties in West Vancouver, British Columbia, although no longer in force, are example of racism accepted and condoned in Canada's recent past. Indeed, the examples are so numerous that one wonders whether the myth of tolerance sprang from one or two isolated incidents, such as the generosity of Canada's participation with the underground railroad when the United States was a slave state. Thereafter, it appears this myth took on a life of its own, growing and expanding despite later and far more numerous incidents of prejudice and discrimination.

Working on the premise that a study of history serves only to teach, the challenge now facing Canadians is to forestall a future that is a mirror image of the past. There is a school of thought that questions why any attention should be paid to the myth of a non-racist Canada. The short answer is that it is not a harmless myth. The prevalence of the myth has caused direct, extensive, and iniquitous consequences to individuals, groups, and society as a whole. The belief in the myth serves as a down-filled comforter underneath which Canadians can snuggle, hiding their heads and denying the reality. It bears a direct correlation to the lack of vigour on the part of community and government in trying to eradicate the evil of racism. If Canadians do not accept the racism evidenced by our history, we will see no need to make massive resource commitments to end it.

Hence, the really debilitating result of the pervasiveness of the myth has been the frustratingly slow and inadequate response of Canadian governments, institutions, and other organizations to racist laws, policies, and practices. The response, when it does occur, is usually uncoordinated, ad hoc, and without focus or vision.

It must be acknowledged that, for the most part (though government's intentions are usually multifaceted or even obscure beyond vote getting), responses have been well intentioned. But social agencies and individuals too often have been left on their own to respond as best they can to prejudice and discrimination, and to the even more subtle forms of racism.

In general, Canadian governments' responses to historic and increasing racism has been to introduce proscriptive laws, such as human-rights legislation, that outlaw the more blatant manifestations of racism. As well, these governments have implemented various multicultural programs. These legal and educational approaches are laudable initiatives. They represent the minimum requirements from which an effective attack on the daunting edifice of racism may be launched.

To make the equality of races a tangible reality a legal and educational framework is essential. The commitment to, and promotion of, racial equality by governments and by the Canadian people is also essential. Many people tried in vain to convince the drafters and signers of the 1992 Charlottetown Accord of this indispensable element in a constitution for a multicultural nation.

The Charter of Rights and Freedoms is a document, a legal support, to which Canadians can turn with pride; so are many of the provincial human-rights codes. The shortcomings of these legislative measures, however, lie in the scope of their purview and the accessibility of their enforcement mechanisms. The cancellation of the Court Challenges Program (under which economically disadvantaged individuals and groups could exercise their legal rights under the Charter) was in our view a substantial step backwards, because it represented a renewed confirmation by governments of the 'truth' of the myth of a non-racist Canada. One might even argue that the cancellation represents a denial of the purpose of the charter itself. For it should be obvious that the primary role of the Charter is to protect and provide redress to individuals harmed or prejudiced by government entities. The Charter exists to level the playing field, but this presupposes accessibility to it. Similarly, the increasing frequency of attacks upon, and objections to, multicultural policies and programs is a disappointing indication of the continuing prevalence of the myth and its insidious effects.

Chapter 2

A Historical Perspective on Racism

Akwatu Khenti

At the dawn of the twenty-first century, Canadians are confronted with 'racist ghosts' that many believed had been buried in the ashes of Nazi Germany. These ghosts, embodied in groups such as the Heritage Front in Toronto and the Liberty Net group in Vancouver, have been springing up all across Europe and North America and are busy recruiting young and old alike.[1] Their 'racist' platforms are gaining ground as growing numbers of Canadians express public dissatisfaction with 'open' immigration, multiculturalism, employment equity, and anti-racism, with little apparent concern for the historical context within which these policies emerged. Indeed, in response to such sentiment, the federal government has downgraded the official agents of multiculturalism policy and put into place restrictive immigration policies that will make it much more difficult for racial minorities to come to Canada.[2]

Canadian members of racial-minority groups also continue to face high levels of racism in their daily lives.[3] A 1991 report of the Economic Council of Canada revealed that employers are more likely to hire White applicants than members of racial-minority groups (Economic Council of Canada 1991). A study by Henry and Ginzberg (1985) found a range of racist responses to Black job applicants in comparison to a control group of White applicants with equivalent skills and résumés. The authors found that when both telephone and in-person contacts were combined, the overall ratio of discrimination was three to one, that is, whites had three job prospects to every one for blacks with equal qualifications. Even faith communities often fail to serve as a refuge from society's racism. It was reported that a national survey of Anglicans showed that 'while most in the church regard multiculturalism as a positive part of Canada's identity, many minority Anglicans experience coldness, alienation and marginalization in the church.'[4]

Of additional concern is the apparent increase in hate incidents over the last few years. The *Globe and Mail* has identified several 'serious incidents' including the 1991 killing of a Cree by Carney Nerland, head of the Aryan Nations group in Saskatchewan, and the repeated brandishing of guns by neo-Nazis at some of their weekend meetings (Makin 1993: 4). An increase in racist incidents comes as no surprise since economic downturns in Canada have historically been accompanied by growing hostility towards racial minorities. Compounding the cyclical economic difficulties is Canada's massive socio-economic restructuring, which is costing thousands of people their jobs and livelihoods.

The growth in racist incidents comes at a time when few Canadians have managed to come to terms with the long-standing and deeply institutionalized racism that has pervaded Canadian life. The idea that Canada has been spared the racism found in such countries as South Africa, Australia, and the United States of America is popular. For example, few Canadians know about either the destruction of the Beothuk natives in Newfoundland or the enslavement of Africans in New France and Upper Canada from the seventeenth to the nineteenth centuries. Many Canadians expressed surprise and horror at the news that Innu children on Davis Inlet, Labrador, had deliberately tried to kill themselves by sniffing gasoline and that 75 per cent of the adults there had been identified as chronic alcoholics. The reaction of the press was also one of surprise. Reporters appeared genuinely shocked to discover that 'Third World' conditions persisted in spite of long-standing government promises to provide the basic amenities: running water, electricity, and sewage systems.

The persistence of public ignorance begs our consideration of the historical background to our problems. Neither long-standing issues nor current increases in racial tensions will be resolved until the causes of our current concerns are properly understood and put in context.

To strengthen our understanding of the current manifestations of racism and assist in developing effective anti-racist strategies, this chapter chronicles the ways in which racism became embedded in the institutional life of Canadians. The roots of racism will be found in the process of global colonization as well as in the domination and exploitation of racial minorities on Canadian soil. The experiences of three groups – Aboriginal peoples, African Canadians, and Chinese Canadians – will be used to illustrate the various manifestations of racism. Racism will be argued to have emerged as a concept of hierarchical categorization of the 'races,' in line with a structured inequality that was established between 'superior' Whites and 'inferior' Natives, Blacks, and Chinese. The experiences of Aboriginal Canadians illustrate the racism that followed from colonialism; that of Africans, the racism that followed from enslavement; and that of Chinese, the exploitation of cheap labour and the use of immigration as a mechanism of racism.

The chapter reports on systemic manifestations such as governments' efforts to destroy Aboriginal culture, the legal acceptance of the enslavement of African Canadians and certain Natives, the restriction of African Canadian children's access to schools, the denial or removal of the citizenship rights of Chinese Canadians, the restrictions on immigration, and the limits on employment opportunities and occupational competition with which racial minorities have had to contend. The chapter also explores the efforts of racial minorities to combat racism and concludes by arguing that because racism has permeated so deeply into the hearts and minds of Canadians over the last four centuries, anti-racism strategies must be based on the historical Canadian patterns of racism if they are to be effective.

THE CONCEPT OF RACE

During the past two centuries race has gradually emerged as the major category used to explain physical differences between groups in different geographical and environmental zones. The ancient and medieval explanation of physical, or what would today be called racial, differences emphasized one's nearness to the sun. These explanations did not imply fixed biological boundaries between 'racial groups' and a distinction among racial (phenotypical or physical) types, as the term implies today. The dominant religious idea in the West of all humanity descending from Adam probably precluded the drawing of biological boundaries within the human family. Thus, for the first three centuries of contact between the 'Old' and 'New' worlds, religious belief determined race distinctions. 'Natives were outside the pale of humanity, but this was regarded as a consequence of the fact that they were not Christians, not of the fact that they belonged to the darker races' (Benedict 1983: 115).

The modern understanding of race as a concept that hierarchically distinguishes and orders human groups on the basis of biological differences only solidified late in the nineteenth century. As Benton and

Howard have noted: 'The career of the race concept begins in obscurity, for experts dispute whether the word derives from an Arabic, a Latin, or a German source. The first recorded use in English of the word "race" was in a poem by William Dunbar in 1508 ... During the next three centuries the word was used with growing frequency in a literary sense as denoting simply a class of persons or even things ... In the nineteenth, and increasingly in the twentieth century, this loose usage began to give way and the word came to signify groups that were distinguished biologically' (1975: 13).

The catalyst that brought about the acceptance of race as a 'biological category' developed during the late eighteenth and nineteenth centuries. During this period, a host of evidence from diverse fields, such as anatomy, geology, and zoology, was compiled in efforts to explain the physical variety of humanity. The key 'scholars' were all of European origin and included such 'eminent' scholars as Johann Friedrick Blumenbach, the French anatomist George Cuvier, S.G. Morton, Charles Hamilton Smith, and Count Joseph Arthur de Gobineau. Whereas colour and other physical attributes were initially the major distinguishing characteristics of race, these scholars began to utilize certain pseudo-scientific data such as cranial measurements (Benedict 1983).

The physical characteristics of choice would vary from racial scientist to racial scientist: some emphasized skin colour, others cephalic index or cranial measurements. The tenuous nature of such choices becomes apparent when one considers that the categories were also used to divide the present 'White' populations of Europe. For instance, the famous essayist Gobineau argued, on the basis of his categories, that the Alpines (a significant part of the French population) were of Yellow extraction while the Mediterraneans (the Greeks, Spanish, and Portuguese) were of Black extraction. The only true Whites, according to Gobineau, were the Nordics (Benedict 1983: 115). In some cases, scholars of race based their racial divisions on purely cultural characteristics such as language. The development of the Aryan race was one such case. Indeed, the statement of one of the foremost nineteenth-century experts on the Aryans, Max Muller, is very revealing both of the extent to which race scientists were prepared to ignore facts in their efforts to establish a superior Aryan race and of the frustration of those who recognized the emptiness of their claims: 'I have declared again and again ... that when I say Aryas (Aryan) I mean neither blood nor bones nor hair nor skill; I mean simply those who spoke an Aryan language. When

I speak of them, I commit myself to no anatomical characteristics. To me an ethnologist who speaks of Aryan race, Aryan blood, Aryan eyes and hair, is as great a sinner as a linguist who speaks of a dolicocephalic (narrow-headed) dictionary or a bracycephalic (broadheaded) grammar' (Benedict 1983: 9).

Common to all racial categories was their descending order of classification from the European (White) to the African (Black), with the Asian (Yellow) and Aboriginal (Red) people somewhere in-between (Bernal 1987: 240). As a result of the pre-eminence of Darwinism, it also became an accepted canon that Europeans, Asians, Aboriginals, and Africans were at different stages of evolution, with Europeans at the top of the evolutionary ladder. Those scientists who strived to prove that a hierarchy of races existed also employed new Darwinist ideas such as the 'survival of the fittest.'[5] Such ideas gave great comfort to racists because of the implication that Africans and Aboriginal Americans would eventually disappear on account of natural selection (Franklin 1991: 45–6). One prominent British exponent of such ideas, Thomas Huxley, wrote: 'No rational man, cognizant of the facts, could deny that the Negro was inherently inferior. Consequently, it is simply incredible "to believe that" he will be able to compete successfully with his bigger brained and smaller jawed rival, in a context which is to be carried on by thoughts and not by bites' (see Franklin 1991: 45).

As a result of Darwin's work, however, physical characteristics could no longer be utilized to distinguish 'races.' Darwin established that sterility, that is, the production of sterile offspring, was the criterion that distinguished species. As Benedict has aptly described: 'Nothing was more obvious than the fact that fertile children were born from the mating of even the most extreme type of the White race with the most extreme type of the Negro or Mongolian ... The idea of species, however, underlay all the thinking of the period, and if human varieties could not be separated one from another by mutual sterility, the criteria must be found in some physical characteristics' (Benedict 1983: 22).

Through no coincidence, the dominant scientific notion about race that emerged by the late nineteenth to early twentieth century held that biological and cultural diversity was the result of basic genetic differences between racial groups. A shift in emphasis also took place, away from the extrapolation of racial inferiority or superiority on the basis of physical or phenotypical characteristics to a focus on genetics and the intelligence of members of different racial groups. As a result, intelligence testing came into vogue among 'race' scientists and became firmly entrenched by the 1920s. Popular acceptance occurred in spite of the problems of defining 'intelligence' – a social construct with no concrete physical existence – and the cultural, class, and gender biases of so-called intelligence or IQ tests (which bring into question their validity as measures of intelligence however intelligence is defined).

To a large extent, this is the form of theorizing that continues to be pervasive in the 1990s. Indeed, it is the main premise of such works as Richard Herrnstein and Charles Murray's *The Bell Curve: Intelligence and Class Structure in American Life* (1994). That many still believe that intelligence differences can be established between the 'races' on the basis of genes or biology, in spite of scientific evidence to the contrary, reinforces the notion of racism as a belief system or ideology.[6] This belief continues even though there is ample evidence that intelligence testing is fraught with deficiencies. Indeed, it has, at different times, identified and labelled all kinds of people as deficient in intelligence, people who later excelled and became successful. For instance, at one time, on the basis of the Stanford-Binet intelligence tests, it was concluded that '83% of the Jews, 80% of the Hungarians, 79% of the Italians and 87% of the Russians were feeble minded' (Franklin 1991: 47).

Clearly, then, racist beliefs have had less to do with objective truths than with subjective constructs. As DuBois explained: 'Every device of science was used: evolution was made to prove that Negroes and Asiatics were less developed human beings than whites; history was so written as to make all civilization the development of white people; economics was so taught as to make all wealth due mainly to the technical accomplishment of white folks supplemented only by the brute toil of colored peoples; brain weights and intelligence tests were used and distorted to prove the superiority of white folks' (1985: 37).

The Global Context

The race research, and racist conclusions drawn, were not undertaken in a global vacuum. The expanding colonization of the Americas in the mid-seventeenth century generated an ideological need to rationalize efforts to eradicate many Native American peoples, as well as exploit enslaved African labour. 'In tropical countries Europeans wanted cheap labour and markets and slaves; in temperate countries they wanted the land to occupy as settlers. Wherever they went, Europeans were bent on extirpating the native religions. The natives were regarded as outside the pale of humanity, without religion, law or morals. Bounties were placed on their heads, and they could be freely kidnapped or massacred' (Benedict 1983: 106–7).

During these early years, it appears that Europe was confronted with a major moral dilemma: how to couple the growing belief in personal liberty and the equality of all men before God with the inhumane treatment of Aboriginal and African peoples. The Spanish may have murdered some 10 million Aboriginal Americans by the end of the eighteenth century. Unknown millions of West Africans were also decimated by the slave trades of the Portuguese, Dutch, and British, which lasted through to the early nineteenth century (Du Bois 1985: 30–1). This moral dilemma was resolved by disparaging dogmatically these peoples. One of the first explicit ideological defences was provided by the late-seventeenth-century philosopher John Locke, who argued that Christian assaults upon 'heathen' Africans and Americans were just because these people were occupying land to which they were not entitled. According to Locke, entitlement derived from cultivation only and indigenous (continental) Americans and Africans were not seen to be cultivators (Bernal 1987: 202–3). This argument was utilized quite widely to justify the expropriation of Aboriginal land. Such beliefs were so tenacious that it was only recently, in 1972, that Aboriginal people in Canada won legal recognition of the concept of Aboriginal title to land.

The anthropologist Ashley Montagu has pointed out how, as a result of the new patterns of servitude, new justifications were needed to rationalize the unequal social order. These new rationalizations were subsequently developed when 'the alleged inborn differences between peoples were erected into the doctrine of racism ... a melange of rationalizations calculated to prove that the Negro was created with articulate speech and hands so that he might be of service to his master the white man' (Drake 1987: 20–1).

Racist ideology matured during the nineteenth century as a direct result of expanding European colonization of the world. By century's end, Europe had attained near complete domination of the 'Coloured World.' This domination was reflected in the political power of direct rule, as with colonies, or in indirect economic power backed by military pressure, as in Central and South America (Du Bois 1987: 26–7). The Canadian experience is reflective of this overall pattern of domination.

Dogmatic theories about race and racial hierarchies, which were the intellectual vogue of Europe and the United States, would gain tremendous currency in Canada from the earliest days of the nation. They would find receptive ground because slavery and effective domination of Aboriginals required structured inequality between 'superior' Europeans and 'inferior' Aboriginals, Africans, and Asians. Moreover, in restricting the political and civil rights of racial-minority groups, the effective result would inevitably be to curtail the groups' ability to generate greater income or advantage from the society. The direct consequence would be the impoverishment of racial minorities and a different labour price for similarly skilled members of different racial groups. This has been described most poignantly by Du Bois: 'Extreme poverty in colonies was a main cause of wealth and luxury in Europe. The results of this poverty were disease, ignorance, and crime. Yet these had to be represented as natural characteristics of backward peoples. Education for colonial people must inevitably mean unrest and revolt; education, therefore, had to be limited and used to inculcate obedience and servility lest the whole colonial system be overthrown' (1985: 37).

HOME-GROWN RACISM

Canada's Colonial Legacy: The Case of Aboriginal People

In Canada, the need to dominate the Aboriginal people provided the stimulus that eventually led to race being employed as a rationale for oppression. The establishment of the fur trade on the shores of Hudson Bay during the seventeenth century generated labour demands that could only be met by the Native population. 'To tap the fur resources of America, the merchants from across the seas could not sweep aside the Indians with the sword and loot secret places of the continent. Indians were necessary to the fur trade and their skill had to be utilized' (Bourgeault 1991: 134). Aboriginal people were not willing, however, to make fundamental lifestyle changes in order to satisfy European demand. They were intent on trading but only in so far as they were able to acquire trade goods that they wanted (Rich 1991: 163). In order to increase Native production and the exchange of fur, therefore, European traders set about the task of altering traditional Aborginal lifestyles. In this deliberate way, European trade was made to play a greater role in the socioeconomic life of Aboriginal people.

A variety of strategies were tried, but eventually the approach of giving away liquor was used, with all the destructive consequences for Aboriginal life that alcoholism would entail (Rich 1991: 175). The efforts of the European fur traders eventually generated the fur-trade society, in which there prevailed a social division of labour, with the 'Indian as a primary producer and the European as a wage labourer' (Bourgeault 1991: 141). In this system, the economic opportunities of wage labour were largely denied to Aboriginals so as to maintain them in the important role as procurers of the fur. The system, however, was not only economically asymmetrical. The correspondence of the traders revealed racist beliefs. For instance, in remarks forwarded by British merchants to their employees in Canada, it is stated: 'Wee do strictly enjoyn you to have publish prayers and readings of the scriptures ... that wee who profess to be Christians may not appear more barbarous than the poor heathens themselves who have not been instructed in the knowledge of the true God' (Bourgeault 1991: 141).

By the late eighteenth and early nineteenth century European efforts to fully incorporate the Aboriginal people into the fur trade were largely successful. During this period, European Canadians had also begun expending considerable energies upon developing ways of 'helping the Indian.' The main idea that had arisen amongst White people, many of whom were well meaning, was that the 'Indians' were incapable of dealing with persons of European ancestry without being exploited. Of course, this lesson had necessarily been extrapolated from the destruction being inflicted upon Aboriginal peoples by White people. European Canadians thus concluded that Natives were in need of White paternal guidance and protection. Governmental authorities assumed the responsibility for 'protecting' the Natives. By 1815 it became the accepted opinion that Native people needed to be civilized and should be encouraged to settle on reserves, where they could be equipped to cope with European civilization. More particularly, a 'reserve system, which was to be the keystone of Canada's Indian policy, was conceived as a social laboratory, where the Indian could be prepared for coping with the European' (Tobias 1991: 128).

By the 1850s, a new strain of racist thought had emerged: the 'Indian' would no longer be prepared to deal with the White man, but would be made into one. Such a belief was institutionalized in the Upper Canadian Act of 1857 – an act to encourage the gradual civilization of the Indians in this province and to amend the laws respecting Indians. The consequences of this act have been succinctly noted by Tobias:

After stipulating in the preamble that the measure was designed to encourage civilization of the Indian, remove all legal distinctions between Indians and other Canadians and integrate them fully into Canadian society, the legislation proceeded to define who was an Indian and then to state that such a person could not be accorded the rights and privileges accorded to European Canadians until the Indian could prove that he could read and write either the French or English language, was free of debt, and of good moral character ... Thus, the legislation to remove all legal distinctions between Indians and Euro-Canadians actually established them. (1991: 130)

The Gradual Civilization Act of 1857 represented the core of an overall offensive to transform Aboriginal people into citizens of British North America and to have them repudiate their 'negative' Native lifestyles. The premise of the act was that acceptance of private property (individual tenure) and enfranchisement would bring the Indian closer to civilization (Milloy 1991: 147). The racism that underlay such acts can be gleaned from statements such as those of the Superintendent General, David Laird, who proclaimed that it was his duty to 'prepare him [sic, the Indian] for a higher civilization by encouraging him to assume the privileges and responsibilities of full citizenship' (Milloy 1991: 152).

Enfranchising Aboriginals out of Their 'Real Political Rights'

By 1869 the Canadian government, with its Act for the Gradual Enfranchisement of the Indians, had once again defined for Aboriginal people their place. This act reflected the prevailing White belief that traditional forms of Aboriginal government were inferior and uncivilized. Aboriginals could elect chiefs and councillors, but only at a time and place and in a manner that was suitable to the Superintendent General of Indian Affairs. Government agencies could also remove any elected Native official for dishonesty, intemperance, or immorality, which again fell to definition by non-Natives (Milloy 1991: 151).

In addition to determining the nature of Aboriginal government, Canadian legislators also sought to define an 'Indian' (Miller 1991: 325). They also unsuccessfully sought to bribe Aboriginals into becoming 'regular' Canadians with allotments of individual plots of reserve land as well as the federal vote, which was withdrawn once the government realized that Aboriginals were not enticed by such offers. The ultimate goal of the Canadian government has been to destroy the reserves over time as well as to eradicate the Native way of life by undermining the collective basis of Native organization and self-government (Miller 1991a: 326).

Assimilation Efforts

The Canadian government, and its Indian Department, resorted to the banning of Aboriginal practices in its efforts to assimilate Aboriginal people. Officials believed that Native rituals and dances sustained pagan beliefs as well as economic practices that were antithetical to private property. The government banned the Sun Dance, Potlaches, and Give Away ceremonials (Tobias 1991: 135). It also 're-educated' Aboriginal children as a central part of its assimilation strategy. It established residential and industrial schools away from reserves so that Native children could be removed from the 'uncivilized environment and traditions' of Aboriginal communities (Miller 1991a: 326).

The goals of these schools were to inculcate Western values – Christianity, individualism, and acquisitiveness – in Aboriginal children (Miller 1991a: 332). The children in attendance at these schools were not allowed to converse in their Native languages or maintain and practise traditional rituals or celebrations. They had their hair cut and were dressed like Europeans. The residential schools represented the ultimate misuse of education: it was a tool of destruction rather than enlightenment. The Canadian authorities also established a system whereby Aboriginals in Western Canada needed a signed pass to leave the reserve (ibid.: 326). This system predated the pass system that apartheid South Africa institutionalized to restrict the movement of its Aboriginal population.

Current Dilemmas

Aboriginal people found their situation becoming more precarious after the Second World War, largely because many resources needed by the dominant society were found on their land. For instance, the land of the Woodland Cree of Saskatchewan had uranium deposits. Many development projects, like the U.S. Alaskan highway, could only proceed by way of their reserves. The pattern of European domination persisted as 'most of Canada's native peoples who were in the path of development found that they were ignored in the process of going after the resources and left out of the division of the proceeds of their sale' (Miller 1991b: 407). The communities of the Lubicon of central Alberta and the Cree of north-central Saskatchewan were two groups that were devastated in this manner.

Government bureaucrats continue to alter the destiny of Aboriginal people with little consideration for either the impact of their actions or whether they have a right to make profound life-changing decisions for an entire population of people. An example of such decision making was the 1964 federal-government-directed move of the Ojibwa of Grassy Narrows in northern Ontario to a new reserve on the English-Wabigoon river system that was polluted with mercury (Miller 1991b: 407).

CANADA'S LEGACY OF ENSLAVEMENT: THE CASE OF AFRICANS

White society institutionalized the enslavement of both Aboriginals and Africans from the seventeenth to the nineteenth centuries. Although Africans would eventually become the predominant victims of this institution, by the late eighteenth century Aboriginal people known as 'Panis' were also enslaved. In 1709, an ordinance was read by the intendant of New France, Jacques Raudot, which declared that 'all the panis and Negroes who have been purchased and who will be purchased, shall be the property of those who have purchased them and will be their slaves' (Winks 1971: 6). This idea of Black people and Aboriginal Canadians as 'mere property' was maintained in the 47th article of the Capitulation of Montreal, which stipulated that French slave-owners would not lose their 'Black and Indian property' under British rule (Bertley 1977: 35).

Before the American War of Independence, the majority of Black people in Canada were enslaved. Those who endured slave status in Canada (a few right up to the abolishment of slavery in 1834) bore no 'human' or 'citizenship' rights for the duration of their enslavement in Canada from 1628 to 1834. As Winks has reported: 'If owners appeared to have used their slaves well, they used them nonetheless, for the slaves continued to die young, as parish records show, and to yearn for freedom, as advertisements for runaways demonstrate. Most wills treated them purely as property, together with furniture, cattle, and land' (1971: 53). It was this pre-eminent socio-economic position that sustained images of Black people as innately suited for service deep in the consciousness of White Canadians.

When 4,000 free Black Loyalists came up to Canada between 1776 and 1783 (largely to the Maritimes and Upper Canada) they found few opportunities for them outside of the most menial labouring positions. Indeed, these free Black people were compelled to do road work for life-sustaining provisions which were owed to them and almost two-thirds never received their share of allotted land. Those Black Loyalists who received any of the land promised to them usually ended up with limited acreage of the poorest land. As a result of deliberate omissions and racist treatment, Black people found themselves with little choice but to accept employment at wages almost one quarter that paid to White labourers. Some were even compelled by circumstances to sell themselves back into bondage. (ibid.: 47)

It is notable that Canada's first race riot occurred in the 1780s, when disbanded White soldiers rampaged through the Black section of Shelburne, Nova Scotia, in response to a perception of unfair Black labour practices. The soldiers, compelled to compete for jobs with Black workers while they waited for their allotment of lands (allotments denied to most Black Loyalists), believed that Black people had driven down the wages unfairly. The perceptions and attitudes of these soldiers represented the establishment of a pattern of occupational limits and wage limitations for Black people. The rise of racist sentiment and actions would be repeated whenever White workers were compelled by economic hardship to compete with Black workers or other racial minorities for jobs that they would otherwise not do.

Immigration Restrictions

In periods of economic decline, the treatment of Blacks grew increasingly harsh and immigration restrictions became much tighter. In Nova Scotia around 1815, as a result of abundant (and unemployed) White labour, the Nova Scotia government tried unsuccessfully to end Black entry into the province on the grounds that the province had enough 'labourers and servants' (Walker 1984: 9). In the late 1840s, after several decades during which Black workers had contributed significantly to road construction and land clearance in Nova Scotia and Ontario, the welcome mat also began to be withdrawn as poor Irish immigrants started to compete for jobs held by Black workers. As a direct consequence of the availability of white labour, Black people faced increasing hostility and resentment across Canada (Walker 1980: 86, 102). As the historian Robin Winks has noted: 'If welcome to fell trees, to lay roads, to cut ties, and to introduce tobacco culture in the 1820s and 1830s, the Negro was needed less in the 1840s, when the Irish – willing to work at equally menial and physically demanding tasks and less likely to raise difficult social questions – began to arrive in large numbers' (1971: 144).

Hostility towards Black people, however, existed even when economic conditions did not compel White workers into menial occupations. In the early-twentieth-century wheat production boom, amid an increasing demand for labour, approximately 1300 African Americans moved to Saskatchewan and Alberta. They did so in response to a Canadian recruitment campaign to attract new migrants, but they received a hostile welcome. Ottawa received several public petitions and municipal resolutions from the prairie provinces calling for the banning of further Black migration into Canada as well as the legal segregation of Blacks already there (Bertley 1977: 111–14).

In response to the public pressure, the Canadian government conducted a somewhat covert campaign to end Black immigration into Canada. Government agents were sent to the southern American states to discourage Black farmers from migrating to Canada. Immigration officials at the border were encouraged to use every letter of the law (including medical and financial requirements) to deny Black migrants entry into Canada. These efforts proved to be very successful, for by 1912 few Black persons were entering Canada (Walker 1984: 15).

The Black refugees of the War of 1812, as well as fugitives running away from enslavement and increasing repression during the early nineteenth century, found that they were expected to fill largely servile positions at low rates of remuneration. During the 1850s and 1860s, Black people were faced with consistent denials of access to public facilities. They were confined to such occupations as being waiters, porters, janitors, barbers, laundresses, domestic servants, and labourers (Walker 1980: 132). In many cases they found themselves confined to poverty and forced by circumstances to rely upon government relief or charity to survive. This African Canadian experience was rooted in the earlier era of enslavement. A direct result of this nineteenth-century ordeal was a reinforcement of the image of African Canadians as 'natural' servants. As well, new stereotypes of Black people as helpless and shiftless emerged. By the early twentieth century new racist images had developed constructing Blacks as fun-loving, superstitious, and sexually aggressive (Walker 1984: 10, 14). Winks concluded:

By the twentieth century, then, a once vague mythology about what the Negro could and could not do had taken on a more exact form. Language, literature, the theatre, science, and even history had informed generations of Canadians of the Negro's inability to adapt to the north, of his love of pleasure, of his sexual appetites, his unreliability, laziness, and odor. There were enough of these people in Canada without adding to the problem ... If Canadians did not wish to follow the Americans in giving segregation the force of law, or if Canadians did not want Black ghettoes to develop in their cities ... they would be well-advised to block the problem at its source; the border. (1971: 298)

Denial of Citizenship Rights

The citizenship rights of the free Black Loyalists, refugees, and fugitives were also severely circumscribed. Black arrivals in the late eighteenth and nineteenth centuries were not free to live wherever they wanted nor were most of their children able to attend the same schools as White children. The few churches and schools that allowed Black people in kept them in separate sections of the church (referred to as 'Nigger Heaven') or in designated rooms or desks in the classroom. The denial of equal access to public or common schools became legally enshrined in several provincial education acts through the nineteenth century – such as Ontario's Common School Act of 1850. Black people also found opposition to their voting, sitting on juries, and enjoying the use of public facilities (such as steamers).

Although African Canadians were never exempt from paying taxes, they were consistently denied access to public recreational facilities such as pools, skating rinks, and theatres. That such restrictions were considered acceptable is demonstrated by the 1919 case involving Loew's Theatre in Montreal, whose practice of confining Black patrons to balcony seats was ruled to be perfectly legal (Greaves 1930: 57, 62–3).

Even when responding to their citizenship calls, Blacks were treated in a demeaning and stereotypical manner. During the First World War, many (if not most) Black volunteers were actually turned away because of a racist stereotype that they would be a disruptive influence in addition to being poor soldiers. Moreover, the few that were accepted (especially the members of a special battalion called the Nova Scotia No. 2 Construction Battalion) were destined to provide support services to White soldiers. In addition, Black soldiers in uniform were physically attacked by their White colleagues in both Europe and Canada. White Canadians soldiers believed that the colour of the Black soldiers was a disservice to the uniform (Walker 1980: 96).

Canadian Prime Minister Sir Robert Borden made comments that reveal the deep strain of racism in Canada. He noted that uniting with the West Indies would strengthen Canadians' sense of responsibility because they would have to administer areas that were 'largely inhabited by backward races.' T.B. Macaulay further observed, some time later, that to allow 'the heterogeneous and unassimilated population of [British Guiana] equal votes with the people of Ontario in controlling the destinies of Canada would strain our faith in democracy' (see Winks 1971: 320).

CANADA'S LEGACY OF LEGISLATED INEQUALITY: THE CASE OF THE CHINESE

Chinese people began to arrive in Canada from about 1858, with the largest influx occurring between 1881 and 1885.[7] Many migrants initially came to work in the mines during British Columbia's gold rush in the Fraser Valley, but the majority eventually found work on the construction of the Canadian Pacific Railway. They were recruited directly to that work. During this period the Canadian Pacific Railway imported 15,000 indentured Chinese labourers for railway work (Creese 1991: 34).

The Chinese workers faced gross exploitation because many were bound to collective contracts that allowed recruiting companies to receive their pay while assuming responsibility for their needs. These workers were segregated from other workers, worked long hours, and were made to pay the contractors for needs that had barely been attended to. In addition, they were controlled and disciplined by these contractors. This kind of group exploitation was also used in the canneries of British Columbia.

The Chinese were confined to menial jobs where White labour was not immediately available. People of Chinese origin could only secure work at unskilled labour, in the farming, lumber, and fish canning sectors, or in such service roles as domestics, grocers, launderers, and tailors (Creese 1991: 34). By 1931 little had changed: the majority of Chinese men, 80 per cent, worked in the agriculture, service, and unskilled-labour sectors, in comparison with only 43 per cent of the overall male labour force of British Columbia (ibid.). The extent of the exploitative conditions that confronted them was reflected in their destitute state, which was vividly described in a provincial-government report of 1885 (Li 1988: 18).

Chinese workers also found that they received less pay than their fellow White colleagues for the same work. Indeed, it has been estimated that Chinese labourers earned on average one-third of the wages of White workers for similar work (Creese 1991: 34). In one case, the provincial government put into place a minimum wage that was higher than the rate of pay for Chinese workers in the lumber industry, simply to attract more White workers and reduce the numbers of Chinese in the market (ibid.: 33). As Creese has noted, 'For the most part, the white labour movement excluded Asians from their trade unions, boycotted businesses employing Asians, pressed for legislation to protect jobs for white men, and were at the forefront of the movement to end further Asian immigration' (ibid.: 36).

Immigration Restrictions

Treatment of the Chinese migrants appeared to depend, as it had for the Black migrants, upon an economic need for unskilled labour. More particularly, it depended upon the availability of work that White workers did not want. As a chief justice commented in the late nineteenth century: 'I do not see how people would get on here at all without Chinamen. They do, and do well, what white women cannot do, and do what white men will not do' (Li 1988: 24).

When the Chinese began arriving in the 1860s, few were opposed to their presence. The welcome mat was extended primarily because their labour was needed in such sectors as mining, railroad construction, forestry, and canning (Li 1988: 35). Once an economic downturn set in, however, that welcome mat was withdrawn. When the Canadian Pacific Railway was completed in 1875, Chinese labourers were confronted by federal-government efforts to restrict their entry into Canada.[8] During that period, Chinese people were prevented from voting in provincial or municipal elections. In 1879 a petition was presented to the Dominion House, with the signatures of 1500 British Columbia workers, that sought to secure the exclusion of Chinese workers from several provincial industries. Even Sir John A. Macdonald, Canada's distinguished Father of Confederation, expressed the view that 'a Mongolian or Chinese population in our country ... would not be a wholesome element for this country' (see Barrett 1987: 316).

Denial of Citizenship Rights

Notably, several important professions such as law and pharmacy, as well as logging work and securing liquor licences, were effectively denied to the Chinese through legislation. The fact that most Chinese employees were controlled by labour contractors rather than employed as individuals also points to the tremendous disdain for the individual rights of Chinese workers. In 1885 the federal government passed an

Anti-Chinese Bill that violated the basic citizenship rights of the Chinese. It imposed a head tax of $50 upon all immigrants of Chinese origin. By 1900 the head tax was increased to $100, and in 1903 to $500 (Li 1988: 29-30). The Chinese Immigration Act of 1923 would prevent Chinese immigrants from coming to Canada for almost a quarter-century. Chinese people also lost the right to vote until after the Second World War (ibid.: 2). Not surprisingly, it became difficult, if not impossible, for most Chinese to become naturalized citizens. Indeed, between 1915 and 1930 only 349 Chinese managed to become naturalized citizens.[9]

The experience of Chinese workers reflected a major characteristic of racism: the tendency to treat individuals on the basis of their group identification whenever negative issues or costs were involved. By contrast, when positive things were attributed to minority individuals, they would be seen as exceptions. In this way, contradictions between belief and practices – which are bound to happen with individual interactions – were minimized and racist views could be maintained in spite of contradictory evidence.

The Canadian government's treatment of the Chinese was never unrelated to the politics of global domination. It is notable that Chinese people were not generally disparaged during the seventeenth and eighteenth centuries when they maintained autonomy in their country and were not the object of colonial designs. They were usually described by seventeenth- and eighteenth-century writers as being of 'a distinct but not necessarily inferior race.' However, by the mid-nineteenth century, with the onset of the Opium Wars with Great Britain, the Chinese people began to be cast as 'racially contemptible' (Bernal 1989: 279). The structured inequality in Canadian society, coupled with the colonial efforts in China, undoubtedly fuelled the intensifying racist attitudes in Canada towards the Chinese. Thus it was that Chinese people could, in the eyes of many if not most Canadians, legitimately be treated with the utmost disdain. Li has pointed out the fact that during royal commission hearings of 1885 and 1902 'the Chinese were commonly equated with no more than a piece of machinery or a horse, something with use value, to be maintained when other labor power was not available' (Li 1988: 250).

No Limit to the Number of Victims

In fact, the racism directed at Aboriginals, African Canadians, and Chinese Canadians was never confined to these groups. For instance, South Asians were also invited to work on the railways and then confronted with similar anti-Asian hostility once their assignments had been completed. And as Matas points out in chapter 4, the federal government introduced a 'continuous passage' rule in 1908 that made it practically impossible for East Indians to get to Canada (except by proving that their voyage to Canada was non-stop and direct from India). Jews fleeing from the Nazi Holocaust were also denied entry into Canada during the Second World War at their most vulnerable hour of need. Jewish Canadians also faced denial of access to services, as well as specific occupations and professions and certain public facilities during the 1930s and 1940s. One of the most horrific acts of structural racism, undoubtedly, was the detainment of Japanese Canadians during the Second World War (from 1942–7), depriving them of their property and the most basic of human rights. Families were separated, some were encouraged to accept deportations, and parts of the country (British Columbia) were made off-limits to people of Japanese origin.

CHALLENGING THEIR SITUATION: THE ROOTS OF ANTI-RACISM

Fighting Back

Aboriginal people consistently resisted the various racist measures described earlier. Their responses included outright rejection of the various legislated agendas. They also fought legal challenges, strived to maintain their cultural traditions – especially their dances and potlaches – by covert means, and openly defied some of the restrictions. Many people refused to adhere to travel restrictions imposed upon them. Several tribal councils rejected the subdivision of their reserve. Indeed, as Milloy has pointed out: 'A general Indian position emerged in the 1860s. Councils across the colony remained pre-development. They wanted education and agricultural and resource development but would not participate in a system designed, as an Oneida petition said, to "separate our people." Civilization, which they might define as the revitalization of their traditional culture within an agricultural context, they would have; assimilation, the total abandonment of their culture, they would not' (1991: 149).

Aboriginals also fought to prevent the destruction of the land as well as to secure Aboriginal title. One method of advocacy was legal arbitration. Their legal efforts brought about court recognition of Aboriginal title. In 1972, the Cree and Inuit of northern Quebec secured court recognition of Aboriginal title[10] for the first time, which represented a tangible as well as a symbolic rebuff to centuries of racism built on the extrapolations of those such as John Locke. Aboriginal title was a defeat for the racist rationale that 'discovery' or intensive agricultural use was superior to Aboriginal occupation of an area from time immemorial. This Lockean notion had served to justify the deprivation of many Native peoples of their essential land base. As a direct result of that deprivation Aboriginal people continued to suffer unemployment rates of up to 90 per cent on many reserves and the proportion of Natives living 'above' the poverty line had never been more than 40 per cent (Frideres 1990: 110).

Although Aboriginal children still fare much worse than the national average, there has been a dramatic increase in the number of children acquiring an education since 1967: graduates rose from some 500 students in 1967 to 15,000 in 1989. This increase has been directly attributed to the recent efforts to develop relevant education and to the direct role that Aboriginal people have played in the process for the first time (Frideres 1990: 109).

Despite its pervasiveness African Canadians have also consistently fought against oppression. Their efforts to acquire their freedom began with running away from enslavement in the eighteenth and nineteenth centuries, and included fighting in court for freedom, voting rights, eligibility for jury duty, and access to common schools. They organized strikes and walk-outs to gain civil rights as early as the nineteenth century. In Upper Canada they published their own newspapers, the *Provincial Freeman* and the *Voice of the Fugitive*, which consistently defended the integrity and image of Black people against racist attack. They also organized self-help associations such as the True Band Society in Ontario and the chapters of the Universal Negro Improvement Association across Canada. It was not until the middle of the twentieth century, however, that African Canadians began to make tremendous strides. For instance, during the Second World War, Black residents of Toronto compelled the National Selective Service to end discrimination against Blacks in essential industries. Railway workers, under the mantle of the Brotherhood of Sleeping Car Porters, also won access to senior positions within the railway by the 1950s. This victory was the result of a battle that lasted decades. Black people have led protests against immigration restrictions, denial of service in restaurants, and employment discrimination right up to the present time (Walker 1980), in particular when even the authorities of the state could not be counted upon to help. For instance, in October 1937, an African Canadian family who insisted upon purchasing a home in Trenton, Nova Scotia, had to witness the destruction of their house and property while the RCMP stood by and the mayor refused to order them to prevent the destruction (Winks 1971: 419). It was their stoic determination to keep on struggling that emboldened others to come to their assistance.

Chinese Canadians also resisted exploitative labour conditions – low wages, long hours, and the contract labour system – by organizing themselves as workers. About twenty-four times between 1921 and 1931, hundreds of Chinese workers went on strike for better working conditions. During this period, they formed several unions: the Chinese Canadian Labour Union, the Chinese Shingle Workers' Union, the Chinese Cooks' Union and the Chinese Restaurant Workers' Union. The Chinese shingle workers fought a long-standing battle for equity in their industry and won wage increases that benefited both Asians and White Canadians. Chinese people also fought injustices in other arenas: as, for instance, when Chinese vegetable hawkers struck to protest against an increase in their licensing fee or when fellow factory workers demonstrated solidarity with a Chinese worker who was assaulted by a White foreman in a Vancouver factory by walking out (Creese 1991: 37–40). As Creese has pointed out: 'Chinese workers were not absent from the history of working class confrontation in British Columbia, although they remain largely absent from the annals of history' (ibid.: 44).

In the 1990s, awareness of the historic roots of 'White Privilege' and of the need for mechanisms to ensure racial equity is evident in the language of most policy makers; rarely, however, will evidence of such commitment be found in concrete changes (for example, in hiring patterns). For instance, although many government ministries and boards of education have adopted race-relations policies, there are few significant changes to indicate that such policies are making a meaningful difference in the lives of racial minorities. Aboriginal and African Canadian student alienation and drop-out rates in schools do not appear to have markedly declined in spite of the widespread adoption of race-relations policies. There is still a dramatic lack of meaningful racial representation among fire-fighters, police, teachers, human service workers, and the staff of government bureaucracies.

CONCLUSION AND IMPLICATIONS

The colonial experiences of Aboriginal people remain the most horrific manifestation of structural racism in this country. The experiences of

African and Chinese Canadians illustrate further the manner and extent to which racism became deeply imbedded in Canadian life through our institutionalization of slavery as well as the exploitation of immigrant workers. This discussion also points out the continual resistance of racial minorities to the racism and discrimination that confronts them.

The ideology of racism has deeply permeated the hearts and minds of Canadians – on account of once-perceived economic needs and the subsequent systemic/institutional efforts to dominate and exploit racial minorities over the past four centuries. To address this situation, anti-racism strategies must be implemented in all sectors of our society, and must be based on a knowledge of Canadian patterns of racism if they are to be effective. Canada functioned as a colonial power vis-à-vis its Aboriginal inhabitants. Canada's early period of slavery, like that of Europe and the United States, set the stage for the social confinement of Africans to servile roles. The treatment of Chinese Canadians is a vivid illustration of how legislated racism manifested itself in Canada. Canada's treatment of African and Chinese migrants illustrates that xenophobia here was fully in sync with the xenophobia institutionalized by other colonial powers.

We can never be complacent about the rising tide of racism outside our borders. Attitudes and actions in Canada have always been related to external forces, so it should come as no surprise that an increase in hate activity in Europe is spurring similar activities in Canada. Moreover, our history demonstrates that we have been avid proponents of racist ideas and ideology and have seldom demonstrated a consistent determination to 'do the right thing.' For instance, we had no abolition movement when slavery was imbedded in our soil and there was no outcry when Chinese and Japanese were denied their basic citizenship rights; nor have we demonstrated any sustained commitment to righting the wrongs that continue to be perpetuated against Aboriginal people.

The spectre of a society that can tolerate extreme forms of structural racism as well as the more subtle ones remains with us. A historical approach would enable anti-racism practitioners to contextualize present circumstances. For instance, they would benefit from knowing that there was a time such as the following: 'When Callender's Colored Minstrels filled every seat in Academy Hall in Halifax in 1884, when J.W. McAndrew, the Watermelon Man, Haverly's Mastodon Minstrels, A.G. Fiel's troupe, or Jack Diamond the Dancer toured Canada, they purported to speak for the Negro – on occasion with compassion and even with affection, but usually with ridicule and low humor ... In time those wooly-headed uncles, Remus and Tom, and the faithful mammies,

Lize and Chloe, were part of the mythology that was the heritage of smalltown Canada as well as rural midwestern America' (Winks 1971: 294–5). Knowing about this kind of tradition would enable anti-racism workers to be clearer about why certain images will never be welcomed by racial minorities.

The global nature of racism demands that Canadians committed to anti-racism work be fully cognizant of global conditions as well as our own history and that we work against racism externally as much as we do at home. More particularly, however, it means that human services workers must never assume that we are not like those bad people, the Americans. There is still a lot of work to do in simply getting Canadians to equate our pervasively White jury system and the consistent pattern of pro-policing verdicts in Canada with the kind of verdict that the Los Angeles jury reached in the Rodney King case. In addition, we have a White education system, a White judicial system, a White sociopolitical system, and a white economic system that maintain the same inferior position for Aboriginal, African, and Asian people vis-à-vis people of European descent as do the systems of America and Britain. The primary role of the anti-racism worker must be the provision of a relevant social education to all Canadians. For only such a balanced and complete education will give widespread public legitimacy and support to the efforts of those who are fighting to improve the education, justice, and human service sectors. To bring about such a profound shift in society's behaviour patterns, Canadians of all backgrounds must come to terms with the 'racist' facts of our history and our national life. As well, we have a moral obligation to ensure that access to the economic, political, social, and cultural life of this country is available to all. As Brand and Bhaggiyadetta have observed, the task is all encompassing: 'The culture of racism is such that white people need not be actively engaged in racist acts. Racism has become so embedded in the way (Canadian) society operates, it has become as commonsensical as sleeping and waking. All white people have to do is go about their daily lives ... and racism is perpetuated' (1986: 83). Racism is so entrenched in the 'Canadian way of life' that only a sustained and conscious effort to rid our society of its evils will bring about the shift that is needed. Let us not just go about our daily lives.

NOTES

1 On 6 February 1993, Kirk Makin reported, in a cover story for the *Globe and*

Mail: 'White supremacists are attracting younger recruits and more women than ever before. Those who monitor the movement say a higher proportion are well educated. Recruitment drives specifically target students. In Ontario and British Columbia, ultrarightists have caused outrage by distributing pamphlets at high schools and stuffing introduction cards into library books.'

2 For instance, the historical avenue of employment as domestics has been narrowed by using secondary-school education as a new criterion for domestic work. The amendments to the Immigration Act contained in Bill C-86 will also make it more difficult for racial minorities (who constitute a large proportion of new immigrants and refugees) to gain entry to Canada; those already here will also have a more difficult time in securing family reunification because of a new points system that increases the importance of skills. See Gerald Owen's 'The New Immigration Rules' in the 12 February 1993 issue of *The Lawyers Weekly*. In addition, the agency responsible for multiculturalism has been gradually downgraded from a government ministry to a department, and finally (at present) to a section of the Department of Canadian Heritage.

3 A variety of studies have documented the pervasive impact of racism on the lives of various members of racial minorities. See S. Ramcharan, *Racism: Nonwhites in Canada* (1982), and B. Ubale, *Working Together: Strategy for Race Relations* (1982).

4 Michael McAteer, *Toronto Star*, 31 January 1993: A12. Notably, when a highly respected Black resident of Toronto, Jean Augustine, asserted that the church was not doing enough to fight racism, this caused quite a stir.

5 A list of such scientists include many famous names such as Thomas Huxley, Herbert Spencer, and Paul Broca.

6 The distinction is made because while 'belief' is merely the conviction that something is true, or exists, or is right, and denotes an opinion to the best of one's beliefs, as best as one knows. 'Ideology,' by contrast, 'denotes any set of ideas and values which has the social function of consolidating a particular economic [and social] order, which is explained by that fact alone, and not by its inherent truth or reasonableness ... The function of ideology is to naturalize the status quo, and to present as immutable features of human nature the particular social conditions which currently persist ... It therefore has three functions: to legitimate, to mystify, and to console' (Roger Scruton, *A Dictionary of Political Thought* [London: Pan Books 1983]. In other words, 'ideology' is *systematic* in a way that 'belief' is not. However, a 'belief system,' as opposed to 'belief' alone, denotes 'ideology.'

7 It has been estimated that 15,701 Chinese arrived between 1881 and 1884 (Li 1988: 17).

8   Although economic problems in the 1860s had already motivated the BC
     government to pass legislation disenfranchising the Chinese and preventing
     them from securing employment upon government projects, it was not until
     the designated tasks of the Chinese labour had been completed – the railway
     project – that actions were stepped up against them.

9   In fact, a deeply rooted disinclination to view Chinese people (as well as
     other racial minorities) as Canadians could be extrapolated from the preced-
     ing actions. In 1979 a CTV *W5* program called 'The Campus Giveaway' was
     aired. Obviously intelligent reporters left the impression that all the Chinese
     were foreign students and that because of 100,000 such students, universities
     were denying entry to 'Canadian students' (Barrett 1987: 299).

10   One key area of public education for human service workers could be this
     issue of Aboriginal title.

Chapter 3

Manufacturing Racism: The Two Faces of Canadian Development

Valerie Bedassigae-Pheasant

The European invasion of Turtle Island (North America) launched powerful economic and social currents that created and ultimately shaped the contemporary situations of First Nations people. Responding to the social, economic, and political situation of First Nations people requires an understanding of the manner by which Natives are governed. Traditionally, the original inhabitants of Turtle Island were organized as autonomous nations, were self-regulating, and maintained intricate and sophisticated forms of government that supported women as decision makers (see Allen 1986, Robbins 1992). Complex systems of consciousness developed science, medicine, astronomy, philosophy, egalitarianism, and religions that supported ceremonial and ritual aspects of female power. As stated by M. Dorris (1987: 102), Native American societies rested upon intelligence and had developed and maintained usable, pragmatic views of the world. Those of their systems that had survived long enough to be observed by fifteenth-century Europeans were dynamic and had clearly worked for millennia.

The occupation and domination of Turtle Island and its inhabitants was dependent upon seizing control of the land and resources, annihilating the people or corralling them at best, and instituting a foreign government. The development and maintenance of the new oppressive lifestyle took centuries to perfect. It operated under the guise of state-supported or -operated services such as religion, education, social services, military and law enforcement, and anything else that could impact upon the People. The modern riders of the apocalypse stormed into our lives. They burned our villages, raped women, murdered our leaders, kidnapped our children, and stole our land. 'Civilization' had come calling; no invitations were necessary. The Grim Reaper was hosting the party, and was sparing no expense. This was the beginning of the racial oppression of Aboriginal peoples by white colonialists.

Bolaria and Li (1988) identify racial oppression as having a number of dimensions, ranging from physical coercion to ideological control. These levels of oppression are means to control the subordinate group, with the ultimate purpose being to exploit its labour power, or to remove its sovereignty from land and resources, rather than to educate its people in the pure sense. This certainly was the case in North America / Turtle Island. Bolaria and Li further state that ideological control is a means to indoctrinate the subordinate group to be subservient. It is after the initial assertion of authority (frequently accomplished by force), when all resistance has been pacified, that the dominant group is in a position to resort to other means of social control, including the use of the law and ideological domination (1988: 22–4).

This chapter will examine the racist tactics that were used to colonize Turtle Island while simultaneously developing a system shrouded in deceit to control the lives of First Nations people, 'for their own good.' Since education was a key weapon in the colonialists' war against First Nations people, it is appropriate that it is highlighted in this discussion. From this examination it will be seen that, after initial contact, the ever-expanding world market of the Europeans and the expansion of capitalism created a situation where unequal relationships developed and the exploitation of people and resources became the norm.

HISTORICAL CONTEXT: FEEDING THE ADDICTION TO GREED

The arrival in North America of the Europeans during the sixteenth century secured a position of authority for the French and British in Canada. New patterns of land ownership were instituted. The official translation of ownership of the land was a foreign concept to the Aboriginal people. In precontact times, land was the basis for all things. It was the Earth Mother who provided for and took care of her children. The relationship of the People to the land defined the Nation: its identity, its culture, its way of life, its fundamental rights, its methods of adaptation, its patterns of survival (Cahn 1970: 68); the land was synonymous with existence.

The Royal Proclamation of 1763 officially segregated the First Nations into separate territories. The area outside Upper and Lower Canada, and beyond the northwest area granted to the Hudson's Bay Company, was to be the exclusive 'hunting grounds' of the tribal groups. In this way the Crown encouraged participation of the European fur traders with inland tribes, using the Hudson's Bay Company to work out specific economic arrangements. These arrangements consisted of trade with no principles or scruples. The primary goal was to secure as much as possible for as little as possible, without regard for the human factor. Obtaining the product, usually furs, was accomplished by trading commodities – alcohol, metal products, mirrors, clothing, and blankets – as units of measure. Guns and traps were items of high value. They would take more pelts to secure; sometimes piles as high as five feet were necessary for a 'ball and shot' rifle, even after the manufacture of the Winchester repeating rifle.

Government Indian policy for that period revolved primarily around the regulation of commerce. The position taken by the state in obtaining the land transfers usually involved the First Nations signing land away through treaty, in a language that did not translate or evoke the same meaning for both sides, or via 'quit-claims' signed under the influence of promises or alcohol. As a result, the early colonial leaders were able to monopolize timber and mining land. By taking and advancing personal interest in early investment, the members of the new British order solidified the establishment of a mercantile economy. The development of the open market bonded colonization with capitalism. The European colonizers brought about a formal process of economic development at the expense of the original inhabitants. The uneven development of the dual economy in the so-called modern (European) and traditional (Aboriginal) sectors fundamentally destroyed the capacity of the indigenous people to be self-sufficient, and created a dependency on the metropolis of the colonizing countries (see Bourgeault 1988). The transformation was beginning; the autonomous societies that once existed were slowly being undermined and exploited for commodities, while feeding the frenzied need for furs and capital accumulation in Britain.

With 1867 came the confederation of the east and west of Canada, and the establishment of the British North America Act. The BNA Act divided the powers and responsibilities of the federal government of Canada and those of the provincial governments. Under the jurisdiction of this Act, Indians are the responsibility of the federal government (section 91, subsection 24). Section 93 of the Act made education a provincial responsibility. A conflict situation arose; the provinces felt they had no duty to educate Indians, as they were the responsibility of the federal government. Further complications arose, as there was no clear-cut definition as to who was an Indian. This decision would rest with the civil servants empowered to write the Indian Act of 1876. In essence, section 91 of the BNA Act removed the independence of the Aboriginal people by making them wards of the federal government.

By the time of Confederation the economy and political powers in Canada were centralized. Control was effectively administered by the Canadian government to minimize investment risks. Since Canada was a resource-based hinterland, dependent upon industrialized countries, it was of prime concern for the government to have access to 'unclaimed' territorial land, while keeping the Aboriginal people subdued. Unclaimed land was land that had not been surrendered for sale or lease by the First Nations. It was land that would be usurped for the good of the growing nation, an act justified by statements that invalidated traditional hunting grounds. This land grab also ensured the protection of the empire's economic base. Concurrently, intense economic development was being pursued by the monopolistic merchant class.

Shifts in the Canadian workforce created a movement away from primary (agriculture, forestry, hunting, fishing) to secondary (industry and transport), to the inevitable tertiary (service and commerce), sectors. The Aboriginal labour force was dismissed as a full participant as the economy was directed towards service-sector developments that espoused a hierarchical, paternalistic, educated Eurocentric workplace. To ensure the submission of the Indians and to maintain absolute control, the federal government affiliated the Department of Indians Affairs with the following departments after its removal from the War Department: Crown Lands Secretary of State, Interior, Citizenship and Immigration, and, currently, Northern Development.

The first comprehensive version of the Indian Act was officially legislated into action in 1876. This Act was a mandate for government administrators to control the lives of Indians. It provided the legal basis for federal administration. The legislation defined who was an Indian and, therefore, who was entitled to government benefits. What the Act actually did was usurp the power of the Nation-to-Nation relationship of the treaties, and placed Indians in their own prisons. The restrictions of the Indian Act were the blueprint for apartheid. It restricted the movement of people (you could not leave the reserve without permission and a letter of authorization from the Indian Agent); it did not allow Indians to own land (they could not even develop it without the consent of the Indian Agent); Indians could not hold large meetings or even attend a large gathering; it regulated who could marry whom; it determined the dispersal of personal possessions upon death; and it provided for Indians' education, as well as incarceration if they were not in attendance at school. The legislation eradicated future forms of self-government that would have resulted from the Aboriginals' desire to reconstitute themselves on their own terms after engaging in a war to maintain their rights. The Act also removed powers of finance and financial control and all social services, including education, into the hands of non-Native people, sworn into the service of the King or Queen. The Indian Act was and is the embodiment of cultural genocide, domination, and control. It continues and maintains the process of colonization of First Nations people.

The government operated under sections 113 to 122 of the Indian Act to keep the education of children away from the control of their parents and the Nation. The insidious nature of these sections not only removed parental responsibility, but ensured that the government had total control over the lives of Native children, and could remove them, incarcerate them, or adopt them out by virtue of the Indian agent's authority. Denominational residential schools were still in operation up to the 1950s, and in some cases as late as 1968.

EDUCATION AS WAR: COLONIALISM AND DOMINATION

> Soap and education are not as sudden as a massacre, but they are more deadly in the long run.
>
> *Mark Twain*

It is generally accepted that education is the formal process by which the transmission of culture and world-view are produced in succeeding generations. Therefore, one can assume that the historical experiences of colonization have produced the framework for, and have maintained, a power structure between the Anglo-Europeans and the Aboriginal people, a stucture reproduced and transmitted through the education system. Education transmits systems of thought and ideologies that are created by the value systems of the creators. Education is additionally intended to provide learners with the skills, knowledge, and attitudes to survive in, and contribute to, the world. The nature of these are all culturally defined. Education systems established by Europeans are defined through the lenses and motivations of Europeans in the era of conquest and beyond to the present.

For this reason, the education of Aboriginal peoples in Canada has generally been an area of controversy. This is a result of the manner in which the system of education was developed. The existing character of Indian education finds its genesis in the confines of governmental/state control. The fact that the state determines and controls education is a major reason that formal education and Aboriginal people have not been well matched.

Cultural interaction has existed for the past four centuries between the Aboriginal peoples and the Anglo-European colonizers. This relationship has been characterized by misconceptions, contradictions, and mutual mistrust. The continuance of these factors reaffirms the notion that the official goal of the state is assimilation. The assimilation model encompasses a variety of concepts that generally define the 'success' or 'failure' of a people, based on the extent to which it accepts the value system of the dominant cultural group at the expense of its own cultural uniqueness. As Bolaria and Li (1988) note, the assimilationist perspective has been criticized for its Social Darwinist overtones and its mechanical application to different racial and ethnic groups, as well as for providing the necessary justification for racist policy developments based on biological inferiority.

Although the overall responsibility of Indian peoples lay in the hands of the British Crown, the security of the colonists was of primary concern. As a result, the education services for Aboriginal people, who were considered the daily responsibility of the military force, fell under a directive of the army. During this time the army did little, if anything, to promote the formal education of their charges. The continued presence of military forces, meant to ensure that the conditions of the treaties were adhered to (by the Native people), set the stage for a condition of permanent economic dependency among all Native people (see Robbins 1992).

The education system became the mechanism by which social division would be ideologically reinforced, while simultaneously delivering the word of God. The initiatives of the various churches were intended to civilize the Aboriginal populations. For example, the clergy of New France were to encourage the Indians 'by means of education, to give up their traditional way of life, to become civilized and to adopt the ways of the Frenchmen' (Kaegi 1972: 4). From its onset, formal education of the Native people promoted assimilation as the desired goal.

In 1824, the Government of Upper Canada took a significant step that allowed funding via grants to Indian schools. The schools in operation were controlled by the Church. The provision for funding may have been the result of action previously established in the United States. In 1819, the American government took the initiative in establishing schools for Indians, thereby providing a model to be used in Canada. This was accomplished by utilizing abandoned army posts. Children were removed from families and boarded at the school, which operated in a fashion similar to a military camp (Bodner 1971: 24).

The forced removal of the children created the first generation of Native people not only separated from a knowledge of who they were but also isolated from the dominant Anglo culture into which they were to be assimilated. This marked a large-scale shift to laying a foundation for the destruction of the Aboriginal societies, including their social, economic, spiritual, and cultural life. *The first tremor of the genocidal earthquake rippled through the communities.* These children became adults with no identity association outside of the residential-school experience, which educated the 'Indian' out of them, replacing it with the fear of God, expressed through the abuses of educators and men of the cloth.

The major forms of education were carried out in the various religious residential schools. The residential or boarding schools were built in isolated areas, generally far from the dominant society. Indian children were removed from their families and communities for long periods of time, causing alienation. Instruction was carried out in a foreign language by poorly qualified teachers. The curriculum was strange to the learners. In addition, new forms of worship were imposed on the students. As well as being separated from what they knew, however, the children were also segregated from the dominant society. There were no provisions made by educators to incorporate the foundations for successful adaptation to a different society as the former culture was being eradicated. The lack of connectedness to either group led to extreme forms of alienation or anomie – a state of being without norms. The educated graduate usually ended up outside the circle. The system left him/her as a ghost – a being of no substance. Up to the mid-nineteenth century, the missionaries carried the brunt of the responsibility for Indian education.

By 1940, technology was also effecting changes within the education system. With the escalation in Canadian society of scientific and technological growth and the society's burgeoning socio-economic sophistication, the federal government shifted its position on educating Canadians. With the growing influence of multinational corporations, the government increased educational investment in order to stimulate a corresponding increase in national output, economic growth, and more jobs, inter alia, and marketed the idea that education would thus become a powerful tool for altering the distribution of income (see Rush 1977). With its concerted emphasis on the ideology that the productive capacity of the individual was directly linked to levels of educational attainment, the federal government would be hard pressed to defend the phenomenally high failure and drop-out rates of the Native students.

The education sector of the Department of Indian Affairs reacted to the situation by pursuing a similar course of action to that taken in the United States. The officials in control of Indian education there firmly believed in the merits of integration: that it would provide better education for the Indians, decrease tensions while promoting understanding between Anglo-Europeans and Indians, stimulate the desire to continue on to secondary school, and eventually open the doors that provide economic opportunities. In order to safeguard its economic investments, while promoting the 'betterment' of the Indians, the Canadian federal government began to phase out residential schools and move towards integration.

The decision for full-scale integration in Canada bypassed the First Nations. Participation in decision making and tuition agreements with the provincial authorities did not include the people who would be affected most by this unilateral action. Essentially, the provincial school boards would receive federal funds for the acquisition of educational services for Native children. By virtue of the tuition agreement they would receive per-capita grants for students, construction grants, and student housing funds, textbook evaluation committees, multicultural programs, as well as other interests, regardless of whether or not the level of education was primary, secondary, or post-secondary. The tuition agreement was an economic windfall for the participating school boards. A new player was afoot, but the game plan remained constant.

Not much changed under the philosophy of 'equality of educational opportunity' and 'equality of access.' Native students continued to drop out, the curriculum did not address the Native world-view, sexism abounded, parents were not considered a part of the process, the language of instruction was English, the teachers and the administrators did not represent the Native population, the methods of socialization and discipline were foreign, educational services were still being delivered by a denominational school of the government's choice, and bussing students over great distances or boarding them out was initiated. Education was still being *done to* the Native population. It was not conducted on equal terms. The power remained in the hands of the federal government and was manipulated by the bureaucrats.

FOR GOD AND COUNTRY: RACISM AND THE CHURCH

The religious fervour of the missionaries was encased in a well-established tradition dedicated to the endless task of saving pagans, savages, heretics, and the unholy from eternal damnation. The task became one of civilizing Natives to the notion of Christianity – another form of conquest wrapped up and delivered in the name of God. Some were saved by prayer and others by fire. The ideology of racism can be found in the religious structures of Christianity. As Bourgeault (1991: 45) points out, in the colonial period capitalist expansion was seen as a religious duty – a duty for the good of the nation. Capitalism and education are inseparable when considering the motive to educate the Indian. Christianity supported the accumulation of capital. The division between precapitalist and capitalist forms of labour was defined as the difference between uncivilized and civilized people. Christianity instilled race prejudice as a justification of the exploitation of colonized peoples, thus reinforcing a racial division of labour between European and non-European.

In 1830, the responsibility of Indians was formally transferred from the military to the Government of Upper Canada and into the fledgling Department of Indian Affairs. Concurrently, in Europe an interesting phenomenon was taking place. 'All the attitudes that existed under the previous theological order found their way in the new scientific order, not only unchanged, but with a renewed and revitalized life. By then Europeans started to believe that the reason they were successful in conquest was not just because they were spiritually and militarily superior to those they encountered, but because they were *biologically* superior as well' (see Mohawk 1992: 441). The 'scientific racists' propagated the concept of the superior-inferior status of the races.

Besides the work of anthropologists, there were the writings of the missionaries and scholarly travellers. The accounts of these worldly people were easily accepted as fact, even though in most cases the accounts moved from description to judgments. The writings eventually took on a humanitarian bias, deliberately stirring feelings of guilt. It was guilt that instigated a move to be made towards atonement, which came in the form of bearing responsibility for the 'protection and civilization of inferior and perverse people, for destroying his independence, his manliness, for killing him through war and disease, and demoralizing him with liquor' (Upton 1973: 54). Those who led the crusade gave little thought to the idea of non-interference in Native affairs. The most important form of compensation was to make them into white men. By the end of the 1830s, the stance taken by the Empire was best summed up by Herman Merivale: 'three alternatives faced all natives in the presence of white settlement: their extinction, their civilization in communities isolated from the whites, or their amalgamation with the colonists ... Their inferiority was cultural and could be remedied by training in civilized ways' (Upton 1973: 54).

Obviously, it was necessary to pressure the Indians into changing their lifestyle. The aim would be to increase the activities of the missionaries. Christianity would give them the desires of the white man. The missionaries would be the executive arm of the assimilationist policy. By 1848, funding had been established for the use of Indian education. The funds were made available to the missionaries; the churches received land, per-capita grants, plus other material rewards for their efforts. The churches gained through material exploitation, while the Indians suffered from moral admonishments, cultural genocide, and the indoctrination of conservative attitudes (see Frideres 1990; Kaegi 1972). The missionaries' efforts focused on bringing a new, foreign culture and value system to the Indians.

Each religious sect (Roman Catholic, Anglican, Baptist, United, Presbyterian) held their own particular belief system and opinions, but the basis of each was the drive to convert and civilize. Their attitudes were pervaded by those of the time. Kaegi (1972) quotes Dr Egerton Ryerson, that the goal of the churches was 'to essentially destroy the customs and beliefs of the Indian people; to civilize them and thus to improve and elevate their character' (p. 5). Working under directives that postulated racism, the missionaries set out among the Indians with the 'best of intentions.' The creation of good Christians overshadowed the quality of educational services brought to Indian people.

RESISTANCE OR RESURRECTION

Refusing to identify with the 'vertical mosaic' and upward mobility, as well as being angry over the manner in which education was reproducing racial stereotypes, hatred, and oppression, the National Indian

Brotherhood produced a policy document that was thought to have created an avenue for First Nations people to become involved in the education process of children resident on reserves. The 1972 *Indian Control of Indian Education* identified two educational principles that would be the focal point of Native peoples' advocacy: (1) parental responsibility and (2) local control of education. These were rights that had been historically denied by the state. The document maintained the federal government's responsibility to provide schools, but advocated that only Indian people can develop a suitable philosophy of education based on Indian values adapted to modern living. Indian children must be given a strong sense of identity, with confidence in their own personal worth and ability.

Even though then Minister of Indian Affairs Jean Chrétien supported the document in principle, the federal government did not move to draft the necessary legislation to provide the legal possibility of enacting the policy, and thus ensure the First Nations' jurisdiction over the education of their children. The transfer of authority still has not taken place. Financial control and decision-making authority continue to rest in the hands of the Department of Indian Affairs.

Despite all the problems of continued systemic obstruction, the First Nations realize that, without community support and their validation of the school and its actions, the resulting symptoms would continue to be the alienation and/or rejection of the system by the learner. The People know that, if the present situation is allowed to dominate their life, anger directed towards others and towards the self, apathy, and fear will result in suicides, alcohol/drug/solvent abuse, crimes of violence against women and children, and an intense resentment towards life. It is the control of the person and community (spiritually, emotionally, mentally, and physically) that will challenge the dominant ideologies and will be the impetus to advance the local control of education. Local control means having pride in, and concern for, an indigenous identity that forms the basis for reclaiming autonomy. The education system contributed to the destruction of the identity of Aboriginals, and can serve to create a site where the construction and reconstruction of identity can take place.

The movement towards local control of education was the result of Aboriginal people refusing to accept a marginalized position in their homeland. After years of subjugation, First Nations people are reaffirming the validity of their language and culture, spirituality, music, and arts and asserting their identities in order to claim their position in contemporary society. As a result of the need to address the global issues that affect life and establish resistance to further assimilation tactics, the recognition and the need to manipulate education became a major objective. The action demonstrated by the First Nations can be viewed as a counter-hegemonic response to a continued colonial style of government. It can also be described as a logical solution to legitimized, racist actions enacted by the state to perpetuate the continued social, political, economic, and spiritual oppression of First Nations people.

SAME WAR, NEW WEAPONS

> We took an oath not to do any wrong to each other or to scheme against each other.
>
> *Geronimo*

Our socialization into Canadian society begins the moment we are born into this world. The cleansing starts. Competent doctors and nurses urge us out into the birthing room of the sterile hospital – into its bright lights and loud noises and its cold efficiency. It is hard to hear our mother's heartbeat over the sounds from the fluorescent lights, radios, telephones, and modern machines. Forms are filled out and we are registered with the province *and* with the Department of Indian Affairs. Our numbers are assigned. We are categorized by 'Band' (occupied territory) and by denomination – not by our traditional names, and definitely not by our nation. This is legal trap set to confuse us, to assist in the erasing of our history, our struggles, and our voices as a People, and to erode our spirituality.

The massive assault against our integrity as human beings continues. It surrounds us. It pretends to guide us, to assure us that the actions taken, the policies implemented, are meant to ensure that we have a good life, a life born of equal opportunity and equal access – life in the 'Just Society.' The bureaucracy has grown like a tree. It has roots and branches. It provides a space for those who can become employed there. It casts a long shadow. For what and whose purpose does it exist? This 'tree' was not meant to be played in, nor to be used for creative methods of construction. The bureaucracy is not a creation of ours, but of those meant to control us. There are some within its structural confines who try to humanize their actions, but usually with least effect. Instead, the endless incursions and assaults upon our dignity as individuals and the imposed and/or maintained exclusionary practices perpetuate the existence of racism. The manner in which we treat each other reflects our humanity, or lack of it.

The 1960s were awakened by a generation of people who vocalized their anger against the establishments, their hatred for the war machine, and their demand for a country based on equality. Protests, demonstrations, and the call for peace and love were heard on the radio, seen on television, witnessed on the streets, and worn on the bodies of the 'flower children.'

While the new generation called for peace and love, the Canadian government was busy changing the federal and provincial relationships, as they pertained to Indians. This action would become the precursor to devolution. The provinces would now have a direct say in the lives of Aboriginal people. Again the state did not see fit to seek the input of those who would be most affected by this change – a modern reminder that 'the little children of the forest' were not capable of thinking and speaking for themselves. Clearly, governmental legislation still controlled the situation; a Nation-to-Nation relationship did not exist.

Before 1962, Indians were considered legal minors in Canada. They were wards of the state in their own home. They could not vote in federal, provincial, and municipal elections; they had no status in courts of law; they could not sue a white man or legal citizen; they could not purchase alcohol or firearms; and they could not become involved in real-estate transactions or secure credit for major purchases (e.g., cars, televisions). There was a provision in the Indian Act that made available to Indians the possibility to 'voluntarily' participate in Canadian society, to become a citizen, through enfranchisement. Enfranchisement involved selling your birthright to the government for $750.

Even if a person were enfranchised, how would this ensure access to Canadian society? How would it assure money-lenders of repayment? Where and what was their collateral? What level of education would this person possess? What type of long-term employment could be secured, with a return that included the resources for leisure activities and club memberships, for a family with eight to ten children? How would they obtain a mortgage or manage a space to rent now that they could no longer live within the confines of the reserve? What about the amenities obtained from the land around us? How were these to be procured in the greater society? It all led back to money – money and more money. This situation was an economic and racially motivated nightmare perpetuated during the post–Second World War period, while the rest of Canada revelled in glory. During one of the most prosperous periods in Canadian history, Indians were excluded by legislation from sharing in the successes of Canada's venture into the world economy. It is difficult to believe that life existed in a government-developed, maintained, and economically oppressed world within such a democratic society, where there was no communication, no mobility, and no credit, and no possibility of developing business partnerships or enterprises.

The Diefenbaker legislation (1960) changed the situation, but was powerless to alter the mind-set that drove it. There were no policy changes or subsequent enabling legislation or new dollars made available from the federal/provincial governments to alter the abysmal economic conditions on the typical reserve community; but we could vote – if we could read, if we could get to the polling station, if we understood the process, it we could trust the system that continued to legislate safe, covert ways to ensure our demise.

VULTURES AND VAMPIRES

The educational, economic, and social gap between Native societies and the dominant society began to widen by quantum leaps. To complicate this scenario, the federal government signed a number of transfer-payment arrangements with the provinces. These agreements allowed children's aid societies, provincial police forces, education and health services, who had previously been unable to do so, to intervene with and on behalf of economically deprived family groups. The influx of new helpers was influenced and driven by the enlightened, liberal politics of the 1960s. The call for help went out to the general public, and was carried across the country by organizations like the Peace Corps, Frontier Foundations, Company of Young Canadians, and Canadian Youth Corps. The gap had to be filled now that the 'Church' had fallen into disfavour as the protector of Indians. The atrocities committed by the churches and their alternative replacement, children's aid societies, are now being exposed. Meanwhile, Aboriginal people are actively working at healing their wounds and seeking peace for their spirits.

The Nations have lost three generations of children through residential schools, adoptions, short-term foster placements, and the juvenile detention system. Our education was substandard in curriculum, resources, and quality of teaching, our families were shattered, and our lifestyle exposed as 'from the bush, the backwoods, like hill-billies.' We were without electricity, therefore no television; that we were without water service, therefore no indoor plumbing; that we were without a furnace, therefore we had to cut wood. We had to hold on; our rescuers were on the way. There were no concerted attempts to address the racial oppression and socialization that had been administered in magnanimous doses since 1885, when the last successful Native leader – Louis Riel – was hanged.

PAINFUL RE-VISIONS

Revisionist history has presented the same Mr Riel with a posthumous Order of Canada and proclaimed him one of the Fathers of Confederation, as well as apologizing to his family. It is now widely accepted that Riel was a victim of racism, anti-Catholicism, and expansionist zeal, a victim of Canada's growth period. However, every First Nation, Métis, and Inuit community on Turtle Island has also suffered from religious persecution, economic oppression, and social degradation. This is the other face of Canada – the reality that has created the anger that led to the occupation at Kanasatake. But it is the dream of freedom that is the backbone of the black-market economy, the bible of the Bingo and Casino movement, the overture that propels the Native artists, actors, writers, and musicians to create.

The federal and provincial governments continue to control the land and the resouces that are held 'in trust' for First Nations, and consort with multinational corporations to modernize imperialistic tactics and colonization. While the demands of the economy take on the aura and rules of high-tech Cowboys and Indians, a battle is being waged over spirituality, the fibre that holds the People together. It is promoted under the guise of the New Age, White Shamanism, 'wannabes,' and 'plastic medicine-men,' who take and offer back something that never was, something bastardized into their own making, something promoted and paid for from coffers that are never empty. Were they not happy with taking our land? Our children? The water? They see out of their commercial eyes, tinted green from the colour of money, the commodity value of legends made visible, of cloning and prostituting the ceremonies for their own net worth.

The misrepresentation of Aboriginals by Whites takes the stereotypes to another dimension, creating further psychological and spiritual havoc in Aborginals. This confusion extends into all peoples' minds and affects their judgment about who speaks for and represents the Indian reality. Once again we are faced with Tonto, Running Brave, and Lovely White Dove. Our legitimacy is challenged, our lineage questioned. Other people get paid large sums of money, an honorarium, to deliver their topic on 'Native Whateverness' while we are expected to share and give, of our thoughts, our time, because it is a part of our culture. Not only are we insulted, but our voices are silenced.

The appropriation of Native arts and ceremonies by the 'culture vultures' is a direct attack on the strength and vibrancy of Aboriginal people. It is racism dressed up in its best linen suit, smelling of Obsession, with shiny black hair compliments of Lady Clairol, and the tawny skin that easily identifies members of the Coppertone tribe. Beware of false prophets.

Our stories of growing up, of loving, of laughing, of crying, of dancing, are reflected in the mirrors of our soul. When we look into the mirror, we see ourselves. We see our happiness. We see our hurt. We tell these stories, or ones of similar nature, so that we may learn from them. As Buffy Sainte-Marie wrote in her song 'Coincidence and Likely Stories,' it is like looking into a three-way mirror of a one-way world.

ANTI-RACISM AND YOU AND ME

It does not require many words to speak the truth.

Chief Joseph

Anti-racism as a way of thought, action, and spirit can become a prism. It can refocus the energies of those who wish to make positive the physical and spiritual realities of Aboriginal peoples. It urges the development of a new view of our history that has been blurred by social and economic dominance. Refocusing can begin within this rounding circle with the seven teachings of the Creator:

1 To cherish *knowledge* is to know *wisdom*.
2 To know *love* is to know *peace*.
3 To *honour* all of creation is to have *respect*.
4 *Bravery* is facing the foe with *integrity*.
5 *Honesty* in facing a situation is being brave.
6 *Humility* is knowing yourself as part of Creation.
7 *Truth* is knowing all of these things.

Knowlege, wisdom, love, peace, respect, bravery, integrity, honesty, and humility – all lead to truth. Anti-racism strives beyond the politic and aspires to truth.

When people who work in the area of anti-racism want to know 'how' to work with First Nations people, there is no pat answer. There is no set formula to follow. There is no manual. Whether on-reserve or off-reserve, in urban communities, Aboriginals still experience racism and discrimination to the same degree. The state and their officials did not care where we were located. If the policy had a hidden agenda of 'swoop, scoop, and grab,' then it was made to be so, because the paper-work justified the objective. The genocidal assault created chasms with respect to our voice in history. But it is up to you who want to know to take that first step to ask the question, and *to listen*. It is not up to you to debate the situation based on facts you learned in schools. It is not your place to justify the tyranny and say it could not have happened, because you didn't know. The atrocities cannot be trivialized. Death from plague-infested blankets is murder, just slower than shooting a bullet into the brain.

The riders of the Apocalypse no longer ride horses with fiery breath and sharpened hooves. They arrive on 747s, in chauffeur-driven cars, in BMWs. They've turned in their flowing robes for custom-tailored suits, and adorn themselves with Rolex watches. Everything is timing, and they control the hands – what ticks and what stops.

Chapter 4

Racism in Canadian Immigration Policy

David Matas

Few Canadians know that Canada, which now prides itself on its tolerance of racial and cultural diversity, is a nation with a sad history of racism, or that this racism was until recently enshrined in law. The first
section of this chapter provides an overview of Canadian immigration
law up to 10 April 1978, when the present Immigration Act came into
effect; and the second examines contemporary immigration policies and
initiatives. References are made to some of these laws and policies by
other contributors (for example, Khenti, St. Lewis); however, I will discuss them in relation to immigration.

CANADIAN IMMIGRATION POLICY (1867–1978)

Racist Laws

To talk of racism *in* Canadian immigration policy up to 10 April 1978 is
to be overly generous to the Government of Canada. Rather, we should
talk of racism *as* Canadian immigration policy. The Canadian Immigration Act of 1910 unashamedly gave Cabinet the power, on the basis of
race, ethnicity, and place of origin, to prohibit people from immigrating
to Canada. In 1919, the Cabinet was given the power to bar immigrants
of any race if they were deemed undesirable 'owing to their peculiar
customs, habits, modes of life and methods of holding property and
because of their probable inability to become readily assimilated.'[1] The
Cabinet invoked this power on numerous occasions. On 14 March 1919
it passed an order-in-council prohibiting immigrants of the 'German,
Austrian, Hungarian, Bulgarian or Turkish races' from immigrating to

Canada, except with permission from the Minister of Immigration. In that same year, Cabinet used this power to prohibit the landing of Doukhobors, Hutterites, and Mennonites – groups deemed undesirable because of their 'peculiar customs' and assessed inability to become assimilated. Asians were prohibited from immigrating to Canada in 1923. Although exceptions were initially made for Asian farmers, farm labourers, and domestics, those exceptions were eliminated in 1930. The only loophole in the moratorium against Asian immigration was that enabling Canadian men to sponsor their Asian wives and children. In 1923 the entry to, or landing in, Canada of persons of Chinese origin or descent was prohibited, irrespective of their allegiance or citizenship. Only diplomats, Chinese-born in Canada, merchants, and students were exempted. This statute remained on our books until 1947.

The most extreme form of racism in immigration was directed against the Japanese during and after the Second World War. Regulations passed on 15 December 1945 under the authority of the War Measures Act did not merely restrict entry of the Japanese from abroad, but provided for the deportation of Canadian citizens of Japanese descent who had been born in Canada. The wife, and children under sixteen, of any person for whom the Minister made an order for deportation could be included in the order. Any request for repatriation would be deemed final and irreversible after a fixed delay. This regulation was challenged before the Supreme Court of Canada in January 1946, and before the Privy Council in England in December of the same year, on the ground that Canada could not deport citizens born in Canada, but could only deport aliens. Both courts ruled that Canada had the power to deport its own citizens.[2]

Quotas and Lists

In 1956, the almost blanket prohibition against Asians was replaced by an agreement with the governments of India, Pakistan, and Ceylon limiting annual emigration from each of these countries to 150, 100, and 50 persons, respectively, excluding immediate relatives of Canadian citizens. Although the quota for India was doubled in 1958, the restrictions on South Asian immigration remained in effect until 1962. But the Government of Canada did not need a negotiated agreement to prevent citizens of particular countries from coming here; it could and it did limit admission to citizens of certain listed countries. The 1954 immigration regulations permitted only citizens of the United Kingdom, Australia, New

Zealand, South Africa, Ireland, the United States, and France to immigrate. Citizens of these countries had to have sufficient means to maintain themselves until they secured employment. In 1956, citizens of the other Western European countries were added to the list, provided they had been contracted to work or had an offer of employment in Canada.

In 1962 the lists were replaced with a general entry requirement. To come to Canada, all prospective immigrants had to prove they could become successfully established here. Despite these changes, some groups continued to have an unfair advantage. For example, Europeans, Americans, and people from the Middle East could be sponsored by extended-family members, whereas others, notably those from Africa and Asia, could only be sponsored by members of their immediate family.

Financial Requirements

Besides the power to explicitly bar certain groups of immigrants on the basis of race, the Immigration Act also contained systemic barriers that prevented members of racial minorities from coming to Canada. The 1906 Act, for example, gave Cabinet powers to require certain classes of immigrants to have minimum amounts of money with them as a condition of admission to Canada. This dollar requirement discriminated against poor immigrants and immigrants from countries where wages were much lower than those in Canada. Implicitly, it also discriminated against Asian immigrants 'whose language and mode of life rendered them unsuitable for settlement in Canada.'[3]

This power was first used in a racist way in 1908. Although all immigrants were required to have $25 with them upon entering the country, a June 1908 order-in-council required Asian immigrants to have $200 in their possession. In 1914, the regulations were changed again. While the $200 requirement for Asians remained, Chinese and Japanese citizens and non-Asians were exempted to accommodate the building of the Canadian National Railway.

This regulation became the subject of some bizarre litigation that went all the way to the British Columbia Court of Appeal. Munshi Singh appeared at the Port of Vancouver in May 1914, a few months after the order-in-council had been passed. He had only $20 with him. He was detained and ordered deported on the basis that he was of an Asian race and had less than $200. Munshi Singh appealed this order to the Supreme Court and to the Court of Appeal of British Columbia. He lost at both courts. In a long judgment, BC Court of Appeal Judge McPhillips wrote:

... the better classes of the Asiatic races are not given to leave their own countries ... and those who become immigrants are ... undesirables in Canada. Their ways and ideas may well be a menace to the well being of the Canadian people. The Parliament of Canada ... may well be said to be safeguarding the people of Canada from an influx which it is no chimera to conjure up might annihilate the nation ... introduce Oriental ways as against European ways ... and all the results that would naturally flow therefrom. In their own interests their proper place of residence is within the confines of their respective countries in the continent of Asia, not in Canada, where their customs are not in vogue and their adherence to them here only gives rise to disturbances destructive to the well being of society ... Better that people of non assimilative ... race should not come to Canada, but rather that they shall remain of residence in their country of origin, and do their share, as they have in the past, in the preservation and development of the empire.[4]

Continuous Passage

Besides the power to prohibit entry and impose financial requirements on the basis of race or ethnic origin, the government had a third power, neutral in appearance, but discriminatory in intent. Until 1978, the Immigration Act gave Cabinet the power to impose a continuous-passage rule. The Governor-in-Council could prohibit the landing of any immigrants who had not come to Canada directly from their home country. When this restriction was introduced in 1908, it was impossible to purchase in India or prepay in Canada a ticket for a continuous journey from India to Canada. The continuous-passage power was invoked in 1914 to prevent the disembarkation of four hundred East Indians from the ship *Komagata Maru*. The ship and its four hundred passengers sat in the Vancouver harbour for two months. One of the passengers, Munshi Singh, challenged the entry prohibition in the Canadian courts. The result was that he was ordered deported. Not only did Mr Singh not have the required $200, but he had also stopped in Hong Kong before coming to Canada. Finally, the ship and its passengers returned to India (Cohen 1987: 88).

Head Tax

Aside from the racial provisions in immigration acts, there was a series of Chinese Immigration Acts that specifically discriminated against the Chinese. The Chinese Immigration Act of 1885 required each Chinese immigrant to pay a head tax of $50. That figure was increased to $100 and $500 in 1900 and 1903, respectively.

Extra-legal Discrimination: The Case of the Jews

Discrimination towards Jews attempting to enter Canada presents a frightening instance of extra-legal discrimination. In *None Is Too Many*, Irving Abella and Harold Troper (1983) recount in chilling detail the single-minded determination of immigration authorities to keep out of Canada every Jew fleeing Nazi persecution, the Holocaust, and the aftermath of the Holocaust. The most appalling feature of this systematic and tragic discrimination is that there were *no* laws in support of it.

There was no equivalent to the Chinese Immigration Act legally prohibiting Jews from coming to Canada. Unlike the restrictions placed on Mennonites, there were no regulations saying that Jews were not suitable for settlement in Canada. There were no head taxes imposed on Jewish immigrants or requirements that they have a substantial amount of money with them in order to enter Canada. There were also no continuous-voyage requirements directed against Jews. One searches the laws in vain for signs of blatant discrimination against Jews. Yet the discrimination was incontestable: 'Between 1933 and 1945 Canada found room within its borders for fewer than 5,000 Jews; after the war, until the founding of Israel in 1948, she admitted but 8,000 more. That record is arguably the worst of all refugee-receiving states' (Abella and Troper 1983: vii). There was no need for express legislative powers; the closing of our borders depended instead on abuse of power.

Whatever the immigration requirements were, Jews could not meet them in the climate of anti-Semitism that held sway in Ottawa. The Department of Immigration was headed by an avowed anti-Semite, Fred Blair, who removed the responsibility for processing Jewish applicants from other government offices to his own, where he personally scrutinized each application and decided on its eligibility. In virtually every case the answer was no. But as Troper and Abella (1983) point out, 'to blame [Blair] alone for Canada's response to Jewish immigration would be both overly simplistic and incorrect; after all, he was, although powerful, only a civil servant whose actions reflected the wishes and values of his superiors' (p. 9).

From the perspective of racism in immigration law, the Jewish experience is illuminating. It tells us that we do not need laws to have racist discrimination practices. All we need is unlimited bureaucratic discretion, an unsympathetic or passive public, unmotivated public leaders, or racists in positions of power to make apparently neutral laws racist.

This lesson is particularly important now that all overt racist references have disappeared from our immigration laws. The present Immigration Act has as one of its obligations 'to ensure that any person who seeks admission to land is subject to standards of admission that do not discriminate on the grounds of race, national or ethnic origin, colour, religion or sex' (section 3f). The legal power to prohibit entry by race is gone; the power to impose a financial requirement by race is gone; the power to insist upon continuous passage is gone. Yet the danger of racism remains.

THE PRESENT

We now have a sophisticated enough knowledge of racial discrimination to know that there can be racial discrimination in fact without racial discrimination in form. The Immigration Act may not be intentionally discriminatory, but whether or not it generates systemic discrimination is an open question, and I will try to deal with it by examining four issues – refugees, the points system, visitors' visas, and delays.

Refugees

There is no reason to believe that the Department of Employment and Immigration is motivated today by the kind of rabid bigotry that characterized its behaviour at the time of Mackenzie King and Fred Blair. And I believe that Canada's recent record in accepting refugees and fulfilling its responsibilities under the UN charter has been amongst the best in the world. The government's recent decision to extend the refugee definition to include women who fear for their safety on the basis of their sex has been widely applauded.

But I am not convinced that the refugee-determination system has proved its fairness. There are clear preferences built into the system, and such preferences can, it seems to me, lead to the fact, as well as to the perception, of unfairness. A complete analysis of the deficiencies of the refugee-determination process is beyond the scope of this chapter, but on at least one point the Supreme Court of Canada has spoken very strongly. The Court held the entire refugee-determination procedure unconstitutional, in violation of the Charter guarantee of fundamental justice and the Bill of Rights' guarantee of a right to a fair hearing, because there was no right to an oral hearing in the system.[5]

An unfair system leads inevitably to inequitable treatment. Genuine refugees in Canada are being denied refugee status, while the preferences to which I referred above constantly suggest the possibility of inequity. For example, Eastern European citizens under the 'self exiled class' did not have to prove that they were refugees. They had only to be outside Canada, and outside their country of citizenship, to demonstrate that they were unwilling or unable to return and that they would be able to become successfully established in Canada. The 'Indo-Chinese designated class' permitted citizens of the countries of Indo-China to have largely the same advantageous rules applied to them as the citizens of Eastern European countries. Members of the 'Political Prisoners and Oppressed Persons Designated Class' also do not have to meet the definition of a refugee. They do not have to be outside their country of origin. All they need prove is both that they have been subject to some form of penal control for political expression and that they are able to become successfully established in Canada. Refugees from Guatemala and El Salvador are also in this class.

In addition to the designated classes, there are special procedures for persons from countries experiencing adverse domestic events. There are currently nine countries for which special procedures are in effect. The procedures vary from country to country, but typically they do not permit deportation back to the country of origin. Relatives not in the family class may sponsor persons from these countries.

I do not suggest that these special procedures should end. However, they point out the importance of making our refugee-determination procedure work fairly. With a completely equitable refugee-determination procedure, some of these special rules would not be necessary. Future applicants could simply claim refugee status.

In the summer of 1992, the Canadian government announced that citizens of the former Yugoslavia in Canada could become landed immigrants without having to show they were refugees. At the same time, the government rammed a bill through Parliament amending the Immigration Act to transfer the power to make decisions on refugee-claim eligibility from an independent tribunal to its own departmental officials.

The Points System

An immigrant's admission to Canada now depends on how many

points he or she receives on a scale that rates competence or potential in areas such as skills, education, work experience, and training. In addition, it is important to have a job for which no Canadian is available, be able to buy a business that employs at least one Canadian, or be able to start or buy a business for which there is a significant demand. One could argue that this system seems inherently discriminatory. Were private-sector employers to hire on such a basis, they would almost certainly be accused of discriminatory procedures.

Only the appropriate collection of statistics will make it possible to determine whether or not the present system is discriminatory. If, for example, we were to exclude refugees and the family class and examine only those who applied as independent immigrants, we could determine whether it is harder for a Black than a White, an Indian than an American, to meet the points requirements. I suspect that the points system works in favour of some racial groups and against others, but in the absence of such data no clear conclusions can be drawn. The government's claims that the system is non-discriminatory and non-racist rings hollow until such data is made available; at this writing the government refuses to collect the statistics on which such claims could legitimately be made.

Visitors' Visas

The Immigration Act requires that all prospective travellers to Canada acquire a visa at a Canadian immigration post abroad before coming to Canada. The Cabinet has the power to make exceptions to this rule, and to many other regulations. For example, citizens of certain listed countries do not need visas to enter as visitors. They can simply request a visitor's permit at the border. The arrangement is particularly generous to citizens and permanent residents of the United States.

Imposing a visa requirement for visitors or, more accurately, removing the visa exception, obviously makes visiting Canada more difficult. Requiring visitors from certain countries to obtain visas abroad instead of obtaining visitors' visas at the border is inequitable, because the latter is usually much easier than the former; a person applying for a visitor's permit at the border usually has to wait only a few minutes, while someone applying at a Canadian post abroad typically has to wait months.

For a select group of travellers, visiting is particularly difficult. Citizens of certain countries are required to obtain visas before their departure even if they never intend to leave the Canadian airport or get off the plane. People from these countries are prohibited even from passing through Canada en route to another destination unless they obtain a Canadian visa abroad. In general, the reason for such a visa requirement is that citizens of these countries are thought to have abused the visitor's permit system. The Department of Immigration has found that a significant number of individuals with visitor's permits have overstayed their visits, and that forcible action has been necessary to remove them from Canada. It is felt that such a visa requirement helps reduce abuse.

It is inherently unfair to require immigrants from certain countries to obtain a visa simply because the Department of Immigration believes, on the basis of their nationality, that they may overstay a visitor's permit. The Canadian Charter of Rights and Freedoms guarantees the legal benefit of the law without discrimination based on national or ethnic origin. To say that nationals of one country require visas, and nationals of another do not, seems a clear case of discrimination based on national origin. The Charter guarantee applies to 'every individual.' It is not limited to Canadian citizens and permanent residents as are other Charter guarantees. The Supreme Court of Canada has already said that fundamental justice guaranteed under the Charter applies to persons who claim refugee status in Canada or at a port of entry.[6] It seems clear, then, that this Charter guarantee should apply to visitors at a port of entry as well. At present, visitors without visas who are from one of the countries on the Department of Immigration's 'list' can be ordered deported if they do not have a visa. Someone ordered deported on this basis could challenge the deportation under the Charter.

Those who come from countries for which visas are not required face another problem. They are subject to an examination to determine whether they are genuine visitors. The examination is selective, and there is a common feeling that this selection is discriminatory. The parliamentary Committee on Visible Minorities noted in *Equality Now* that, rightly or wrongly, there is a widespread perception that minorities are discriminated against at the border on the basis of race or ethnic origin. In the words of one witness: 'Turbans attract attention' (p. 57). The Committee recommended that Employment and Immigration Canada take appropriate steps to ensure that members of visible minorities are not unduly singled out for unusual immigration procedures and that all such procedures are adequately explained to arriving persons and their awaiting relatives and friends. The government acknowledged the perception of discriminatory treatment (for instance, more intensive interviews) and has committed itself to developing a cross-cultural training program for its officers as well as to establishing stronger links with ethnic minority communities.

Delays

In some parts of the world, visa delays are relatively short; in others, they are excruciatingly long. A table published in 1992 by the Recruitment and Selection Branch of the Canada Employment and Immigration Commission gives some idea of the dimension of the problem. For instance, in the third quarter of 1992 the mean processing time for family-class applications in London was 84 days, in Birmingham 93 days, in Sydney 120 days, and in New York 176 days. At the same time, the mean processing time in Manila was 380 days, in New Delhi 324 days, in Port-of-Spain 303 days, and in Hong Kong 289 days. In other words, the same application took four-and-one-half times as long to process in the Philippines as it did in the United Kingdom.

A related problem is the number of immigration offices, about which almost nothing substantive has been done in the last decade. In 1983, when we received over 7800 landed immigrants from India, there was only one visa office in that country. Yet in India distances are large, transportation is inefficient, time-consuming, and expensive, and interview requirements are common. In the Philippines, again a large territory, from which we received 4600 immigrants, there was also only one immigration office. On the other hand, the United Kingdom and France, from which we received 5700 and 1500 immigrants, respectively, had three visa offices each. In the United States, from which we received 7000 immigrants to May 1993, we had ten visa offices; now there are four. Although the numbers of immigrants from India and the United States was about the same, there were ten times as many offices in the latter. It is little wonder that processing delays were far longer in India.

The Parliamentary Committee on Visible Minorities dealt with this issue as well. The Canadian Government attributed the lengthy delays to factors such as the lack of reliable systems of record-keeping in the country of origin (*Equality Now*, p. 59). However, the inadequate number of offices suggests that poor record-keeping is by no means the entire explanation. The Committee recommended that the Government conduct a general review of its policy with regard to both the number and location of offices and the procedures for processing applications. In response, the Government said it would open seven new points of service in existing Canadian missions in developing countries, and that it would closely monitor processing times in different posts (*Response of the Government of Canada to Equality Now Report* 1984: 13). Little, however, has been done. At this writing, there is still only one visa office in India, one in the Phillipines, and four in the United States.

CONCLUSION

Canada, now as always, needs immigrants. Like other industrialized Western nations, it has a declining birth rate, an aging population, and the need for skilled and educated men and women who will expand the labour force, invest in Canadian industry, generate jobs, and help sustain our standard of living. Moreover, Canada has a moral and legal obligation under international law to provide a place of refuge to people fleeing war and persecution in their homeland.

Many of those who wish to come here, many of those who are here and wish to stay, and those who by accident of time and place seek asylum with us are amongst the most vulnerable of people. Those in the legal community who represent them, as well as those in the voluntary and professional sectors who counsel and support them, know this all too well.

In the space of a few decades Canada has been transformed from a country with overtly racist laws and practices to one in which respect for human rights, at least in principle, is universally accepted. But our history is a cautionary tale. As we have seen, principle is no sure guarantor of human rights. We must be vigilant to ensure that the principles of racial equality stated in our Immigration Act and in our Charter of Rights and Freedoms are put into practice by our institutions and officials, are given legal force by our courts, and are clearly understood by all those who work with immigrants and refugees.

NOTES

1 Canada, *Statutes*, 9-10 Edward VII, C. 27, s. 28(c)
2 1946 *Supreme Court Reports*, 248; 1947 A.C. 87
3 *Canada Gazette*, Vol. 41, 3276
4 *Western Weekly Reports*, 1347 (1914)
5 Re Singh 17, *Dominion Law Reports*, (4th) 422 (1985)
6 Ibid.

Chapter 5

Race, Racism, and the Justice System

Joanne St. Lewis

This chapter presents a critical examination of race and the Canadian justice system. It starts with a brief review of the legal-historical framework in which racial issues arise, and proceeds to discuss contemporary issues in Canadian law that are related to race. Practical recommendations will be provided throughout the discussion.

Before proceeding, let me clarify the term 'racialized communities,' to which I refer throughout the discussion. 'Racialized community' refers to communities whose members have traditionally been identified as 'racial minority,' 'visible minority,' or 'people of colour,' and whose identities are often constructed with reference to race, racism, and/or exclusionary experiences; all of which result in disadvantage that they suffer (St. Lewis and Galloway 1995).

RACE IN THE LEGAL CONCEPTUAL FRAMEWORK

The Canadian Constitution, through the Canadian Charter of Rights and Freedoms, guarantees every individual the right to be free from discrimination. However, the Canadian Constitution, like all constitutions, is not infallible and does not serve all persons equally. Like history, a constitution is written by the victors (Huggins 1991), and often fails to reflect the concerns of those racialized communities it purports to serve (St. Lewis and Galloway 1995).

The source of most of the legal rights identified in the Constitution can be found in nineteenth-century liberalism (Goldberg 1993: 5). Liberalism emphasized the capacity of every individual to claim rights, which were to be exercised without interference from the state, providing that the exercise of those rights did not impair the rights of another. It does not recognize collective or group rights based on race, gender, or class because of its focus on individuals alone.

The relevance of the above discussion about liberalism is twofold. First, it is the underlying framework for the current debate about rights. As Goldberg points out: 'Liberalism plays a foundational part in this process of normalizing and naturalizing racial dynamics and racist exclusions. As modernity's definitive doctrine of self and society, of morality and politics, liberalism serves to legitimate ideologically and to rationalize politico-economically prevailing sets of racialized conditions and racist exclusions' (1993: 1). Second, reliance on liberalism prevents the recognition of individuals who seek rights that encompass their group identity.

The entire discourse about rights has been fraught with difficulty. Frances Ansley has suggested that 'in the real world of civil rights scholarship no pure models exist. The themes of race and class refuse to keep their bounds. They constantly interpenetrate, converge and reflect on each other' (1989: 1050). It has been suggested that the failure of liberalism to recognize collective rights, despite its espousal of equality as a guiding precept, demonstrates a lack of the analysis that would fully ensure social justice. '"Blind" liberalisms are themselves the reflection of particular cultures. And the worrying thought is that this bias might not just be a contingent weakness of all hitherto proposed theories, that the very idea of such a liberalism may be a kind of pragmatic contradiction, a particularism masquerading as the universal' (Taylor 1994: 44). This debate both within and outside critical race scholarship reflects the struggle for reconciliation of a racialized legal history in a contemporary context where the instruments for social transformation are limited by the law's power to define relationships (West 1993; Crenshaw 1988).

There are a number of observations raised within critical race discourse that are useful to anyone who seeks to understand how the values that inform their discipline/professional responsibilities are reinforced by the law:

1 Objective rules do not create equality; they have a disproportionate impact on the less powerful because their values and perspectives were not part of the rule-making process (Delgado 1992: 818).
2 The experiences of racialized women are a distinct ground of discrimination, not merely a degendered experience of racism (Harris 1990).

3 There is a base of expertise that derives from the specificity of the experience of racialized peoples.
4 The voice of racialized peoples must be contextualized or placed in a cultural framework to understand the multifaceted nature of their experience with racism (Davis 1991).
5 Critical race discourse offers fundamental challenges to the notions of property and the individual, so that broader societal relationships can be understood (Powell 1992).

One of the overarching tools of the Common Law legal system is our reliance on precedent, which enables our legal system to surmount the idiosyncracies of any one judge and provides some certainty about both the reasoning and the outcome of particular cases (Gall 1990: 272). Through the doctrine of precedent, the law is rooted in the past. It becomes difficult to envision a racism-free jurisprudence when the law relies upon concepts derived from a time when chattel slavery existed, women were not persons, and colonization, including the theft of Aboriginal lands, was in full force. We have not yet had an acknowledgment of this conceptual taint, much less an attempt by the courts to revitalize the law within an anti-discriminatory framework. Legal precedents cannot transcend this racist history. It is one of the primary, yet invisible, obstacles within the legal system (Bell 1992).

The other source of law is legislation. While the legislative processes of the provincial and federal governments are open to public scrutiny, the legislative drafting process – how language gets into the document – remains shrouded in mystery. It is not common practice to have the persons who are to be specifically subject to legislation participate in its drafting, though they may be consulted formally and informally. The question in the context of this paper is how representative of racialized peoples are the legislatures? One need only look at the representation of racialized peoples and First Nations peoples to realize that our lawmakers are significantly under-representative of the broader Canadian society.

HOW IS RACIAL DISCRIMINATION ADDRESSED IN THE LAW?

There is a naïveté behind the suggestion that the courts, as the upholders of our constitutional rights, define and protect vulnerable communities (Delgado 1991). But what happens when racial discrimination is the problem? The right to seek remedy directly from the court for racial discrimination was addressed in *Bhadauria v. Seneca College of Applied Arts and Technology (Board of Governors)* by Justice Bertha Wilson, as she then was. In recognizing the right of victims of discrimination to redress, she said: 'I do not regard the Code as in any way impeding the appropriate development of the common law in this area. While the fundamental human right we are concerned with is recognized by the Code, it was not created by it' (*Bhaduria* 1980: 203). However, the Supreme Court of Canada rejected the creation of a new tort of discrimination, hence restricting complainants to seek remedy through human-rights tribunals.

The courts have difficulty responding to racially motivated offences and incorporating race into their analysis. In the case of *Smithers*, the young Black hockey player was found guilty of manslaughter after the death of a white opponent with whom he had an altercation. He had suffered repeated racial slurs from his opponents during the game and was alone when he was accosted outside of arena by three white players from the opposing team. By the time the case reached the Ontario Court of Appeal, and later the Supreme Court of Canada, all mention of race had been removed from the judgments.

The courts have also upheld discriminatory legislation directed towards a racialized community. The Indian Act is part of Canada's colonial legacy. The discriminatory provision (s. 12(1)(b) of the Act) that disenfranchised Indian women of their status when they married non-Indian men, as defined by the Act, was only partially remedied when the impugned provisions were challenged at the International Human Rights Committee (see Berlin, chapter 12). In keeping with the minimalist approach to addressing systemic racism, the residual discrimination of section 6 continues to complicate the lives of First Nations women and their children. The consequence of these and other provisions that have denied First Nations peoples their right to self-determination has been identified as a form of cultural genocide (Strickland 1986).

The failure of the courts to recognize systemic racism and their exclusive jurisdiction in human-rights matters has placed increased expectations on tribunals to provide social justice through the recognition and redress of racist practices at the individual and institutional levels. However, human-rights tribunals are still struggling to develop their understanding of race-related issues in all their complexity. In the case *Pitawanakwat*, the Saskatchewan Human Rights Commission found racial discrimination and ordered the federal Secretary of State to reinstate the complainant in a comparable position. The department was not required to provide a position in the same jurisdiction or return the complainant to the original position. The fact that the Aboriginal woman complainant was a single parent with school-age children was not determinative. The discrimination experienced by the victim was compounded by the tribunal's attempt to balance the institutional interests of the employers with those of the victims.

Human-rights remedies are not always sufficiently broad to encompass the systemic problems that give rise to the individual case. The monetary compensation for loss of dignity is low. In addition, boards of inquiry have imposed a range of remedies – including individual apologies, requiring anti-racism training, reinstatement in the position, requesting racial diversity in advertising, instituting employment-equity plans and developing anti-racism policies to address racist conduct.

The failure of courts and tribunals to effectively address systemic racism provided one context for the work of the Court Challenges Program and for interventions by public-interest advocacy groups, such as the Women's Legal Education and Action Fund (LEAF) and the Minority Advocacy and Rights Council (MARC). These organizations have brought an equality analysis, including one of racism, to courts and tribunals through the use of intervenor status based on a test-case litigation strategy. Their briefs have informed the courts of perspectives and issues that might otherwise have been marginalized or eliminated without question. Their work has challenged the race-neutrality of the law through the explicit recognition of the heightened vulnerability of racialized persons. The newly formed African-Canadian Legal Clinic, in Toronto, is also committed to using a test-case litigation strategy to challenges issues of anti-Black and systemic racism. Through their advocacy, racialized peoples are moving from the invisibility of the periphery to demand full consideration in the courts' deliberations. They understand that as long as we continue to rely on the myth of objectivity and neutrality, our courts will fail to address fully the systemic racism that results from its ahistorical race-neutral stance (Johnson 1988: 1031).

THE SOCIAL ENVIRONMENT IN WHICH RIGHTS ARE BEING DISCUSSED

There is increasing tension between racialized communities and those who see the incursions of rights advocacy as a 'good thing that may have gone too far.' These communities are struggling to maintain the gains that they have obtained in the past decade. In *Backlash: The Unde-*

clared War Against American Women, Susan Faludi discusses the attempts to roll back the progress made by women that are based upon a perception or misperception that too much progress has been achieved (Faludi 1991: xix). Racialized peoples who have yet to experience the swing of the pendulum to the centre are also finding themselves caught in the struggle to ensure that an awareness of the pervasiveness of racism and of its impact on people remains on the public agenda. The debates about political correctness under the guise of freedom of speech mask an increasing intolerance towards those who would challenge the status quo and find it wanting (Greene 1992). Many have lost sight of the fact that the ostensible goal of equality for all is yet to be achieved. All too often the voices of the least enfranchised are not heard in the esoteric debate to determine who is or is not politically correct.

There has been a resurgence of white supremacy that is troubling in its persistence. It is not sufficient to speak about how aberrant such values are from the rest of society. The environment in which they thrive and in which they recruit and seek their support is the one in which we live. It should not be overlooked that the shields that are raised by white supremacists to criticism are those of freedom of association, freedom of religion, and freedom of speech. Courts have uncritically interpreted these freedoms without applying the leavening intent of an equality analysis. The communities who find themselves the targets of the white supremacists are then seen as censors and restrictors of rights rather than persons who are seeking to assert their own rights to peaceful coexistence (McIntyre 1993).

Increasing economic disparity domestically and internationally has meant heightened vulnerability for those communities already disproportionally under-employed and unemployed (Mies 1986: 112). Global capitalism has resulted in more porous borders, whereby the economic policies of one nation can ripple around the globe. In addition, labour has become more mobile as people seek work and flee the economic instability that is fostered in part by policies which do not focus on the needs of the local population. The legacy of colonization, multilateral trade agreements, and the impact of transnational corporations have resulted in a convergence of economic power that continues to disempower the people of the South. It also affects the economies of countries like Canada.

It is important to understand the relationship of global capitalism to the national economic and social situation, since this is the catalyst for the large-scale displacement of people globally. The plight of the domestic worker who leaves her family to care for the children of a privileged middle-class European or North American is not, ironically, unlike the condition of the slave women forced to raise the children of their masters. Simultaneously debased and entrusted with the future, racialized women and their communities must reconcile this contradiction. Throughout this process, it is the law that upholds the relationships – that recognizes freedom of contract, permits unequal treatment under labour law, and interprets multilateral trade agreements that deny the centrality of human rights while they augment commercial interests.

The federal government's recent discussions of social-policy reform, the changes to Canada's immigration policy (see Matas, chapter 4), and the widespread concern about our increasing debt means that conversations about race and racism are no longer viewed as a priority. The fact that we no longer have the luxury of ignoring racial tensions as we seek to build our community is not on the table. Canada's multiculturalism policy (see James, chapter 1), in all its ineffectiveness, remains one of the most powerful assertions of our commitment to multi-racialism. Unfortunately, it has been improperly implemented and reflects much political cynicism about the role of racialized communities in the Canadian state (Bissoondath 1994).

PROVISION OF SERVICES WITHIN THE CONTEXT OF RACE AND
RACISM

Human-service providers are faced with a very diverse clientele. Defining the service to be provided depends in part on who is to be served and how that person/community is identified. The essential issue, in the context of this paper, is how and when race becomes a factor in this decision. There are three basic options – to define the issue as race-neutral, to respond in a race-specific manner, or to contextualize the issue. Quite often the clients themselves have different views about how their cultural values should be defined and what if any relevance they have to the service you are about to provide.

The first question that arises is one of defining culture. Canadian culture is not race-neutral (see James, chapter 1). One of the defining facets of culture is the values and perspectives we hold and the manner in which we regulate them through the operation of the law. Our legal system provides a framework for our understanding of what Canadian culture is. The Common Law has Judaeo-Christian roots and was born within European society. In addition to the class and gender biases present in it, the Common Law inevitably reflects notions of the individual and personhood that operated to exclude racialized peoples. It is the very pervasiveness of these European-based values that makes them invisible. Those who challenge these values are perceived to have 'race,' while all others who adhere to them see themselves as 'race neutral' and accuse others of bringing racism into the discourse. Racialized people are denied the power to both define and reinforce present understandings of Canadian culture and feel excluded from full participation in the society.

Before there can be a commitment to providing culturally sensitive service there must be an analysis of whether culture is relevant. The culture of racialized peoples has often been written of and defined from the perspective of European anthropologists, sociologists, and historians. It is also defined from within, through the eyes of predominantly male élites. Lack of cultural sensitivity can reinforce the discriminatory impact of already pernicious cultural practices. Canadians were shocked to read of cases in the North where judges spoke disparagingly of the impact of sexual assault on Inuit girls and women based upon their understanding of Inuit culture and the different cultural reality of life in the North. For example, a sexual assault where the victim was a virgin was seen as less serious because it was perceived that sexual practices in Inuit culture condoned such behaviour.

The form of newspaper reporting did little to dispel the notion that these statements were anything more than the idiosyncratic statements of individual judges. Teresa Nahanee has noted the pervasiveness of these beliefs and the plethora of cases involving Inuit girls and women that reinforced these stereotyping practices. It was the reliance on this evidence that satisfied the Eurocentric viewpoint on Aboriginal peoples, and served to reinforce the Inuit male perspective that further victimized Inuit women in the courts (Nahanee 1994: 192).

The debate between individual versus collective rights continues to rage on at the international level. There is, however, a practical reality. How can you serve individuals and do so in a context that neither forces their isolation/exile from their community nor makes assistance available only through assimilation to existing service norms? The above discussion about the gendered nature of culture is also an indication of the extent to which Canadian standards of male-female relationships are an acceptable norm. Further, violence against women is pervasive in our society (Canadian Panel on Violence Against Women, 1993).

In discussing the widespread vulnerability of all women to violence, we must recognize that its incidence, context, and impact may vary for racialized women. We must also ensure that in our efforts to address culture we do not create a new stereotype of racialized communities as being inherently more sexist or misogynist that our own. Robert A. Williams Jr, in his aptly entitled article 'Gendered Checks and Balances: Understanding the Legacy of White Patriarchy in an American Indian Cultural Context,' sounded a cautionary note that provides some guidance regarding how to approach a critique of internal cultural norms in a historical and respectful manner (Williams 1990).

The issue of conflicts between racialized communities can be paralysing as you struggle to devise a solution that disempowers neither yet still achieves justice. Resolving an interracial dispute requires an understanding of the history of the relationship between the two communities. In addition to race, quite often the dispute may reflect a legacy of economic and political inequities that have never been reconciled. To approach the mediation process in a historically neutral manner makes the solution more fragile and less attainable.

Mediation is often touted as an alternative to the adversarial process of the court. However, mediation can provide an environment where confrontational characteristics are still present. Furthermore, the informal atmosphere of the mediation can create an atmosphere that can encourage or at least fail to limit sexist and racist practices. It is incumbent on the mediator/human-service provider to ensure that the rights of the participants, as identified under the human-rights legislation and the Charter, are respected and form the environmental context for the mediation.

THE ROLE OF HUMAN-SERVICE PROVIDERS IN THE COURTS

There are two principal roles for human-service providers in the courts that I would like to discuss at this point. The first is the role of expert witness and the second is that of assisting in client preparation for court.

As an expert witness, the human-service provider is expected to provide insights that would otherwise not be available to assist the court in arriving at a just decision. The role of expert witness brings with it credibility and the right to be heard, as well as responsibility. It is incumbent upon the expert to evaluate critically the values that inform the evidence that she or he gives in court. Academic and empirical studies, qualitative research, and anecdotal evidence are not value-neutral. In fact, one

need only think of the impact of systemic discrimination on the participation of persons from racialized communities in the academy to come
to the conclusion that their absence would directly affect the research
that currently defines the experiences of racialized peoples (see Christensen, chapter 7, and Tator, chapter 8). Human-service providers
should reflect upon the evidence that they have to offer and consider
whether there are any aspects of their testimony that may be informed
by individual prejudices, societal stereotypes, or systemic biases based
upon particular fields of study or an absence of accurate/validated
research on the particular community.

It is rare to find a 'trial by combat' of experts. In fact, often the evidence of the experts will be unchallenged. In court, evidence is subject
to two tests – probative value and weight. The first refers to the relevance of the information to the matter at hand. The second refers to the
level of importance or impact that it should have on the deliberations.
Human-service providers should consider how the information that
they have derived about particular communities would stand up to this
double scrutiny. This self-imposed critique is simple to apply and would
have the benefit of strengthening the testimony provided in court while
lessening the vulnerability of racialized communities to further stereotyping.

Human-service providers may find themselves in the position of
informing their clients about the legal system or supporting them
through a judicial proceeding. In addition to the basic issues of language
access and basic literacy in the functioning of the Canadian legal system,
there are concerns that may stem from your client's racialized status. It
should be noted that the lack of literacy in the Canadian legal process
increases the responsibility of the human-service provider to place the
specific needs of the client in a context.

Client preparation in an anti-racist framework may mean the inclusion of a number of specific actions that may not be consonant with a
race-neutral approach. It may mean validating the client's lack of trust
of the judicial system. A number of studies (Royal Commission on the
Donald Marshall Jr. Prosecution, 1989; the Commission on Systemic
Racism in the Ontario Criminal Justice System, 1994) have recognized
both systemic and direct discrimination in the criminal-justice system. A
client's reluctance to cooperate or enter into the system is therefore not
one simply of perception but one of a different expectation or experience
within the broader society. Thus, it may be necessary to validate this
lack of trust while seeking to bridge the gap and providing information

to the client. It may mean that part of the strategy or decision-making process regarding the efficacy of going to court must take into consideration or acknowledge your client's vulnerability to racism. Finally, it may mean engaging in discussions with the client to determine whether racism was a factor in the circumstances that have arisen.

Exchanges with clients over issues of racism may not be pleasant. In addition to the fear, embarrassment, and helplessness of the experience there is often anger. The lack of trust of anyone within the system of power can be compounded by the service provider's membership in the community that the client has identified as the source of his or her racist experience. It is important to acknowledge the source and basis of this anger so that effective communication can be established with the client.

Patricia Williams has spoken of the impact of racism on the dignity of racialized peoples as 'spirit murder,' and has set out the societal context in which anger may legitimately arise (Williams 1987). The daily 'micro-aggressions' of racist experiences may inform the client's attitude towards both you and the court. 'Vigilance and psychic energy are required not only to marshall adaptational techniques, but also to distinguish microaggressions from differently motivated actions and to determine "which of many daily microaggressions one must undercut."' (Davis 1989: 1566). Non-racialized peoples rarely experience or have to respond to such microaggressions. Care should be taken to ensure that the denial of the relevance of racism in any circumstance is not simply a reflection of discomfort or lack of experience. Recognition of the reality of racism may be of assistance to service providers in the court-preparation process.

SPECIAL ISSUES FOR HUMAN-SERVICE PROVIDERS

Culture and the Family

The rights of children have become an issue of increasing importance on the public agenda. Children's rights advocates have pointed out the interrelationship between women's lack of power and the oppression of children. The feminization of poverty has often also meant the impoverishment of children. The vulnerability of women to abuse in the home has frequently meant the vulnerability of children to abusive situations. In this context it is not difficult to both understand and support measures that would serve to protect children who clearly lack the power and autonomy to transform their abusive situations.

In our zeal to protect children and develop policies that would ensure that their rights are respected it is important that we examine how uniform policies can compound discrimination against racialized parents or further the discrimination against racialized women. The first example is that of child abuse where it arises in the area of physical discipline. The second is challenges to the parental decision-making process by children through the use of school guidance counsellors, social workers, and teachers. The third is the uniform charging practices in cases of alleged partner abuse.

There are cultural differences both in the defining of the family and in the relations within families. Many members of Canadian society would contest the efficacy of corporal punishment, but might debate when and what form of spanking of a child (age to be defined) would be appropriate. The determination of whether this practice is lawful is no longer debatable. It is increasingly argued that good parenting skills means that parents should be able to negotiate better ways of dealing with disciplinary problems with the children which do not necessitate physical discipline. Yet, many Canadians are not unfamiliar with the saying 'spare the rod and spoil the child.' This truism is not unique to European culture but permeates many cultures. In seeking to enforce this new standard through the operation of the criminal law we may have a conflict between social understandings and legal reality.

The role of the schools in supporting or fragmenting family relationships has not been discussed extensively. Human-service providers can find themselves the unintentional actors in family disputes when they choose to support children challenging their parents' authority on the basis of violation of their rights. It is not uncommon to find first-generation children of immigrant parents who are conversant in the range of rights provided under Canadian law and social policy challenging their parents' rules on the basis that their individual rights and autonomy are being violated. An application of child-rearing strictures that are inimical to the cultural practises of the family often results in further alienation between the child and the parent and makes it very difficult to build a relationship between the parent and the service provider. It is here that a failure to contextualize the family situation and to respect the possibility of different but equally valid forms of child rearing can result in the criminalization of parents, the fragmentation of racialized families, and the liability of these parents to other legal sanctions.

Human-service providers are concerned about protecting children from vulnerable racialized communities. What is not explicitly stated is the unspoken belief that perhaps certain women in these communities are not 'good mothers.' We define what is good parenting within a specific frame of reference. Non-European families, who may not share the same cultural values as the dominant Canadian society, may find perfectly reasonable practices (such as having an older sibling take care of a younger one) challenged. When this happens we must consider whether we are redefining these communities and their cultures to suit our assumptions about how families should function rather than truly focusing on the protection of the vulnerable.

The consequence of over-scrutiny could be the further disintegration of racialized families and the criminalization of vulnerable racialized women. One need only recall the apprehension of Aboriginal children in Canada by social-service agencies to recognize our own capacity to develop and implement a similarly discriminatory policy. In the ever-expanding consciousness of children's rights it is important that over-scrutiny or racist understandings of non-European families do not inform our practice.

The defining of what is a 'good parent' has risen to new heights in American jurisprudence and has been compounded by the systemic gender and race biases that underlie prosecutorial discretion (Greene 1991: 778). One example is the manner in which poor women, who are disproportionately found in racialized communities, have been criminalized for delivering drugs to their unborn children through their drug addiction. The reason for this is that these women are more often reported to government authorities – because their poverty has brought them into contact with many different social-service agencies.

Another area where a uniform approach may compound the vulnerability of racialized women is that of mandatory charging in situations where partner abuse has taken place. Economic inequalities, fear of ostracism by family or community, and a desire to preserve the family can motivate some women to remain in an abusive situation. Racialized women, however, are faced with issues outside these boundaries that must be acknowledged by human-service providers (St. Lewis and Galloway 1995). The reality of systemic racism means that racialized men have a heightened vulnerability to charging, prosecution, and conviction. Concern has been raised about their vulnerability to higher sentencing. For the racialized woman who is aware of this reality, entering into the judicial process may be very difficult. Violence against women is not unique to any culture. However, it is important that human-service providers acknowledge and support women who wish these contextual issues to be considered in their selection of a strategy to deal with their abusive situation.

Culture as a Defence in Breaches of Canadian Law

The most recent discussion paper of the Department of Justice on the reform of the Criminal Code states explicitly that culture should not be a defence in criminal law. While this indicates that the matter is of sufficient urgency and magnitude in the courts that it has attracted the attention of legal policy makers, there is an assumption underlying this statement that there are cultural practices that are incompatible with Canadian values. Canadian criminal law does not incorporate the values and perspectives of non-European peoples. It is, therefore, unable to respond effectively to their concerns in a non-racist manner. Many of the issues that have arisen in the case law – incest, spousal abuse, sexual assault, femicide – are all present in Canadian society in general. As discussed above, the issue is how Canadian values are determined and who defines non-Canadian culture. To start from the premise that other cultures tolerate incest, do not value life, or do not find violence abhorrent is racist.

What is most disturbing about our preoccupation with culture as a defence is our search for deviant cultural practices in other societies with a concurrent blindness to systemic racism and its impact on racialized peoples in Canadian criminal law. The message is clear – racialized peoples bring with them practices that we must regulate. There is no recognition that we have any responsibility for their cultural practices as a consequence of their experiences of racism within this society. It is this outward focus that is the problem.

The practices identified in this section are not to be challenged because they are part of non-European cultures. They are to be challenged because all cultures find themselves in the unenviable position of devaluing the lives of the most vulnerable within their communities. It is the purpose of law to attain justice for all members of society. We do not need a misleading conversation about culture to deal with the appropriateness of developing laws that would restrict violence and protect women and children.

STAFF REPRESENTATION AS A RESOURCE FOR IMPROVED
SERVICE PROVISION

This brief section is not meant to review the extensive discussion of the operations of employment-equity legislation that is contained in the article by Cynthia Stephenson in this volume. In fact, employment equity properly applied is a significant tool that can assist us in the move towards equity.

Where employment equity may be limited is in its effectiveness to achieve social transformation for racialized communities. Representation of individuals within a given workplace, particularly when it is a token one, does not mean a change in the organization's cultural values. In fact, this is not necessarily an explicit goal of the equity process. There is nothing to prevent the process from operating in a manner that avoids the assimilation or acculturation of the worker to the dominant organizational culture. Without a critical mass at the level of senior decision making and reasonable dispersal throughout the organization, racialized peoples will find it very difficult to negotiate changes in the organizational culture that would adequately reflect their perspectives and values.

Human-service providers are further limited in attaining equity within their workplace since access to educational opportunities are limited for some members of our society. Colleges and universities provide the applicant pool for institutions. Furthermore, the capacity of human-service providers to respond to the changing demographics of their clientele is impaired by the lack of inclusion of issues of race and culture centrally within the curriculum of these educational institutions. The issues of who is trained and what is the basis of the training are an integral part of and precursor to the hiring process (see Christensen, chapter 7; Tator, chapter 8).

Despite its shortcomings, employment equity is currently the best tool for developing a respresentative workforce. It is through a diverse workforce that internal challenges to existing understandings of service provision can take place. Employment equity makes it possible to evolve a service delivery and organizational culture that address the needs of clients.

The responsibility for the implementation of employment equity is often managerial, whereas the accountability for the maintenance of an anti-discriminatory and welcoming environment is individual. Everyone has a role to play in attaining this goal. We need to have frank and open discussions about the implications of employment equity and evaluate what is truly coded behind the notion of the 'innocent white victim' (Ross 1990). Terms like reverse discrimination (see Stephenson, chapter, 13) must be critically evaluated. Recognizing the particular resources that some employees bring to the job is not discriminatory. A diverse workforce in the human-services sector means that there will be a better capacity to serve clients based upon workers' experiences, expertise, and the ability of the client to identify with the worker. There will be less vulnerability to racist practice and an enhanced capacity to identify systemic barriers. Diversity is truly about professional competence and good service.

CONCLUSION

Our commitment to address racism must not paralyse us. We should not be afraid to question, to make mistakes, and above all to learn. We should all commit ourselves to rights literacy for ourselves, our families, and our clients. 'The enabling and empowering response that avoids illusions is to sustain one's hope for social change by keeping alive the memory of past and present victories, and to remain engaged in such struggles owing principally to the *moral* substance of these efforts' (West 1993: 244). We should know the human-rights legislation in our province and how it affects our daily lives. We should examine ourselves and our organizations to ensure that we maintain environments that are hospitable for all racialized peoples. If we have a model of 'working with,' we start out on a path of mutual respect and shared vision. We must work with the community, be flexible, and be prepared to let go of accepted ways of doing things.

The process of naming racism is not an indictment. It is an opportunity for change. It also recognizes the progress that has been made by Canadians working together to realize a vision of our society where all people are treated with dignity and respect. In many ways the law is static – it must be pushed towards social justice, and at some point must respond to the advocacy of individuals and communities. There is power in naming, speaking, and challenging. If we name our vision, it will become a reality. Eventually, words like 'race' and 'racism' will gather dust and lose their power to hurt, victimize, and disempower.

Chapter 6

Anti-Semitism in Canada: Realities, Remedies, and Implications for Anti-Racism

Karen R. Mock

Many involved in anti-racism work would say that anti-Semitism is not racism and that it is not systemic in our society; they argue that Jews, though they can be from many different racial backgrounds, are primarily white and members of the power structure, and thus cannot be victims of racism. While most Jews would acknowledge what can be called their 'white privilege' in a racist society, I believe that there has been, and is currently, a powerful racist component in anti-Semitism, and that anti-Semitism must thus be on the anti-racism agenda.

In addition to dealing with the present manifestations of anti-Semitism, and possible responses to it, this chapter will attempt to trace its history and its change from a primarily religious to a primarily racist phenomenon. An understanding of the meaning and evolution of anti-Semitism, and of its current expression in Canada, should help make clear the relationship of anti-Semitism to other expressions of racism in our community.

THE HISTORICAL EVOLUTION OF ANTI-SEMITISM

What Is Anti-Semitism?

Anti-Semitism can be defined most simply as hostility directed at Jews solely because they are Jews (Anti-Defamation League 1989). In spite of what anti-Semites profess, anti-Semitism is not caused by the actions or beliefs of Jews, but rather is a result of attitudes and behaviour that arise regardless of what Jews do or believe. Anti-Semites are antagonistic to

Jews for who they are and what they represent, and this antagonism has an ancient history.

The roots of anti-Semitism go back to ancient times, when the religion of the Jews first began to distinguish them from their neighbours (Patterson 1982). Indeed, the roots can be found in the Hebrew Bible itself. According to Schoeps (1963), 'the anti-Semitic polemic of the nations of the world goes back to early antiquity – to be exact, to Haman's vexation that here was a nation with laws differing from the law of every nation.' While the other peoples of the ancient Near East worshipped many gods, the Jews (first called Hebrews, then Israelites) had only one god, who was invisible, had delivered them from slavery in Egypt to their land, and created the laws by which they lived. Unlike those around them, the Jews regarded their God as so holy that they refused to make statues or images of God, and dared not speak God's name.

Although the term 'anti-Semitism' is only about one hundred years old, the prejudice it describes was clear in writings dating from as early as 300 BCE.[1] Patterson (1982) points out that one Alexandrian writer of that period even challenged the claim of the Jews that they had escaped from slavery in Egypt, writing that they had been expelled because they were lepers. Alexandrian writers accused Jews of every imaginable offence, claiming they were traitors for not worshipping the city gods, and even accusing them of killing human beings for religious reasons (a practice strictly forbidden in Judaism, even during the times of sacrificial cults). Apion, living in the third century BCE, was the first to accuse the Jews of ritual murder, a charge that was to be repeated, often with disastrous effects on Jewish communities, in later centuries.

Jewish monotheism continued to clash with the polytheistic practices of Rome and other cultures. When Jews were granted certain rights to practise their religion, resentment would often increase, many in the population labelling them 'clannish' or even 'hostile.' Foremost among Roman anti-Semites was the historian Tacitus. Patterson notes that Tacitus called Jewish religious practices 'rites contrary to those of all other men' and claimed that they were 'sinister, shameful and have survived only because of their perversity' (1982: 6). Patterson goes on to suggest that 'like most anti-Semites then and later, [Tacitus] did not seem to know very much about Judaism, and was certain that Jews worshipped donkeys which they consecrated in their temples.' In 135 AD (CE), Jews were barred from their holy city, Jerusalem, and could only approach as far as the outer wall of the temple (the Wailing Wall, now known as the

Western Wall). The Roman emperor banned circumcision, and passed laws to isolate the Jews even further, just as Christianity was beginning to spread through the empire.

The Christian Roots of Anti-Semitism

A detailed history and analysis of the evolution of anti-Semitism is beyond the scope of this chapter, but some mention of the role of the Christian church is essential.

Jesus was a Jew, faithful to the law of Moses and the teachings of the prophets. He was called 'Rabbi'; his last words on the cross were from the psalms. Like other Jews who were religious nationalists, the Roman government considered Jesus a threat because of his preaching and the increasing size of his following. On Jesus' Passover trip to Jerusalem the Roman procurator ordered his arrest and execution. His followers, the Nazarenes, continued to practise Judaism until many years later, when Paul, who had never met Jesus, transformed his teachings, removed most of the traditional Jewish practices, and laid the foundation for a Christianity that became separate from and hostile to the very Judaism out of which it emerged. By the time the Gospels were written they reflected this increasing bias against traditional Judaism, and told the story of Jesus in such a way that it seemed the real enemies of Jesus were not Gentiles, or even the Romans who put him to death, but the Jews. With each successive author of the Gospels, the Jews were increasingly, though falsely, painted as the persecutors of Jesus and those who drove him to his death. According to Patterson (1982) it was in this way that hostility against the Jewish mainstream resulting from the fierce competition in the first century between early Christianity and Judaism (or, until Paul, between two different sects of Judaism) became a permanent part of the Christian Bible and later of Christian teaching and ritual.

Thus, generations of Christians to this day have grown up influenced by the negative pictures of Jews painted in these scriptures (and literally painted as menacing stereotypes of evil in frescos and murals on church walls) – sources that many Christians, with no understanding of either the historical context or the historical facts, consider to be sacred and infallible accounts of history.

Anti-Semitism in the Middle Ages

Repetitive cycles of pogroms, expulsions, and massacres throughout the ages continued to isolate Jews, making them increasingly fearful and suspicious of the Christian world that surrounded them, and forcing them to cling even more strongly to their faith for survival. The Crusaders massacred tens of thousands. England expelled them in 1290 and France in 1306, with many German towns shortly following suit. They were slaughtered in retaliation for their rumoured causing of the Black Death in Europe, and there were countless burnings at the stake for alleged ritual murders.

In spite of forced conversions in Spain, the killings continued there because of suspicions of 'bad blood' and of the secret practice of Judaism. The Inquisition saw thousands burned at the stake or abused, imprisoned, and stripped of their property ('More than one pyre blazed; and the blood sacrifices of the Inquisition are without number' [Schoeps 1963: 36]). Spain and Portugal expelled all Jews in 1492 under penalty of death. Some were welcomed in Turkey and Italy. Continued persecutions and expulsions from Germany and other western European countries meant that the only safe havens for Jews were Poland, Lithuania, Galicia, and the Ukraine, until the Ukrainian Cossacks ravaged Poland and destroyed seven hundred Jewish communities in 1648. The surviving remnants found their way back to some of the western European countries, including Germany, where they lived under lock and key in walled ghettos. Those who did not go to the cities remained impoverished in small farming villages in Eastern Europe.

Enforced segregation strengthened Jewish solidarity and devotion to religious study, but it isolated Jews from the larger society and made them objects of ridicule. They were no longer feared as a danger to Christian society, but were demeaned in art and literature, reviled in sermons, and mocked in public. Locked up in ghettos and isolated in rural towns, they were closed off from the effects of sweeping political, cultural, and religious changes that brought Europe into the modern era between the sixteenth and eighteenth centuries. Moreover, Martin Luther and his followers continued to preach a virulent anti-Semitism. It is not surprising that the first-large scale Nazi pogrom – 'Kristallnacht' – in November 1938 'was performed in honour of the anniversary of Luther's birthday' (Hay 1950: 169). The widespread use of the printing press contributed to the flooding of Europe with anti-Semitic pamphlets and books.

So-called enlightened philosophers advocated equal rights for all people, but advised Jews to abandon their customs and merge with the Christian majority. Voltaire, an avowed Jew-hater, wrote that they were the 'enemies of mankind' and were fully deserving of all the persecutions and massacres that came their way. Nevertheless, the Enlightenment was ultimately beneficial for Jews. Its emphasis on equal rights, and the French and American revolutions, led to the Jews' emancipation from the ghettos to take their part as 'equals' in European society.

Anti-Semitism as Racism

Emancipation was a mixed blessing for the Jews. Previously denied the vote, land ownership, or access to trade, industry, or education, they were now permitted both citizenship and access to the benefits it conferred. Such benefits, however, did not give Jews equality. Rather, Jewish progress inflamed anti-Semitism. Fear and hatred of Jews festered and took on a racial rather than a religious dimension. That is, Jews were now resented simply for being Jews, and even changing their religion did not help. The modern age of 'racial anti-Semitism' had arrived.

As the 1988 document prepared by the Pontifical Commission of the Vatican, 'The Church and Racism,' indicates, the development of modern racist theory can be traced to the attempts by colonial conquerors and slavers to 'justify their actions.' This pseudo-scientific theory 'sought to deduce an essential difference of a hereditary biological nature, in order to affirm that the subjugated peoples belong to intrinsically inferior "races" with regard to their mental, moral, or social qualities. It was at the end of the 18th century that the word "race" was used for the first time to classify human beings biologically' (sect. 3, para. 5).

It did not take long for European racial theorists to apply such ideology to the traditional 'other' in their midst – the Jews. Leading the way were some of the principal figures of the so-called Enlightenment, such as Voltaire, who held that Jews could not be assimilated into European culture. From the perspective of the secular theoreticians of race, there simply was no solution to 'the Jewish problem.' Jews were now no longer simply 'reprobates' or 'unbelievers.' They were subhuman.

Racial anti-Semitism had considerable acceptance in pre–Second World War Germany. The National Socialist totalitarian party made racist ideology the basis of its program to eliminate all those deemed to belong to an 'inferior race,' among whom were Jews, Blacks, and Slavs. As Fisher (1990) points out, one had only to re-define a group out of the category of 'human' in order to lose all bonds of moral hesitancy on what a dominant group could or would do to a minority group.

While the situation in pre-Nazi Germany seems remote from Canada in the nineties, the rise in anti-Semitism and the strengthening of right-wing hate groups across the country permit analogies to be drawn. One is the connection between hate propaganda and the rise in racism and anti-Semitism.

CURRENT MANIFESTATIONS OF ANTI-SEMITISM IN CANADA

Hate Propaganda and Racism

Hate propaganda is unabashedly racist. It portrays selected groups as inferior, as less than human, while at the same time undermining the norms and values of a society. The targets of racist hate propaganda are the traditional objects of prejudice and stereotyping, who are often characterized as taking advantage of the rest of society and posing a threat that must be removed. Hate mongering, now as always, finds its most receptive audience among those who are looking for someone to blame for their problems. Difficult economic times inevitably lead to this pattern of scapegoating, and any identifiable minority group is at risk. At such risk are many Canadians today.

As we have seen, Jews have been the traditional scapegoats throughout the history of the Western world. Indeed, anti-Semitism can be considered the prototype of racism. Denied citizenship, the vote, land ownership, housing, and employment, Jews have been blamed for the Plague, for partnership with the Devil, for ritual murder, for international economic and political conspiracy, and for every form of economic, social, and political upheaval. The proliferation of hate propaganda, in the form of speeches, pamphlets, brochures, and stereotyped cartoons and 'jokes,' was usually the prelude to pogroms or expulsions. The most dramatic example of the impact of hate propaganda was, of course, the Holocaust. The Nazi dissemination of hate propaganda and the promotion of hatred against Jews was so successful that many peoples across Europe participated enthusiastically in the Nazi attempts to systematically murder them.

There are more subtle implications. Hate propaganda promotes a negative self-image in members of the targeted group, often to the point of self-hatred and feelings of worthlessness. Individuals may try to assimilate and 'disappear' as an identifiable group, though hate mongers would suggest that this is impossible. According to avowed racists and white supremacists, the minority traits always remain as a contaminant of the society or pure race, and must therefore be eliminated to whatever extent possible. How well individuals and groups tolerate such abuse depends on the strength of one's self-image and on the group support available. But the effect of singling out the group from the rest of society achieves the hate monger's goal, regardless of the personal effects on the group and its members. As Ian Kagedan (1991) has pointed out, even when the audience is unreceptive, hate propaganda can do damage by playing on people's doubts and fears, feeding on misconceptions, and increasing the barriers to understanding.

Hate propaganda contributes to disunity in society, compromises democratic values, and maintains inequality and oppression. It is ironic that hate propagandists are among the most outspoken advocates of free-speech, while they use that freedom to deny others their freedom. Hate propaganda is most certainly not a free speech issue. It is the promotion of hatred against an identifiable group, and in Canada it is against the law. Legislation against hate mongering existed in pre-Hitler Germany, but because it was not enforced, racism and anti-Semitism went unchecked.

Hate Propaganda and Anti-Semitism: Canadian Realities

Racism and hate propaganda have long been part of the Canadian experience. Many European settlers and clerics held, and propagated, the view that Aboriginal peoples were intellectually or morally inferior to white Europeans, or that they were damned because they were outside the limits of the Eurocentric religious vision. These views were often used to justify the abuses perpetrated on Native peoples. Some of those abuses continue to this day. This campaign of dehumanization, detribalization, and marginalization has been enormously effective. It has largely prevented those who committed the abuses from being punished, and has resulted in profound despair amongst Native Canadians. The high rates of suicide and alcoholism in many Native communities are a direct consequence of the racist attitudes that have prevailed for almost half a millennium.

In addition to the racist attitudes towards the First Nations, there was rampant anti-Semitism in Canada's early history.This is not surprising considering that the early immigrants to this country brought with them the intellectual baggage of Europe, where Jew-hatred was a way of life. Regular attacks on Judaism and the Jewish community appeared in *Semaine religieuse de Québec* and in other religious publications, and the infamous anti-Semitic forgery, *The Protocols of the Elders of Zion*, was promoted by various religious leaders in Canada. From 1910 through the 1940s prominent Canadians like Edouard Plamandon, Adrian Arcand,

Goldwin Smith, Henri Bourassa, and Mackenzie King were associated with virulent anti-Semitism, taking such stands as justifying Russian pogroms against the Jews, openly praising Hitler, and denying safety in Canada to Jews fleeing Nazi persecution. During this period many other minority groups were also victimized by hate propaganda, most notably the Sikhs and Chinese.

Canada also witnessed the rise of hate groups during the pre-war years. The 1920s and 1930s saw the development of the Ku Klux Klan and the formation of the Western Guard and Aryan Nations (Barrett 1987). Such groups promoted hatred against, among others, Catholics, Blacks, and Jews. It was not uncommon in those days to see signs along the beaches or other 'restricted' areas in Toronto or Montreal that read 'No Dogs or Jews Allowed.'

There was a postwar decline in overt racism and anti-Semitism in Canada. However, with recent increases in immigration, the reduction of systemic racism in the immigration regulations, and the development of policies of multiculturalism and bilingualism, there has been an upsurge in hate-group activity and hate propaganda. Recently, the Klan has been implicated in the anti-Mohawk agitation in Quebec; Klan propaganda has been distributed in some Montreal schools and the Eastern Townships; anti-immigration white-supremacist telephone 'hate lines' have attracted attention in Vancouver, Winnipeg, and Toronto; racist skinheads have rallied regularly and have been implicated in or convicted of a number of racially motivated crimes; there have been various KKK-style cross-burnings; and Holocaust denial has become a new form of anti-Semitism in schools and public venues across the country. There is evidence of active recruitment by racist organizations of young people in high schools.

The League for Human Rights of B'nai Brith began documenting reported incidents of anti-Semitic vandalism and harassment in 1982. Over the last several years there has been a dramatic increase; the 1993 total was the highest in twelve years, and represented a 200-per-cent increase since 1988. In 1994 there were 290 reported incidents of harassment and vandalism, representing a 12 per cent increase over 1993. This was the highest number of such incidents reported by the League in thirteen years of documentation. The League's annual *Audit of Anti-Semitic Incidents* serves as a barometer of racism in Canada. Members of the Black, Chinese, and South Asian communities also report an increase in racism directed towards their communities, and both the increase in the number of cases before the Human Rights Commission and the courts and reports from various multicultural and anti-racist organizations, as well as statistics from recently created police hate-crimes units, corroborate our findings.

Yet another disturbing trend has emerged in recent years. There are more reports both of anti-Semitic workplace harassment and of the indefinable feelings of marginalization and alienation that occur when systemic discrimination exists. This kind of anti-Semitism is much more difficult to document and to resolve than overt incidents, but the emotional stress and personal anguish are palpable.

ANTI-SEMITISM / ANTI-RACISM – WHAT CAN BE DONE?

I believe that there is no one effective way to fight hatred and hate mongering, but that we can and should use whatever strategies we have at our disposal. The three most important tools we can use are the law, community action, and education.[2]

Anti-Racism Remedies in Law

Hate propaganda, defined as 'the promotion of hatred against identifiable groups,' became a criminal offence in Canada in 1970, when laws against it were adopted as amendments to the Criminal Code (sections 318–20). In that same year, Canada ratified the International Convention on the Elimination of All Forms of Racial Discrimination, which had been adopted by the UN in 1965 and signed by Canada in 1966. The Canadian Human Rights Act and various provincial human-rights acts also address the issue of hate propaganda. While the League for Human Rights and several other organizations, as well as many studies and commissions, have proposed changes to strengthen the effectiveness of the existing legislation (a summary and analysis of which are beyond the scope of the present chapter), there is almost universal agreement on the need for effective laws to deal with hate propaganda.

The catalyst for such legislation was undoubtedly the Holocaust. It showed the world that unchecked racism and hate propaganda could lead even a highly educated and cultured society to justify the most heinous crimes against humanity.

The Canadian anti-hate laws in the Criminal Code are the result of years of debate concerning the balance between individual and group rights. The premise underlying Canada's hate-propaganda laws is that in a democratic society identifiable groups must be protected against racism, including its verbal manifestation, so that those groups' basic freedoms and thereby their full participation in Canadian society are not limited. This notion is not only consistent with our international obliga- tion under the United Nations Convention, but is based on our vision of a multicultural society, a vision entrenched in the Canadian Bill of Rights (1960) and articulated clearly in the Charter of Rights and Free- doms (1982), sections 15 and 27.

Keegstra in Alberta and Andrews and Smith in Ontario were charged and convicted under the hate-propaganda laws. Although the respec- tive provincial Courts of Appeal reached opposite conclusions on the constitutionality of section 19 of the Charter, in 1990 the Supreme Court upheld the constitutionality of the hate-propaganda legislation, albeit by the narrowest majority. Concern for the values inherent in sections 15 and 27 of the Charter, and for those in the international agreements to which Canada is a signatory, played a significant role in that decision, which underscored the need to preserve the delicate balance between individual and group rights that is the mark of a free and democratic society.

There are those who insist that taking hate mongers to court gives them a platform, and who thus discourage such prosecutions and their attendant publicity. Such detractors need to be reminded that had the hate laws on the books in pre-Nazi Germany been implemented with effective penalties, the hate propaganda that led to the most violent rac- ism in history might have been halted. It is essential to continue to pros- ecute hate mongers and to impose penalties that will serve as deterrents. When the Alberta Court of Appeal overturned the Keegstra decision, there was a dramatic increase in hate-group activity and in the dissemination of hate propaganda in Western Canada. By the same token, it is possible that the recent decline in the severity of anti-Semitic incidents is a direct result of the Supreme Court's decision, of the increased awareness and vigilance of police, and of longer sentences for those convicted.

Community Action Against Racism and Anti-Semitism

The League for Human Rights of B'nai Brith encourages legal action to combat hate propaganda, but has also demonstrated during recent years that coordinated community response is effective in fighting racism. In 1989 the first Canada Day Aryan Fest took place in Minden, Ontario. The citizens of Minden stood up against racism with a campaign spearheaded by Reverend Edward Moll of the United Church, supported by the *Minden Times* and the League for Human Rights, all under the supervision of the local police. The League assisted the residents to create a human-rights committee to develop local policies and guidelines to combat hate mongers in the future.

A year later, the 1990 Canada Day Aryan Fest attracted close to 250 skinheads and white supremacists to Metcalfe, a small town near Ottawa. The League gathered a multicultural coalition of concerned citizens to rally against racism on the steps of the Parliament Buildings and to march out to the property to protest the rise of racism and the distribution of hate propaganda. Once again, the police monitored the activities of the racists, and the League's presence was felt. Because of the adverse publicity, the property owners did not allow the white supremacists to return the following year. Instead, the League for Human Rights sponsored a Multicultural Anti-racist Youth Leadership Camp, and made anti-racism, rather than racism, newsworthy. Young people learned how to stand up against racism in their schools and community organizations.

In 1992 in Toronto, the Heritage Front opened an anti-immigration 'hate-line' that included racist diatribes against the Black and Native communities. They spread hate pamphlets throughout Toronto's downtown Riverdale neighbourhood to recruit members. The League for Human Rights responded to a request for help by assisting with the filing of a complaint with the Canadian Human Rights Commission (similar to one filed by the League against the KKK in Winnipeg) and by putting a group of concerned citizens in touch with the police, the Urban Alliance on Race Relations, the Native Canadian Centre, and others. Neighbourhood Watch issued a counter-pamphlet, advising their neighbours to report any suspicious people and to take action against efforts at recruitment, particularly of young people. An ad hoc working group, calling itself Citizens Against Racism, met regularly and planned a 'Rally Against Racism' to commemorate March 21st, the International Day for the Elimination of Racism. A rainbow coalition of speakers from the First Nations, Black, Chinese, Jewish, and Sikh communities, among others, exemplified the motto on the B'nai Brith banner: 'We will not be silent.'

Coordinated community action not only raises awareness and increases vigilance, but it also reduces fear and promotes security and solidarity in the fight against racism and anti-Semitism.

Anti-Racism Education Is the Key

The battle against racism and anti-Semitism will ultimately be won through increased efforts to incorporate multicultural, anti-racist, and human-rights education in our schools and to start this training as early as possible. Many school boards have race and ethnocultural equity policies on the books, but lack of in-service training of teachers and administrators often leaves staff powerless in knowing how to handle incidents of racism, and may even result in the staff being as much part of the problem as part of the solution. There is a need for education and awareness at every level of the educational system, from early childhood through post-secondary, from teachers' federations to the ministries and departments of education. Students must be helped to stand up to racism instead of being either victims or perpetrators of harassment. Teachers must be given the skills to identify and handle expressions of racism and to develop a curriculum that is both pro-active and anti-racist. We must turn Holocaust denial into Holocaust education, and cries of 'reverse discrimination' into advocacy for organizational change, employment, and educational equity.

Through human-rights and anti-racism workshops, the League has seen children's behaviour change; its Student Human Rights Achievement Awards have demonstrated what they are capable of understanding. Organizations are clearly grappling with change through policy development and implementation. The effective leadership of dedicated principals, teachers, managers, and workers is evident. But there has also been tremendous resistance and backlash. We have a long way to go.

But there is room for optimism. Recently the Ontario Anti-Racism Secretariat of the Ministry of Citizenship declared unequivocally that anti-Semitism is on its agenda. The Secretariat is increasing its networking efforts with local police to monitor hate-group activity, and has published the League for Human Right's 'Combatting Hate' guidelines on actions to be taken against racism and anti-Semitism, along with the League's Incident Reporting Form, which is designed to encourage groups to work together and to come forward without fear to report racist and anti-Semitic incidents.

The Department of Immigration has recently prevented the notorious Holocaust denier, David Irving from entering Canada for his annual hate-promoting tour. The Solicitor-General has issued guidelines for gathering statistics on racially motivated crime, and policing services across Canada are creating hate-crimes units to monitor such crimes, assist victims appropriately, and conduct public education in schools, on campus, and throughout communities. The Ontario minister of education agreed to thoroughly investigate Paul Fromm – a known white supremacist and neo-Nazi who has hurled racial slurs against Aboriginal peoples at public meetings, whose hero is Hitler (he has celebrated his birthday at a meeting of the Heritage Front), and who continues to teach history and English for the Peel Board of Education (though he has been taken from the regular classroom and placed in adult education). There are signs of progress, however slow.

CONCLUSION

Is anti-Semitism racism? Yes and no. Attacks against Jews come from two distinct sources, religious *and* racial. Therefore, the word 'racism' is not wholly applicable; but neither is the term 'religious intolerance' sufficient.[3] Clearly, neither the attacks nor the basis on which they are made are acceptable. Though it is true that people of colour are more often subjected to racist attacks and systemic discrimination than are Jews (regardless of their colour or their visibility by virtue of dress), it is also true that, because of its religious dimension, the hatred directed against Jews differs from that directed against visible minorities. But racism is racism, and, as has been pointed out, racism has been, and continues to be, a clear component of anti-Semitism. Coming up with a satisfactorily precise term for discrimination against Jews may be difficult, but the accepted term *is* anti-Semitism. That it is a consequence of racist hate-mongering is not in question.

And racism is rarely limited to one group. It usually doesn't come in the singular. Someone who is anti-Black is also likely to be anti-Jewish. If a school system marginalizes children of colour, it is not likely to have an inclusive curriculum that values children of all religions. When we have both individual and systemic discrimination to fight, quibbling over terminology is divisive and destructive. It's time to stop arguing about the wording and to get down to ending racism, anti-Semitism, and all forms of discrimination once and for all. Policies and practices designed to eliminate racism must also be applied to eliminating anti-Semitism and to raising awareness of its continuing existence – in order to eradicate it.

We can look back to our own past and to world history to see how far we've come, but let us recognize that we still have a way to go. Legislation and enforcement have taken us a long way, and will continue to be essential in the battle against racism and anti-Semitism. Because of our laws and codes, the restrictive signs on our beaches are gone. But legislation is never enough. Community action and education will reduce prejudice and promote understanding and unity. I believe that we will overcome hatred and bigotry only when the vision that to be Canadian is to be part of a uniquely multicultural society is universally shared.

NOTES

1 Since BC means 'before Christ,' and AD 'anno Domini,' the year of our Lord, it has become inclusive practice to use the abbreviations BCE (Before the Common Era) and CE (the Common Era).
2 Portions of this section have been adapted from: Karen Mock, 'Combatting Hate – Canadian Realities and Remedies,' *Canadian Human Rights Forum* (Ottawa), Summer 1992.
3 This concept is elaborated in Lorne Shipman and Karen Mock, 'It's Time to Stop Playing with Words and Fight Racism,' *Canadian Jewish News*, February 1992.

COMMENTS:

Racism and the Issue of Voice

Kass Sunderji

The CBC is sometimes called the guardian of Canadian culture. Yet, if CBC-FM were the only radio station I listened to, I would never know that there were people of non-European origin living here. Occasional concerts of sitar music on 'Arts National' or well-meaning references to the multicultural Toronto scene on 'The Arts Tonight' would not change that perception. I once pointed this out to a CBC program director attending a national conference on visible minorities and the media. His response was that as a national radio network, the CBC had to reflect the 'core' cultural make-up of the country in its program content. When asked to explain 'core culture,' he answered somewhat vaguely but his response carried a categoric message: 'core culture' refers to the two founding cultures, and in the case of the CBC, English Canada. When I drew his attention to the changing make-up of 'English' Canada, pointed out that the core culture of the larger urban centres was tangibly different from that of the rural areas, and asked which of the many core cultures he meant, he seemed perplexed. To him 'core Canadian culture' meant white Anglo-Saxon/European culture. Had I continued to challenge this construct by making references to the First Nations of this country and their place in Canada's history, he might have accommodated this group, albeit with some uncertainty about the implied programming implications. 'New Canadians' and non-European immigrants would be placed at or outside the margins of the 'core culture.'

This manner of thinking is more the norm than the exception in terms of who becomes part of Canada's cultural life. Exclusionary ideas effectively keep Canadian artists and writers of non-European backgrounds from taking their rightful place in the country's central cultural milieu. A number of national and provincial arts funding agencies systematically deny financial support to writers and artists of certain communities by hiding behind legal statutes and program criteria; in doing so they rob these communities of a voice.

What does the above debate have to do with racism? As has already been shown in chapter 1, racism is not confined merely to racially derogatory remarks or stereotypes. While those can damage self-esteem and the ability to participate meaningfully in society, the systemic denial to racial minorities of a voice in the affairs of the larger communities is a far more effective way of making them powerless. In this sense, voice is defined as a significant and meaningful presence in the social, political, cultural, and economic institutions of society. This systemic exclusion is the consequence of a status quo that bestows on the white majority power and privilege – birthrights not always obvious to those blessed with them.

The white majority commonly uses three arguments to defend that status quo:

1 It takes time – usually a generation – for newcomers to integrate into Canadian society. Once integrated, immigrants can participate equally. Proponents of this view cite the ill-treatment of various groups at different points in history as evidence that Canadians adapt and grow to accept others and that new groups eventually become an integral part of our society.
2 Legal equality, or freedom from racial discrimination, ostensibly guaranteed under the federal Charter of Rights and the corresponding provincial human-rights legislation, provides minorities with potentially unrestricted access to power and material wealth. Occasionally, individuals of racial-minority backgrounds, such as the former lieutenant-governor of Ontario, Lincoln Alexander, or Premier Joe Ghiz of Prince Edward Island, are used as 'proof' of this argument.
3 Immigrants, particularly those from the so-called Third World, invariably racial minorities, should accept the status quo because Canadian society, imperfect though it may be, is none the less a lot better than that of the immigrants' countries of origin. By tying the human rights of racial minorities and those born outside of Canada to external factors that have no relevance to the rights to which all Canadians are entitled, this position advocates differential and discriminatory treatment.

A cursory look at the reality of the lives of racial-minority community members shows how these arguments, and the assumptions that reinforce them, are fundamentally flawed. They perpetuate racist and discriminatory structures, and help keep intact the structures of privilege enjoyed by the majority simply because they are white. The experiences of Aboriginal peoples, Black Nova Scotians, and others should dispel any notion linking equal participation in Canadian society with the length of stay in the country. If this notion were valid, both groups would have achieved equality long ago.

We must also put to rest the myth that the presence of the occasional racial minority person in a position of prominence and power shows that discrimination does not exist. Token appointments are often used to deflect attention from systemic barriers.

The third position defies both common sense and common decency. To argue that immigrants should accept discriminatory behaviour because they are 'better off' here than 'where they came from' is to perpetuate systemic injustice and to risk breaking the many provincial and federal human-rights enactments that make no distinction between Canadians who may have experienced prior hardship and those lucky ones who have not.

I started by highlighting the conspicuous absence of non-Europeans (racial minority) peoples and cultures in Canadian cultural life and institutions. In my view, this absence of 'voice' is indicative of the exclusion of racial minorities from the structures of power, where important decisions are made. Symbols drawn from a nation's cultural fabric form an integral part of a country's national consciousness. When groups cannot find themselves represented by those symbols, they are excluded from full participation in the life of their country.

In Canada, racial minorities, in spite of multiculturalism policies and programs, are still outside the national consciousness. The term 'Canadian,' although sometimes used (and inaccurately so) to refer to Aboriginal peoples, is still largely synonymous with white people (see James's discussion in chapter 1). As long as racial minorities remain outside the realm of the national consciousness, the issues of voice and representation will remain high on the agenda of racial minorities. While overt demonstrations of racism are no longer socially acceptable, racist structures continue to rob racial minorities of a voice and a sense of belonging.

PART THREE

Racism and the Human Service Sector

COMMENTS:

Social Services Agencies' Role in the Fight against Racism

Rosemary Brown and Cleta Brown

Social service organizations have to be in the forefront of challenging the myth that racism does not exist in Canada, and in combatting its debilitating effects on individuals. In their role as protectors of the most vulnerable members of society, social service agencies have a special obligation to strive ceaselessly to deal with the impoverishing impact of racism. The interrelationship and exacerbating interaction of racism and poverty cannot seriously be denied, especially when one remembers the economic roots of racism and the economic need that relies on its continuation. Since the two invariably coexist, social service agencies cannot hope to achieve any meaningful or long-term success so long as the existence and impact of racism as a contributive social ill is not recognized and acknowledged.

Social service agencies are a microcosm of our society. Obviously, therefore, these agencies' perception of their mandate, of the problems they must address, and of the approaches they have to adopt, is formulated by the larger society's definition of their purpose and by the allocation of resources to this purpose. From what is and is not taught in social work, education, and health curricula, to the legal and policy parameters within which social service agencies must operate, society's imprint cannot be avoided. Part of the challenge for social service and community workers is to recognize this social imprinting and to question, in particular, the assumptions and values upon which it is based. When one undertakes this examination, even in a most superficial way, one returns full circle to the myth that Canada is basically a non-racist country.

Chapter 7

The Impact of Racism on the Education of Social Service Workers

Carole Pigler Christensen

For some time, Aboriginal peoples and Canadians of minority ethnic and racial backgrounds have voiced concern about the impact of racism in both education and social services (Head 1977; Mawhiney 1995). Although the two may seldom be connected in the minds of the general public, I believe that the lack of access to social services experienced by members of minority and Aboriginal communities is directly related to the way social service workers are educated. This paper explores the nature of that education, indicates how insufficient attention to race, culture, and ethnicity hampers workers' ability to provide sensitive and appropriate services, and suggests remedies for the current crisis in access to social services.

I use the term 'social service workers' to refer to professional social workers with university degrees such as B.S.W.'s or M.S.W.'s, those who have been trained in the human services at the college level, those holding associate degrees or diplomas in the social services, such as child-care workers, and others who fill job descriptions with the title 'social service' or 'human service' worker, whatever their background preparation may have been.

The discussion below is based on two premises: that those working in social services are in contact with society's most vulnerable people, both individuals and groups, and that all Canadians and residents of Canada are entitled to effective, non-racist, and culturally appropriate social services.

Those, particularly in the cultural 'mainstream,' who find that social services are relevant to their needs, are often dismayed by calls by minority communities for greater access, and by the Aboriginal peoples' movement for the right to take over services in and for their communities. Their dismay reflects a vision of Canada as a monoculture – white, Christian, and Eurocentric. In light of such concerns about the nature of Canadian society, some facts and trends should be noted:

- Many non-white Canadians are not 'new'; they have been here for a century or more.
- Aboriginal Canadians were here first and have been here longest; archaeological estimates of their earliest presence in the land *begin* at about 40,000 years ago.
- Since the 'non-racist' immigration policies of 1967 were introduced, increasing numbers of immigrants have originated from non-white and Third World countries; their children know no other home than Canada, and will expect to enjoy all of the rights, privileges, and opportunities of majority-group Canadians.
- Because of a decreasing birth rate and the increased longevity of its citizens, Canada will continue to need immigrants in order to maintain its current standard of living.
- Given current world conditions, large numbers of immigrants and refugees will continue to come from developing countries, whose inhabitants are visibly distinct from Euro-Canadians. Undoubtedly, social work graduates will be called upon to serve an increasingly multiracial and multicultural clientele, who will continue to demand competent and relevant services (Christensen 1986).

A NOTE ABOUT TERMINOLOGY

Since those without power seldom have the privilege of defining themselves and of deciding what they will be called, the terminology used in connection with minority and Aboriginal groups is often controversial. Hence, before exploring the subject-matter at hand, I wish to briefly review some of the terms that have already been discussed in earlier chapters and that appear frequently in this discussion.

As a European folk concept associated with colonial expansion and oppression, race is a term in which skin colour and other visible, socially selected, traits are used to arbitrarily classify populations of the world into a hierarchical order in terms of human qualities. In this classification Europeans believed themselves superior to all others (Green 1982: 6). Although it is now generally acknowledged that the concept of race is not scientifically defensible, as long as people continue to be identified in terms of 'race,' and to act on belief systems connected with this term, simply suggesting that the term is irrelevant (as many suggest at present) is not helpful. *Racism* exists when (because of the belief that people are born with unequal and unchangeable levels of intelligence, industry, morality, and human potential) those classified as inferior are given unequal access to society's goods, services, privileges, and resources, including higher education.

Ethnic groups are often confused with races, but they actually comprise people who *choose* to associate with each other to maintain common bonds of language, ancestry, or attachment to a geographic location. Although often placed in a single ethnic category and believed to be all the same, people of 'Black,' South Asian, and Chinese ancestry, for example, come from many parts of the globe and represent many ethnic groups and cultural backgrounds, as do those of European origin. Religious communities can also form ethnic groups.

Culture is another term about which there is confusion, especially because many Canadians seem to believe that the cultures of immigrant populations remain the same despite many years spent in this country. But in a multicultural society, culture should be recognized as being shaped by the common experiences that lead people to develop values, norms, behaviours, and lifestyles in response to social, economic, and political realities in Canada, rather than only in an ancestral homeland (see chapter 1).

Those whose skins are not white (referred to as 'visible minorities' in Canada) and who are of neither British nor French ancestry are generally in a *minority* position in terms of power and influence, and may experience varying degrees of oppression. Should they have no accents or distinct forms of dress, white ethnic and cultural minorities cannot be distinguished from the dominant groups. Unless they choose to segregate themselves, immigrants of European background may become integrated into the dominant or majority group (French or British) culture within one or two generations. Most of the power and decision making belongs to the *majority* group, whose culture is legitimized in schools, religious institutions, the media, and other socializing agents.

HISTORICAL FACTORS

To be thoroughly understood, the factors affecting the educational experiences of social service workers must be considered in a historical context. Historically, racism has been, and remains today, a taboo topic.

Canadians have long prided themselves on being non-racist, and tend to resist any discussion of even the most obviously racist aspects of our history. This sanitized myth of Canadian history has been powerful enough to keep out of our schools until very recently any multiracial or multicultural content. And even where such content exists, it all too often takes the form of a passing mention of the 'quaint' traditions and customs of minority groups, which differ from those of the dominant cultures (see also Khenti, Jetté, Bedassigae-Pheasant, St. Lewis, Matas). As a result, students generally graduate from high school without having learned anything meaningful about the historical and present realities of people other than those of British and French origin. The impact of racism in peoples' daily lives is seldom discussed at any point during the educational process. Indeed, most graduates of post-secondary institutions, including schools of social work, have never been asked to consider the impact of ethnicity, culture, and race on social service delivery or on society as a whole.

Philosophically and historically, social work in Canada is rooted in the English Poor Laws and in the benevolence of the French Catholic Church, modified by the North American social welfare movement. The belief that the wealthier classes should be charitable only to the 'deserving poor' set the stage for subjective judgments to enter into assessments of personal problems that have systemic roots (Christensen 1995).

During the formative years of the development of social services, few workers attempted to respond to the plight of oppressed racial groups such as Aboriginal peoples, Blacks, or Asians. Social services were segregated on the basis of race and religion (Christensen 1990). Those with limited access to the financial market were unable to amass the capital necessary to establish adequate separate, or parallel, services. The role of language (other than French and English) in limiting accessibility was not usually considered. At the same time, negative myths and stereotypes about racial and ethnic groups were incorporated into social-science literature and social work theories (Giordano and Giordano 1975). The theoretical base of the profession has traditionally been monocultural, middle-class, and assimilationist, and has assumed that Anglo–North American norms are a standard that Aboriginal peoples and immigrants would, or should, eventually adopt. Evidently, social-policy decision-makers and educators were no less prone to racism and discriminatory practices than were other segments of society (Campfens 1981).

The poor of the pre-industrial era have been replaced by many of today's refugees, migrant workers, immigrants from developing nations, and racial minorities. Along with the indigenous population, they often experience oppression in a multicultural society that professes equality of opportunity but practises discrimination. It remains to be seen whether the growing power of the 'third force' (those of neither British nor French background) and the movement towards Aboriginal self-determination and self-government will eventually lead to lasting changes in the status of oppressed groups.

MORE RECENT DEVELOPMENTS

The present status of social service education and the services offered to various groups are a consequence of sociocultural, political, and economic factors.

Government-sanctioned social work programs at universities and colleges are the major training grounds for professionals employed in the health, education, correctional justice, and welfare systems in Canada. All such programs depend on the financial support of the dominant society. Not surprisingly, curricula have been designed to reflect the social perspectives of middle- and upper-class majority-group Canadians. Students and faculty have also tended to be drawn from the mainstream British and French constituencies.

In addition, the development of the welfare state has meant that a majority of social workers are employed in bureaucratic institutions funded, at least in part, by taxpayers. As government employees, workers and their boards are socialized to be accountable to various levels of government. Thus, remaining 'in business' does not depend on satisfying clients but on satisfying budgetary and policy requirements established for specific services.

Although blatant forms of discrimination are no longer socially acceptable, it has become increasingly clear that ethnic and racial minorities have been unable, or unwilling, to make use of monocultural social services. However, rather than encouraging a critical examination of social service theories and practices, social service workers have incorporated widespread myths and stereotypes to explain the lack of voluntary clients from minority and Aboriginal populations. For example, many minorities have been labelled resistant, non-verbal, incapable of abstract thought, and unmotivated for social work treatment (Christensen 1986). Such myths, stereotypes, and labels mask racist attitudes and allow institutional racism, often referred to as 'subtle' or 'polite,' to continue.

It is now widely acknowledged that social 'science' disciplines are neither objective nor free of cultural bias. Western-based authors developed models and theories based on their particular life experiences and on social realities in Europe or North America. Similarly, the values underlying social services are those of the western European and North American middle classes. These values emphasize the individual above the group or collectivity, the nuclear rather than the extended family, and independence as a good in and of itself. Students are now taught that they should be non-judgmental about all people, including those about whom they have little or no factual knowledge. Educators need special training if they are to help students to explore and understand the life-experiences of Aboriginal peoples, of minorities of long standing, and of recent immigrants and refugees from developing nations.

BIAS AND OMISSION IN CURRICULUM CONTENT

Those preparing for careers in the social services are generally exposed to courses in the areas of human behaviour and the social environment, social service practice and methods, social welfare policies and services, research, and field practice. The following is a brief review of what is now included in such courses, with some suggestions about what I believe should be included.

Human behaviour and the social environment courses are designed to help students understand the interaction between individuals and the surrounding community or wider society. Such courses should allow students to analyse critically the differential impact of internal and external forces on persons from diverse ethnic, racial, and cultural backgrounds. In addition, students should become aware of the need to adapt dominant-group theories about how people move through the life cycle and relate to their families, peer groups, cultural organizations, and institutions representing the dominant society.

Curriculum content should attend to the effects of oppression and institutional racism on people's life chances, family life, social behaviour, and mental and physical health. The implications of bicultural identities and generational differences among various population groups should be considered, as should the processes of adaptation, acculturation, accommodation, and integration experienced by immigrants and refugees. An appreciation of variations within groups (for example, the discussion of social class) and differences among ethnic or racial groups is very important.

Social welfare policies and services courses are designed to help students become familiar with current human services and to analyse the policies underlying their operation. Such courses should use scientific methods to examine the effects of social-welfare policies and services on various ethnic, cultural, and racial groups in our society. They should include an overview of the history of organized mainstream social services, including the study of such issues as institutional racism, which has resulted in the exclusion of racial and ethnic minorities from access to effective services. The historical and current effects of immigration and refugee policies should be included. Students should be helped to understand that a worker's use of a particular theory, model, or level of intervention when dealing with clients from various backgrounds is, in effect, a policy decision. For example, helping individual families cope with poor housing conditions rather than helping them collectively plan a cooperative housing unit is an imposed policy rather than a response to the best interests of the clients.

Social service practice and methods courses are meant to prepare students to use various methods and levels of intervention (casework, family intervention, group work, community organization and development) appropriate to their clients' problem situations. Courses in this area of study should provide opportunities for students to consider carefully whether certain methods are relevant and appropriate for particular individuals or groups. In many cases, methods such as advocacy, mediation, community development, and systems change are more helpful to Aboriginal and minority populations than are reflective therapies. It is important that students learn to recognize how their lack of self-awareness regarding prejudices, stereotypes, and biases affects clients, interferes with empathy and rapport, and limits intervention outcomes.

Research courses are designed to help students appreciate and apply scientific methods for the purpose of examining current issues and problems. Such courses should give students opportunities to become familiar with how scientific methods can be used to document the special needs and experiences of minority populations. Students should learn methods of evaluating the effect on minority and Aboriginal populations of social service theories, practice models, and policies and programs. Opportunities to identify bias in research and to understand the political implications of research studies should be provided. The suggestion that the impact of racism in social services is difficult to research should be challenged.

The *fieldwork practicum* allows students to apply what is learned in the classroom to actual clients in agencies and in the community. Fieldwork should ensure that all students acquire the necessary attitudes, values, knowledge, skills, and experience that will enable them to work competently with people from a variety of ethnic, cultural, and racial backgrounds. Before this objective can be met, field supervisors themselves must possess the knowledge and skills that they are to teach. Social service agencies should fund opportunities for in-service training that emphasizes self-awareness and the application of culturally appropriate intervention skills. It is particularly important that students learn to assess the role of racism, discrimination, and oppression on the life-chances of minority-group members.

CURRENT STATUS

A recent exploratory survey indicated that most accredited schools of social work in Canadian universities with B.S.W. and/or M.S.W. programs do not have required courses dealing specifically with multicultural and multiracial issues (Canadian Association of Schools of Social Work 1991). And though several schools suggested that they are attempting to include issues concerning diversity in all courses, they report varying degrees of success. The Canadian Association of Schools of Social Work's delegates recently took the encouraging step of voting (on two occasions) to implement the recommendations of the Task Force on Multicultural and Multiracial Issues in Social Work Education at the Annual Assembly (in 1991 and again in 1992). Based on interviews with relevant constituencies – students, faculty, field instructors, administrators, and community representatives – the Task Force that I chaired recommended changes to accreditation standards pertaining to organizational structures, policies, curriculum content, student body, faculty, fieldwork, and community accountability. Less is known about the current status of multicultural and multiracial issues in junior colleges and diploma programs.

THE IMPACT OF RACISM ON SOCIAL SERVICE STUDENTS AND THEIR CLIENTS

Minority-Group Students

Racism discourages many minority and Aboriginal students from applying to social service programs. Students who might otherwise be attracted to a profession promising to alleviate human distress and help people reach their full potential must overcome several barriers to enter the social service field (Christensen 1994).

In primary and secondary schools, the special educational needs of Aboriginal, immigrant, and minority children are generally unrecognized and poorly met; those from certain backgrounds (such as Black and Aboriginal children) are often labelled as being 'slow' or having 'behaviour problems.' Many feel that they are streamed into non-academic courses that hamper the likelihood of their attending college (Burrell and Christensen 1987).

If students meet the criteria and are accepted in a social service program, they often describe the educational institution as an alien, or uncomfortable, environment where there are few students of colour and fewer, if any, teachers of colour. Students are generally without sufficient psychological and social support when they experience racism in educational institutions and fieldwork settings – as, for example, when they are assigned only clients of their own racial or cultural group. In addition, it is often difficult for those with limited financial resources to remain academically competitive because they must hold one or more jobs while studying.

Course material is generally inadequate to help minority and Aboriginal students understand problems experienced by their communities. Attempts by the institution to provide culturally sensitive material are often seen as biased and stereotyped because they are delivered by teachers without proper training or experience.

Majority-Group Students

When presented with anti-racist material, majority-group students, consciously or unconsciously, are often preoccupied with the need to prove that they, and Canadian society in general, are not racist. This defensive stance hampers learning and personal growth. Because they do not recognize that the experience of minority groups differs from that of the dominant culture, students may try to 'treat everyone exactly the same' when they deal with minority and Aboriginal classmates or clients. When 'cross-cultural training' deals with increasing factual knowledge alone, students are not challenged to become aware of the existence of their prejudices, stereotypes, and racist behaviours, and of the potential impact of these factors on clients.

Social work continues to train people, implicitly and explicitly, for effective practice with white, middle- and upper-class clients, born in

North America or conforming to Anglo-Canadian norms; moreover, the majority of students are drawn from those social strata. Students may decide that they will try to work only with people like themselves, even though urban centres no longer reflect in any way such a vision of society.

Students from both minority and majority backgrounds may find it difficult to establish rapport, and provide satisfactory interventions, with minority or Aboriginal clients if they have not learned to adapt traditional theories, skills, and models to the task. As a result, clients may find social service interventions (which do not involve concrete services) irrelevant to their needs; be engaged on a superficial level only; drop out of treatment after one or two sessions; come to agencies mainly as involuntary clients; or find the experience negative and degrading. Minority clients are becoming increasingly aware that they pay taxes to support mainstream social services to which they have limited access owing to the culturally and racially insensitive policies, practices, and procedures of these services (Christensen 1986).

CONCLUSION AND RECOMMENDATIONS

Those working in the human service sector are in an excellent position to influence the educational policies and programs of schools of social work. Unfortunately, this power is neither sufficiently recognized nor acted upon, and as a result educational institutions are not forced to deal with the implicit racism of their programs and curricula. Human service organizations can exert pressure on schools of social work to pursue diligently methods of improving accessibility to Aboriginal peoples and minorities who are currently underrepresented. This pressure can be applied in the following ways:

1 Schools are dependent on agency personnel with B.S.W. and M.S.W. degrees to train and supervise students. Agencies with mission statements and policies promoting anti-racist, culturally appropriate services should ensure that schools that ask them to train students adhere to CASSW accreditation policies and standards relating to preparing students for multicultural and multiracial practice (Canadian Association of Schools of Social Work 1991).
   (a) Supervisors should insist that the curriculum content to which students are exposed is relevant to the population groups actually served at the practicum agency or institution.

(b) When students are evaluated competence should be defined and measured in terms of the extent to which students have gained the knowledge and skill necessary to work effectively with a multicultural and multiracial clientele.

2 Ethno-specific and mainstream agencies should become familiar with the admissions policies and criteria of schools of social work serving their geographic area. Involvement on a school's admissions and curriculum committees, and on local chapters of social-work associations, can help to achieve this end.

(a) Where admissions policies and criteria serve to discourage or disqualify students from Aboriginal, immigrant, and minority backgrounds, agencies should identify the restrictive clauses, such as criteria based mainly on high academic averages earned in a Canadian institution. Agencies should try to work cooperatively with schools' admissions officers and committees. If this approach fails, they can collectively lobby schools and universities for change.

(b) Human service organizations should establish methods to identify people in various ethnic and racial communities who have the 'non-professional' work, and/or voluntary, experience that clearly indicates their ability to perform well in a helping role. Such people should be encouraged to apply to schools of social work, and their progress should be monitored.

3 Human service organizations should seek to identify ways of giving moral and, where needed, academic and financial support to social work students from Aboriginal and minority backgrounds. The moral support is essential because many students of colour report that attending a social work educational institution is an alienating and emotionally difficult experience (Canadian Association of Schools of Social Work 1991).

(a) Role models who have successfully completed social work programs, or who are working in the social service field, should be asked to serve as mentors to minority students during their social work training. Often, immigrant and minority students simply do not understand the 'culture' of the university or of the profession and need help from those who have been successful.

4 Human service organizations should make known their expectation that schools of social work provide opportunities for in-service training for agency personnel and supervisors needing to upgrade knowledge and skills in order to be able to provide effective services to a multicultural and multiracial clientele.

5 Educational institutions should provide opportunities for in-service training for their own faculty and field instructors needing upgrading so that they can teach multicultural and multiracial content.
6 Human service organizations and educational institutions should define competence for social service practitioners in terms of their ability to work effectively with a multicultural and multiracial clientele.

I am sure that social service workers who are dedicated to the ideal of alleviating distress and helping all people to reach their full potential in harmony with their environment will give these recommendations their immediate attention.

Chapter 8

Anti-Racism and the Human-Service Delivery System

Carol Tator

The cultural and racial diversity of Canadian society creates significant challenges to our human-service delivery system. Social and health-care agencies are experiencing growing pressure from a wide range of external constituencies (funding bodies, government agencies, and community advocacy groups) to adapt their policies, programs, and practices. Schools of social work, nursing, and medicine are being asked to include cross-cultural and anti-racism training in their curricula. The overall goal of these changes is to develop more effective, accessible, and equitable human-service delivery systems. Recent legislative decrees and public-policy enactments such as the Charter of Rights and Freedoms, employment-equity legislation, the Canadian Multiculturalism Act, anti-racism policies, and human-rights codes are powerful incentives to provide services free of bias and discrimination.

This chapter examines the dynamics of individual, institutional, and structural racism as they are reflected in the policies, practices, values, and norms of traditional mainstream human service organizations. Included in this analysis are a wide range of services including family and child services, mental-health programs, child-care facilities, and child-welfare agencies. It provides an examination of some models of organizational response to service delivery within a multicultural, multiracial society. It briefly explores some of the deficiencies in social work education and training, identifies the barriers faced by racial-minority practitioners and clients, and concludes with some suggestions for improving the current system.

RACISM AND RESPONSES TO IT

Personal, institutional, and systemic racism affect the kinds of service, training, and employment opportunities available to members of racial minorities throughout the social and health-care system. Racism also has an impact on the relationship between social and health-care agencies on the one hand and minority communities and ethno-specific service agencies on the other.

The 1987 Social Planning Council of Metropolitan Toronto comprehensive study *A Time for Action! Access to Health and Social Services for Members of Cultural and Racial Groups* (Doyle and Visano 1987) points out that while access to basic social and health-services is a universal entitlement, mainstream agencies across the human service delivery system have failed to provide accessible and equitable services. The researchers identified linguistic, cultural, and racial barriers and an absence of strategies to address them. Studies in other regions of the country indicate similar barriers to universal access (Sanga 1987; Chan 1987; Bambrough et al. 1992; Bergin 1988).

Despite evidence of barriers, human service organizations have been slow to change. As Tim Rees observes: 'Organizations providing services to the public and members of the "helping" professions are generally appalled by the suggestion that their own efforts, the policies and practices of their agencies, and the institutional arrangements and structures within which the human service system functions, may knowingly or unintentionally, contribute to racism. Well motivated, highly skilled practitioners, dedicated to providing caring and competent service to clients/patients, find it difficult to believe that their professional norms, or the practices of their agencies, may serve to disadvantage their clients, fellow workers and minority communities' (1987: 1).

In 'Social Work and Ethnicity,' Cheetham (1982), writing from the perspective of her extensive work in the United Kingdom in the area of race, ethnicity, and social work, argues that mainstream social service workers have generally been unwilling to acknowledge that the way they provide services can actually ignore or work against the interests of racial and cultural minorities. White social workers, for example, are often oblivious to racism as a powerful social force and generally lack an understanding of the daily struggles of racial minorities to deal with prejudice and discrimination (Dominelli 1989). At the same time, a preference for homogeneity and assimilation is deeply embedded in Canadian social institutions and is woven clearly into the human-service

TABLE 1
The Monocultural/Assimilationist Model

Key assumptions and practices

1 Equality is best achieved by treating everyone the same. Despite the obvious differences in cultural or racial identities of clients, all people share common needs and desires and therefore require similar modes of service or intervention.
2 Too much attention paid to differences will only perpetuate them to an undesirable degree; the social goal is conformity with mainstream Anglo-Canadian values, standards, and codes of behaviour. The onus is on the individual to adapt to this norm.
3 The collective history of a group – which may include experiences of prejudice, discrimination, and political or racial violence, or the particular problems and traumas associated with immigration and integration – is not a significant factor in working with clients.
4 Staff is competent to provide services to anyone, and the door is open to anyone. Since needs are universal, and cultural differences largely irrelevant, highly trained professionals already possess the necessary knowledge and skills to provide appropriate service whatever the client's racial or cultural background.
5 Racism is an aberration; prejudice, bigotry, and discrimination are limited to a small number of people (rarely found among human service professionals) and have no impact on the organization or the service provided.
6 The values of the dominant majority culture are reflected in all aspects of the daily routines and life of the organization including its policies, programs, employment practices, language, and media of communication and delivery of service.

delivery system. Thus, the organizational change that is necessary to put anti-racism human service programs in place is often very difficult to initiate.

A body of literature describing this change exists; it identifies a wide range of organizational responses to racial and cultural diversity (Cox and Nickelson 1990; Jackson and Holvino 1989; Thomas 1987). Drawing on the research literature from Canada, the United States, and the United Kingdom, tables 1 to 4 summarize the primary assumptions underlying these approaches to racial and cultural diversity. However, they also represent the stages through which some organizations pass as they attempt to become more accessible and equitable (for a more detailed discussion of organizational stages, see Minors, chapter 11).

THE MONOCULTURAL/ASSIMILATIONIST APPROACH

This is the model for human service organizations that has prevailed for most of this century and that, in varying degrees, continues to shape and influence the delivery of service in many agencies. It is based on an

TABLE 2
The Add-on Multicultural Model

Key assumptions and practices

1 The hiring of a few 'ethnic' workers will help deal with the needs of immigrants and cultural/racial minorities who seek service from the agency. Generally, these workers are not expected to interact with other clients. Therefore, their role and contribution are marginalized within the agency.
2 Most communications continue to be in English and reflect a monoculture-mainstream perspective. Sometimes, however, there is multi-lingual translation of literature if there is a significant demand by specific minority communities. Lacking 'ethnic' staff, linguistic (and, in rare instances, cultural) interpreters are used to help in the provision of services where required, and based on the limited resources available for such programs. The racial implications of communications are often ignored.
3 Training is needed to help mainstream workers to become more 'sensitive' to cultural differences; to develop a greater understanding of 'other cultural norms, values and lifestyles.' However, there is no need to alter fundamentally the way in which counselling, therapy, or service is offered. Cultural awareness is seen as an end in itself.
4 Some effort is directed at recruiting minorities (in 'token' numbers) to serve on boards and committees and there is a limited attempt to initiate outreach programs to the community. But the organization requires no fundamental alteration in its operations.
5 Racism is perceived to be an issue of concern, but mainly in minority client–mainstream professional interactions and relationships. Therefore, the primary responsibility of the agency is to provide opportunities for human relations–race relations sensitization programs targeted at front-line staff.

assimilationist, monocultural (Anglo-Canadian) perspective. Organizations based on this model view racial and cultural diversity as an irrelevant factor in determining agency policies and practices. The multiracial-multicultural nature of the community has no impact on the services delivered, the constituencies served, the professional staff hired, or volunteers recruited. In monocultural organizations, language, cultural, and racial barriers to service delivery are neither identified nor addressed. Thus, the services provided by these agencies remain largely inaccessible to members of multicultural and multiracial communities.

THE ADD-ON/MULTICULTURAL APPROACH

An organization based on this model is willing to address the issue of diversity and to develop programs designed to increase the access and participation of minorities. They introduce new initiatives, such as the translation of documents or the recruitment of staff, board members, and volunteers from minority communities.

TABLE 3
The Integrated Multicultural/Anti-Racism Model

Key assumptions and practices

---

1 Change is a systemic process involving every level and constituency within the organization as well as consultation with external groups.
2 Racism and discrimination are social phenomena as much as they are behaviours arising from personal belief. They are reflected in social conditions that serve to disadvantage people because of their race or ethnicity, and are manifested in institutional policies and in the allocation of social, economic, and political rewards and resources.
3 Advocacy is an important aspect of the fight against racism. Advocacy involves acting as a broker among the community, institutions, and government – identifying unfair and unjust practices, advocating for new policies and programs, supporting external alliances or coalitions, working collaboratively with ethno-specific agencies, and lobbying for changes in education, policing, justice, and employment.
4 Human service workers must re-examine their core values and practices to find out how they may be inappropriate or ineffective.
5 Recognition of the state of powerlessness experienced by racial minorities in almost all aspects of their lives is fundamental in developing appropriate strategies and interventions. For example, the status of and relationship between the worker or professional and the client or patient are fundamentally unequal. Clients not only function within an environment over which they lack control, but the combination of gender, class, and race barriers limit their self-determination. Therefore, efforts are directed towards empowering both clients and communities to help identify those strategies that are most appropriate to their own needs and circumstances.
6 Cultural and racial communities, other community and ethno-specific agencies, the extended family, clergy, and others are all seen as important resources to be tapped wherever possible.

Multicultural and anti-racism issues, while important, are separate concerns from the day-to-day life of the organization. The needs, issues, and interests of minorities are dealt with on an ad-hoc basis, rather than integrated into the structure and practices of the organization. Barriers facing minority groups can be identified, but the responsibility for change is often delegated to the front-line worker, who may function in a totally non-supportive environment. Concrete action to promote effective change is sometimes lost ordeferred as the organization attempts to juggle competing demands and priorities.

THE MULTICULTURAL/ANTI-RACISM INTEGRATED APPROACH

This model involves a wide range of racial and cultural groups in all areas of organizational life. Issues of minority access, participation, and

TABLE 4
The Ethno-Cultural Community-Based Model

Key assumptions and practices

1 Cultural and racial diversity are defining characteristics of Canadian society, and the commitment to maintaining them must be realized by equitable access to, and participation in, all areas of the social service and health-care delivery systems.
2 The primary barriers to equitable access to mainstream services are language, race, culture, gender, and class. Other barriers are limited access to information about the nature of the services provided, confusing bureaucratic and administrative procedures, unnecessarily complex forms, limited office hours, and inappropriate office locations.
3 Ethno- and racially specific community-based services provide critically needed services such as settlement and integration programs; culturally appropriate family counselling models; and advocacy and mediation for minority populations within other institutions (e.g., police and the courts, education, government agencies).
4 Funding needs to be allocated on a more equitable basis to reflect the enormous contribution that ethno-specific and community-based organizations make in the delivery of services.

equity are given a high priority throughout the organization. Systems of responsibility and accountability are established to ensure that multiculturalism and anti-racism training are implemented throughout the organization.

THE ETHNOCULTURAL COMMUNITY-BASED APPROACH

Ethnocultural, community-based agencies are a crucial part of the human service system, and have traditionally filled the huge gap created by the failure of mainstream institutions to serve the needs of minority and immigrant populations. These agencies have in most cases operated separately from the mainstream system and have generally provided service to people who are members of a particular racial or cultural group. While there have been some efforts in recent years to establish linkages between the mainstream and ethnospecific delivery system, they continue to function largely as 'two solitudes' (Doyle and Visano 1987).

In the short term at least, many observers feel that it is more effective to maintain alternative agencies to address the particular needs of minorities than to integrate services for minorities into mainstream agencies. A longer-term approach could take the form of a Duality model such as suggested by Agard (1987) in a paper prepared for the Ontario Social Assistance Review Board. In this model, the mode of ser-

vice requires ethnocultural, community-based organizations to be contracted on a purchase-of-service basis. Using this approach, the
mainstream agency maintains traditional service-delivery responsibilities but contracts ethnocultural community agencies to undertake specific assigned service functions, based largely on referral. This model
serves to create a set of support programs based on the needs of minority communities. Simultaneously, mainstream agencies are expected to
continue to develop their own organizational multicultural and anti-
racism orientation. Variations of this model are being attempted, but at
this stage have not been described or evaluated in the literature.

The major problem with the present system of ethnocultural agencies
has been a serious lack of financial support for them from government
and other funding bodies. In recent years, funders like the United Way
of Greater Toronto have attempted to rectify this chronic under-funding,
but this effort has clearly been inadequate to meet the staggering
requirements of minority and immigrant communities.

EDUCATION AND TRAINING

While many undergraduate and postgraduate educational programs in
human services provide some cross-cultural and multicultural learning
opportunities, they are generally either fragmented ad-ons or isolated
interventions in the curriculum (for a more detailed discussion of this
issue, see Christensen, chapter 7). There is virtually no anti-racism training offered. Those few courses that are offered tend to focus on 'cultural
sensitization.' These programs are rarely mandatory and they have not
been evaluated (Canadian Task Force on Mental Health Issues 1988).

In recent years cultural awareness and cross-cultural training programs have come under significant criticism. Critics of these programs
argue that teaching anything meaningful about the over one hundred
racial and cultural groups living in Canada is impossible and that while
these courses are well intended, the study of the history, values, and
norms of minorities often leads to stereotyping and to erroneous generalizations.

Furthermore, the relevance of this kind of information is seen as questionable because ethnic or racial groups are not homogeneous entities.
Individual variation within each group is as great as within the mainstream population. The results of acculturation or socio-economic differences (or differences in religion, age, and class) would render the
generalizations inherent in such approaches problematic in dealing with

individual needs. Critics also argue that this approach provides neither the knowledge nor the skills required to deal with racism.

For agencies and organizations, the in-service training emphasis has been on cross-cultural learning. Dr Ralph Masi, Multicultural Health Coordinator for the Ontario Ministry of Health, says: 'We've been sensitized to death over the last 5 or 6 years. The time has come to move beyond the raising awareness about cultures to the development of specific systems that truly reflect the needs of the Canadian population as it is today – its ethnic and racial diversity' (Lechy 1992: 2212).

United Way of Greater Toronto has recognized the importance of training in assisting organizations to confront and eliminate racism. Its workshops generally target senior managers and board members who, by providing leadership, developing appropriate policies, and shifting resources, have the power to make significant changes. Unfortunately, the emphasis of most workplace training continues to be on personal rather than organizational development.

THE RACIAL-MINORITY PRACTITIONER

Members of racial and cultural minorities working in human service organizations confront a number of barriers, conflicts, and pressures unknown to mainstream practitioners. A recent study in Nova Scotia (Bambrough et al 1992) revealed that Black social work graduates from the Maritime School of Social Work found fewer desirable jobs than others, including limited or term positions and more part-time jobs. Moreover, once they obtained work, they found that opportunities for advancement were relatively limited and salary levels were low. The report concluded that Black graduates were less successful than the majority group in accessing the more prestigious social work jobs, such as those to be found in family counselling, in hospital social work, and in administrative/supervisory positions.

Another formidable barrier frequently encountered by minority new Canadian workers is that their knowledge, skills, and experience acquired in their home countries may not be recognized or is significantly undervalued. Degrees earned abroad are often not accredited and foreign-trained graduates have no access to retraining (Doyle and Visano 1987).

Minority-group social workers and other practitioners may experience serious conflicts between their own cultural values and norms and those of the dominant culture that influences the practices and priorities of their organization. Minority workers commonly function from a dual perspective. They are positioned to understand both the particular needs and issues of concern within their own respective communities and the limitations of the programs and treatment modes offered by established human service organizations. As suggested earlier, mainstream practitioners in social work and health-care delivery are trained and socialized in a professional subculture inclined to view their services as having universal applicability and accessibility.

Minority workers are frequently isolated and marginalized in their agencies. They are concentrated disproportionately at the entry levels or in front-line positions. Their primary role is to serve those clients who share the same cultural background, but they tend to have limited power and status within the organization. This practice can result in a kind of ghettoization of minority workers within organizations, where all 'problems with Blacks' are referred to the Black worker (Thomas 1987).

This practice, however, is not without some merit (as a short-term organizational strategy), in that minority clients are more likely to use the service if they can communicate and interact with someone of the same or similar cultural background. In the case of racial-minority clients, it is quite likely they will feel more comfortable with a worker of colour, who understands the experience of racism. However, 'ethno-specific workers'[1] in some agencies have raised strong objections to this approach.

RACIAL AND CULTURAL BARRIERS IN SERVICE DELIVERY

As we have seen, the human-service delivery system has, to a significant degree, failed to adapt its programs and services, its administrative systems, and its organizational structures to the reality of a multiracial society. The consequence of this neglect is inadequate and inappropriate services to members of racial, ethnic, and cultural minorities. The following section provides some examples of how this failure affects the actual delivery of services.

Family Services

A 1991 study, *Family Services for All*, prepared by John Medeiros for the Multicultural Coalition for Access to Family Services in Metro Toronto highlights some of the problems. It found an 'appalling lack of services' in ten ethnocultural and racial-minority communities. Less than 8 per cent of staff at established agencies speak a language other than English. Just 14 per cent of front-line staff are from the ten communities studied. While $14.6 million is allocated annually in Metro Toronto for family services, only $900,000 goes to ethno-cultural agencies. 'The issue is not just lack of money, but rather a complacent disregard for the needs and the rights of ethno-cultural and racial communities who collectively represent 60 per cent of the population of Metro' (Medeiros 1991: 7).

The study indicates that 62 per cent of the established family-service agencies had no formal or informal policies or practices to address the concerns of ethnic and racial-minority communities in Metropolitan Toronto communities. The data lead to one conclusion: systemic barriers, first identified in the early eighties, continue to operate in the delivery of family services to these communities. These barriers have a significant impact on the process of family counselling, from assessment and diagnosis to intervention and treatment. Mainstream family-service agencies continue to deliver services on the assumption that 'immigrants shed their values, religion, language and colour as they enter Canada and ... pass nothing on to subsequent generations. The reality is that they cannot relinquish their cultural and racial heritage without risking major personality conflicts' (ibid.: 10).

Clinical models of treatment and intervention offered by mainstream human services commonly ignore or dismiss the strength and significance of ethnocultural group identity and fail to recognize the supportive role such groups play in helping ethnocultural and racial minorities confront discrimination. This attitude is largely due to the underlying assumption of mainstream agencies that the family is a nuclear unit and that its problems can be dealt with as if the pressures placed on it from the external environment were largely irrelevant. Indeed, the most influential literature on family therapy makes recommendations for family treatment based on the nuclear model.

Yet, one cannot consider family dysfunction without at the same time considering the larger, sociopolitical context of family life (Thompson 1993). Among the most important elements in that context, and one that is largely disregarded by mainstream agencies, is the experience of racism by minority families. 'Therefore when one is contemplating working with Black (or other racial minority) families it must be acknowledged that they experience this society as racist and that this experience affects every aspect of their lives' (James et al. 1991).

The fact that multicultural and anti-racist policies have been established in many family-service agencies appears to have made little difference in the dominant cultural values or the professional norms underlying organizational practices (Bridgeman 1993). Research in Canada, the United States, and the United Kingdom has shown that, as a result of the continuing racial and cultural barriers within these organizations, many clients underutilize or terminate their involvement with an agency, finding the manner of service delivery too institutionalized and culturally/racially insensitive (Agard 1987; Sue and Sue 1990; Cheetam 1982).

Mental-Health Services

A national task force established to conduct hearings on access to mental-health services by immigrants and refugees, in its report *After the Door Has Been Opened*, found that health and social services for immigrants are highly fragmented and that they have been developed without coordination with the mainstream service-delivery system. The task force identified several cultural and linguistic barriers that prevent effective use of mental-health services. Ethnic and racial-minority groups and service-providers agree that language problems are the most significant barrier to assessment and treatment.

The scarcity of trained interpreters is a serious problem. In Ontario the provincial government, through the Ministry of Citizenship, has made some limited efforts to support the training of interpreters, and interpreters have been hired by some major hospitals. However, the majority of social and health-care agencies rely for interpretation on volunteers, on family, or on their own unqualified employees. Not only can this lead to embarrassment for clients or patients forced to reveal private matters to non-professionals to whom they may be related or with whom they may work, but translations may be inaccurate and render proper treatment problematic (Canadian Task Force on Mental Health Issues 1988).

The formal and bureaucratic atmosphere of some social and health agencies is another significant barrier to service. Sterile reception areas, often staffed by culturally insensitive staff, complex and confusing administrative forms, information printed only in English, and lack of flexible office hours create an alienating environment that discourages members of certain groups from using needed services (Doyle and Visano 1987).

The difference in perceptions between mainstream and ethnic and racial minorities about the role of the family in the treatment of individual problems can be another barrier to effective treatment. Many ethnic and racial minorities assume that emotional and health concerns are a collective problem affecting both the immediate and the extended family. As a result, family members, especially elders, expect to be involved in the assessment of the problem and to play an active role during the course of treatment. So, while the centrality of the individual is an indispensable foundation of mainstream social work, it is, for some minorities, an incomprehensible concept (Cheetham 1982). In many cultures, independence from one's family is less important than interdependence, cooperation, and family loyalty. The family's needs are seen as more important than the needs of the individual (British Columbia Task Force on Family Violence 1992).

Minority professionals have pointed out the profound difference in world-views that typically separates the white interviewer from the racial-minority client (Sisskind 1978). Racial stereotyping often skews the initial assessment by the therapist, who may view a client's aggressive or passive behaviour as indicative of a personality disorder when it may in fact be an appropriate response to living in a racist society. There is a constant danger that majority-culture and class-bound values will be used to judge normality and abnormality in clients.

One study found that when therapists interview patients, they tend to assign diagnoses of depression more often to whites and of schizophrenia to Blacks. When they used a standardized interview form, diagnostic differences disappeared. A submission to the task force by Harambee Centres of Canada identified racial stereotyping as a potential factor in making biased assessments (Canadian Task Force on Mental Health Issues 1988).

Several studies in the United States (Sisskind 1978) identify racial and cultural barriers that damaged the counselling relationship between white therapists or counsellors and minority clients to the extent that there was a high drop-out rate from treatment. One researcher proposes the term 'equal but unresponsive services' to describe the inadequacies of the social/health-care service delivery systems (Sue and Sue 1990). She suggests that minority clients require different services to provide a better 'fit' between professional technique and the particular needs of clients. Assumptions that counselling is based on universal principles can conflict with the values of many minority groups. Self-disclosure and discussion about intimate aspects of life and relationships with 'strangers' is viewed as inappropriate among some groups.

Traditional interviewing techniques emphasize a professional distance between client and therapist, a non-directive style, an emphasis on verbal, emotional, and behaviourial expressiveness, and self-disclosure. Stress is laid on the client's ability to assume responsibility and on examining the client's past experiences. These techniques are rooted in a North American value system that may be in direct conflict with the client's cultural values. For racial-minority clients whose lives have been marked by racism there may well be a reluctance to be entirely frank with a white professional. For some cultural groups, sharing intimate aspects of one's experiences is only possible, if at all, after a long relationship has been established, and not after only a few fifty-minute sessions with a stranger.

Children's Services

The white ethnocentrism so deeply rooted in our institutions has a significant impact on child-welfare policies and programs. It also has a profound effect on the self-image of children who are members of racial minorities.

A recent study by Chrysostom Louis (1992) of African-Canadian children (the term is used to refer to all children of African heritage in Canada, regardless of place of birth) under the care of child-welfare agencies identifies several ways these children are affected by racism. He outlines the cumulative effects of the racism experienced by children at the hands of bigoted peers, by teachers and other adults, by media, and by fellow African-Canadians. He argues that the child's self-esteem is distorted and that feelings of positive racial identity are undermined extremely early. Other studies reinforce this finding and suggest that children begin to develop racial awareness as early as three to four years of age. These children are aware of differences between racial groups, possess the ability to recognize and label these differences, and can identify themselves in racial terms (James and Muhammad 1992; Milner 1975).

Other researchers point out that children from oppressed racial or cultural groups tend to have different preoccupations than their white peers. In order of concern, they have questions about their own identity, about racism, about whites, and about other groups. For white children the order seems to be questions about people of colour. Their comments reflect stereotyped or negative attitudes, and questions about their own identity (Derman-Sparks et al. 1980). These findings have significant implications for current policies and practices involving racial-minority children, from day care to child welfare.

In the study on African-Canadian children and the child-welfare system, Louis (1992) observes that when African-Canadian children are removed from their natural families, they enter into an almost exclusively white world – white social workers, lawyers, counsellors, doctors, judges, and court officials. In addition, African-Canadian children tend to be placed with white families. This uprooting of children from their natural family and community and their placement in all-white environments can have a negative effect on both their self-image and group identity. They often feel insecure and unable to discuss their experiences with racism. So, however well-intended the caregivers and the agencies responsible for child-welfare services may be, there is a general failure to recognize the unique problems facing these children and an absence of appropriate programs to address their particular needs (Louis 1992; James and Muhammad 1992). Many studies in the United Kingdom have made similar findings (Ahmed 1981).

Women's Services

Racism and sexism operate together in the lives of women of colour and affect both their day-to-day experiences and their access to services. For example, in the case of sexual assault or family violence, women of colour may be under even more pressure than white women not to report the incident so that the solidarity of the community is not breached (British Columbia Task Force on Family Violence 1992); they may be totally isolated and without the traditional family support networks. Furthermore, many immigrant and refugee women are unaware of their legal rights. For example, they fear that if they report their husbands for abusing them they might lose their status as landed immigrants and be deported.

Lack of English proficiency is another serious problem. It is difficult for non-English speakers to even find out which services are available. Linguistic, cultural, and racial barriers make it more difficult for women when they seek help from social workers, police, counsellors, doctors, and religious leaders. In an Ontario study, 62.2 per cent of battered immigrant women interviewed cited 'fear that I will lose everything (house, children, reputation, everything I worked for) once I involve the police' (ARA Consultants 1985: III:3 and IV:19). In the same study, 42.2 per cent of the women cited 'fear that husband/partner will be brutalized/victimized by police' as a 'somewhat important' or 'important' reason for not calling the police (ibid.: IV:19).

Women of colour may experience discrimination in their relationships with police, the courts, and shelters. Social workers or judges may be racially biased. The woman of colour may not be believed, particularly if she is describing the conduct of a white person (ARA Consultants 1985).

These racially determined barriers to equitable treatment lead some researchers to conclude that victims of family and sexual violence from minority cultures confront not only the trivialization and denial that are the by-products of sexism, but the additional denial that stems from the invisibility of racism in Canadian society (BC Task Force on Family Violence 1992).

CONCLUSIONS

Racism within the human-service delivery system deeply affects members of racial minorities. Racial and cultural barriers continue to influence both to whom services are provided and the quality and appropriateness of those services.

Racial discrimination is reflected in the allocation of resources by funders who continue to ignore the dramatic rise in the number of immigrants and refugees in recent decades and the particular needs of racial and ethnocultural groups and the agencies that serve them. Racism operates within organizational structures, shaping organizational culture, policies, programs, and procedures. Racial bias and institutional discrimination affect the employment opportunities of minority social workers and health-care practitioners.

Racial and cultural bias is reflected in the modes of treatment and approaches to problem resolution developed by mainstream social workers, which frequently ignore the effects of systemic racism on the client or fail to take into account group values, community norms, and indigenous resources. Racism is reflected in the common assumption that racial minorities are a 'problem' – either they have problems or they are the cause of problems. It is seen in the attitudes and behaviours of practitioners who engage in stereotyping.

The disempowering effects of racism are compounded and reinforced when a person of colour is also from another group that experiences discrimination. For example, when a person is from a racial minority and is also an immigrant or refugee, the effect is even greater marginalization and disempowerment. Women of colour or older people who are also immigrants are particularly vulnerable.

Social work (and health-care) educational programs have generally failed to address the issue of racism in either theory or practice. Nor, as we have seen, do workers in the human-service delivery system acknowledge that their activities are frequently in support of a discriminatory status quo.

Anti-racism principles must be incorporated into the education and training of human service workers if change is to occur. To be effective, such training must achieve the following:

1 Begin with an analysis of the ways in which racism manifests itself in individual attitudes, values, and behaviours.
2 Identify (a) its relationship to the practice of social work or health care, and (b) its impact on both organizational norms and culture and institutional policies and practices.
3 Enable learners to analyse those social values that serve to sustain the advantages of the dominant group and subordinate the interests of minorities.
4 Provide both historical and current perspectives on the social, economic, and political conditions that have had an impact on racial minorities, on the responsibility of mainstream institutions for racial discrimination, and on the impact of racism on the daily experiences of minority-group members.
5 Provide an opportunity to analyse the different ways of dealing with racial diversity, from assimilation and ethnocentrism to anti-racist cultural pluralism.
6 Help learners to
  (a) develop an understanding of the cultural values by which they interpret their world;
  (b) identify which of those values may conflict with a client's cultural perspective and world-view;
  (c) see all cultures as having integrity, validity, and coherence; and
  (d) understand the complexities of cultural and ethnic identity, the ways in which cultural distinctiveness is either asserted or abandoned, and how cultural identity changes and evolves over time (Green 1982).
7 Make the distinction between cultural and racial group-identity formation.
8 Encourage learners to
  • develop new approaches that can lead to fundamental changes in organizational mandates, policies, program delivery, and methods of counselling;

- build new relationships with minority communities;
- use indigenous sources of help such as lay and professional practitioners in the client's community; and
- identify more pro-active strategies in addressing and eliminating racial bias and discrimination in the organization, in the human-service delivery system, in other institutional arenas, and in the broader society.

9 Move learners from being passive observers to active participants in social change.

10 Lead to the creation of a new social agenda based on the goals of participation, power-sharing, access, and equity.

The task of dismantling racist institutional or organizational practices while they remain invisible to those who are responsible for those arrangements presents an enormous challenge. It requires heightened awareness, deeper understanding and knowledge, the acquisition of new skills, and the translation of that learning into comprehensive and ongoing series of actions. It demands individual, organizational, and institutional commitment. It requires that everyone involved in the delivery system, including educators, managers and administrators, front-line workers, volunteers, members of boards of directors, unions, and professional associations, be full participants in a transformative social-change process. There is no neutral position possible in a society in which discrimination and oppression operate.

Anti-racism involves more than altering individual attitudes or even redefining the roles of practitioners. Anti-racism is an ideology that reflects a vision of a society without discriminatory barriers. It involves a long-term commitment to the empowerment of minority communities and a carefully planned process of organizational change. It requires the development of new patterns of behaviour and a new relationship with clients, colleagues, and the community.

Anti-racism challenges all of us to become advocates for social change. The process of eliminating racism must include the participation of those who suffer from its consequences – minority clients, patients, colleagues, and members of ethnic, cultural, and other communities.

In the change process, the minority professional has a powerful role to play in helping the organization identify the barriers to access and equity. As the change process proceeds, minority workers become part of a collective effort. They can help not only to meet the needs of minority clients but also to support the efforts of the organization to transform itself. However, their special contribution to the process must be recognized and rewarded by full participation, mobility, and integration in the organization.

Funders and statutory agencies can also play a critical role in ensuring that the policies, programs, practices, and resources of the agencies and institutions that they support have anti-racism policies and practices in place. At the same time, the lack of access to adequate funding for ethnocultural community agencies is a profound barrier to equitable service.

In recent years, there have been signs of change within some mainstream agencies that are largely due to new multicultural and anti-racism policies established by funding agencies. However, in many cases, the nature of the change has been cosmetic rather than substantive; ad hoc and isolated rather than integrated and systemic; involving short-term interventions rather than long-term strategies. Organizational policies have been developed, but not implemented, monitored, or evaluated; training has been provided, but not in the context of anti-racist organizational change; community outreach has been initiated, but power has not been shared; recruitment of board members and volunteers from minority communities has increased, but in largely token numbers. Thus, racial and cultural barriers to access and equity for people of colour continues to operate within most human service organizations. White social workers within mainstream agencies continue to resist significant changes in their professional values and practices. Administrators demonstrate a preference for the assimilationist approach or an ad-on multicultural model rather than fully integrating and institutionalizing anti-racism change within the day-to-day life of the organization. Ethno-racial community-based agencies still struggle to provide services with limited financial support and token recognition for the essential contribution they make.

Thus, this analysis leads to the conclusion that the human-service delivery system and the organizations and practitioners that work within it require a more systematic, pro-active, and organized anti-racist stand. The alternative is that social work practice will contribute to and reinforce existing systems of oppression and discrimination in Canadian society.

NOTE

1 The very word 'ethnic' is objectionable because it is commonly applied to all but the dominant group / culture. Thus, workers from the dominant culture

are not required to develop the skills and knowledge necessary to help minority clients; and minority workers, locked in administrative and supervisory positions, remain locked out of the decision-making process (Thomas 1987).

Chapter 9

Immigrant Service Agencies: A Fundamental Component of Anti-Racist Social Services

Dawit Beyene, Carrie Butcher, Betty Joe, and Ted Richmond

The roots of racism in this society are very deep, extending back to the genocidal treatment of the Aboriginal peoples in the occupation of their lands. The adoption of multiculturalism as federal and Ontario government policy held out to various ethno-racial groups a promise of increased equality that went beyond the official rights accorded to the English and French languages and nations. But multiculturalism to date has turned out to be more of a philosophical goal than a reality, particularly in relation to the problem of racial discrimination.

One dimension of racism in Canadian society is our immigration policies – the selection of those who get into the country as immigrants and refugees and the ways they are treated after their arrival. The discrimination and racism experienced by the approximately two hundred thousand immigrants and refugees who arrive in Canada each year is the focus of this chapter. We present an anti-racist perspective on social service provision from the point of view of immigrant-serving community agencies.

THE GROWTH OF IMMIGRANT SERVICE AGENCIES

That the Canadian government has a major responsibility for social support services to immigrants and refugees is a relatively recent concept; and interpretations of what that responsibility entails are still evolving. Traditionally, the federal government departments that have assumed some fiscal and jurisdictional responsibility for this matter have thought in terms of a relatively brief period of 'settlement,' lasting no more than two or three years. During this settlement period the new arrivals would receive such support as initial orientation, language instruction, and citizenship classes, and would then move on to receiving the required general social services from existing mainstream[1] institutions such as schools, hospitals, and government offices. (See also Tator, chapter 8, for another discussion of mainstream institutions' role in social service delivery).

The 1970s across Canada, especially Ontario, saw a continuing high level of immigrant arrivals. Some groups such as Vietnamese and Latin American refugees had acute needs. Many ethno-racial communities began to provide services to the new arrivals, initially on a mainly volunteer basis. Government recognition of the need for settlement services, in the form of limited funding, allowed the fledgling community agencies to hire their first paid staff and begin to plan and coordinate their activities better . This period marked a turning point in the eventual development of a large and diversified network of immigrant service agencies (ISAs).[2]

As work developed at the agencies and valuable experience was gained, it became clear that the integration of newcomers was not progressing in the way that government had imagined it would. In the first place, it was not possible to say that the settlement process was 'completed' after two or three years. It became clear that the need for language training, labour-market adjustment, and culturally sensitive individual and family counselling continues throughout the life of the immigrant and for their children.

Second, immigrants and refugees are unable to get culturally appropriate services from mainstream Canadian institutions and often require extensive assistance and intervention from immigrant service agencies. A number of different studies, including those of Doyle and Visano and Madeiros, have documented the failure of traditional Canadian social service institutions to provide access for various ethno-racial groups. Language is one of the problems identified in these and other studies. In addition to this more obvious barrier, immigrants and refugees seeking services from mainstream institutions have had to deal with racist policies and practices, as well as staff and programs that lack a fundamental understanding of their culture and life experiences. Faced with these barriers, immigrants and refugees have turned increasingly to the immigrant service agencies, where they felt a sense of ownership, comfort, and involvement.

Thirdly, the rapid development of immigrant service agencies was due to the fact that immigrant and refugee clients preferred to receive social services from organizations and staff rooted within their own communities. Clients that had first used the agencies for English-language instruction or citizenship classes were returning for services as diverse as employment-skills training, health education, and support groups for immigrant women. In fact, it is through the provision of anti-racist, culturally and linguistically appropriate services that ISAs have become part of, and are changing, social-service delivery systems. These services are combined with advocacy to eliminate racism as a barrier to settlement. It is this combination of settlement services and advocacy, the result of which is anti-racist community development, that makes the ISA a fundamental component of anti-racist social services.

Fourth, the existence of the agencies is also due to increased funding from various levels of governments, along with funding from other bodies, such as foundations. Some of this funding is provided for projects designed to address specific needs of these communities. While the funds have been limited, they have been achieved at the price of endless hours of work and advocacy by the immigrant and refugee communities.

All these factors contributed to the development of immigrant service agencies as we know them today. The Ontario Council of Agencies Serving Immigrants (OCASI), founded in 1978, represents more than one hundred and thirty such agencies, which together serve an estimated half a million immigrant and refugee clients annually. About 90 per cent of these clients receive assistance from the staff or the volunteers of these agencies in their own language; in total, services are provided in more than fifty different languages (OCASI 1990a, b).

IMMIGRANTS' EXPERIENCES WITH RACIAL DISCRIMINATION

Immigrants and refugees, particularly members of racial minorities, face many barriers to settlement. Consider, for example, the Ethiopian or Somali refugees who have arrived in Ontario during the past several years. They will likely be highly educated and skilled, but their education and experience will usually not be recognized as valid by Canadian employers, trades and professional associations, or educational institutions (white immigrants from the United States or Britain face the same barriers). They will not be able to afford to attend English- or French-language instruction if there are no training allowances or access to affordable child care. If they are women, they will face sexism as well as racism.

Experiences like these are not unique to any particular racial-minority immigrant group. Without equal opportunities to earn an income or acquire communication skills in one of the official languages, immigrants and refugees are denied access to fair and equitable participation in Canadian society. This is systemic racism. The lack of recognition of education and skills (trades and professions) acquired in other countries has been documented by McDade (1988), by the Task Force on Access to Professions and Trades in Ontario (1989), and by the Working Group on Immigrant Credentials for the Government of Manitoba (1992). Practices of racial discrimination in employment (including hiring, firing, and promotion) have been substantiated by Henry and Ginzberg (1985) and by Billingsley and Muszynki (1985). These discriminatory pressures combine to reproduce a stratified labour force in which many immigrants, particularly immigrants of colour, women, and those with fewer economic resources are locked in the lower strata. Studies of labour-force data show that immigrants as a whole take about twenty years to achieve wage parity with their Canadian-born counterparts, and that many specific groups of immigrants (especially women and people of colour) never fully catch up (Beaujot et al. 1988; deSilva 1991). These findings are confirmed by Ho-Lau's (1992) studies of the employment prospects and social participation of adult Chinese immigrants in the area of Metropolitan Toronto. The survey respondents in her study tended to have higher rates of unemployment than the provincial average and reported serious difficulties, including racial discrimination, in advancing in their chosen careers. The problems were most severe for the most recent immigrants. Labour-market discrimination is just one of the manifestations of racism faced by the typical immigrant.[3]

Immigrants and refugees also suffer a lack of access to culturally appropriate, anti-racist services, as discussed by Tator in the previous chapter. Here we wish to make two points. First, mainstream institutions such as hospitals, family support agencies, and welfare offices are funded by public taxes. These taxes are also paid by those same immigrants and refugees who have great difficulty in gaining access to these essential services. In the early 1990s, funders and policy makers began to require these institutions to be more accessible to diverse, traditionally underserviced groups. The effect of this apparent focus on equal access to publicly funded services has not been as significant as it could have been. Many organizations have made token gestures such as providing cross-cultural sensitization training to staff or hiring one racial-minority staff member. Without fundamental changes – such as having immigrants and refugees represented on boards of directors, eliminating racist policies and practices and adopting explicitly anti-racist ones (for example, offering services in the languages of immigrants and refugees, adopting employment-equity policies and practices, and ensuring community participation in strategic planning, needs assessment, program planning, and evaluation) – lack of equitable access will remain the norm.

Second, denial of access to programs and services necessary for the process of settlement is discrimination. Inaccessibility of funding for settlement services is directly linked to structural barriers rooted in racism. ISAs that provide these essential services face severe public-funding discrimination. In spite of some improvements in the early 1990s (in Ontario at least), their level of sustaining funding (long-term renewable funding, including administration and operational costs) continued to be quite marginal. Enormous amounts of human energy are essentially wasted each year in re-justifying and re-packaging their activities to suit the changing political priorities of a multitude of funders. Considering the range and value of the services provided by the ISAs, their share of the public monies available for social services remains a token response.

These injustices – the labour-market discrimination and the lack of access to appropriate services -- operate in ways that are still considered completely 'normal' within the dominant institutions of Canadian society. It is still generally 'business as usual' for an educational institution to be unable to evaluate the worth of a university certificate from Teheran or for a hospital to have no ability to offer translation and interpreting in Chinese. These things are 'normal' in the same sense that it was 'normal' to deny the vote to Asians in Canada for the first half of this century. It is only when we realize that such daily occurrences are neither normal nor inevitable, and we start to see, and act upon, the depths of injustice behind them, that they will start to change.

THE ROLE OF COMMUNITY AGENCIES IN ANTI-RACIST SERVICES

What do immigrant service agencies do to combat the forms of discrimination and racism described here? First and foremost, ISAs are governed by community boards of directors that come from or are accountable to the communities they serve, are established on the basis of an assessment of community needs, and are instruments for anti-racist community development and the achievement of equal participation.

Within this framework, ISAs provide a broad range of essential services that would otherwise not be accessible to immigrant and refugee clients.

Much of the work of ISAs is done within the context of the settlement services that provided their initial funding and service framework. The term 'settlement services' itself is one that encompasses a host of interrelated activities, delivered within the language and the cultural viewpoint of the client, to help immigrants and refugees settle into and take control over their new environment. Programs such as language training are developing in increasingly specialized forms related to the specific language needs and immigration experiences of the different client groups. Some ISAs offer first-language literacy programs and English-as-a-second-language instruction in the workplace.

Other programs are related to the specific needs of immigrant women, such as women's support groups, women's health education in the workplace, and specialized forms of labour-market skills training. Many ISA activities are geared to respond to the severe difficulties faced by their clients in the current economic restructuring and prolonged recession: employment counselling, assistance with securing unemployment insurance and welfare, and skills retraining for displaced workers and those whose skills and qualifications are not recognized by Canadian employers. The delivery of culturally appropriate individual and family counselling services has developed in response to the multiple stresses experienced by immigrants and refugees, as have community-based initiatives for physical and mental health services responding to the needs of specific ethno-racial groups.

Legal assistance on issues like immigration status, access to housing, income maintenance, and employment rights is provided by a number of ISAs and community legal clinics. Other agencies provide such specialized services as therapeutic counselling and group support activities for refugee victims of torture, assistance from trained cultural interpreters, advocacy for the rights of immigrant domestic workers, and support services for immigrant and refugee youth.

Immigrant service agencies also assist their clients in gaining access to 'mainstream' institutions by providing cultural interpretation, information, and referrals, and by making the appropriate interventions with those institutions to ensure that the service is accessible. As well, the ISAs are increasingly working directly with larger institutions to improve general access to services. This work may take the form of providing consultations to mainstream organizations on anti-racist organizational change or on the development of accessible programs.

A third field of activity for ISAs is community education and development. The scope of these activities is very broad. Most ISAs publish newsletters addressed to the communities they serve and regularly organize public forums on topics of concern such as violence against women, housing, AIDS, and employment standards. Many also maintain small reference libraries in the languages of their clients. As well, the needs assessments conducted by ISAs within different immigrant and refugee communities provide essential information to the agency, to governments, and to broad-based advocacy organizations such as OCASI.

The fourth and final field of activities is advocacy for changes in the policies that perpetuate discrimination and racism. At present, much of the advocacy work in this area done by community agencies is directed at government policy makers. OCASI, for example, is involved in regular consultations with numerous federal, provincial, and municipal departments and sub-departments, sometimes on a monthly or even a weekly basis.

OCASI is only one of the organizations involved in advocacy. In Metropolitan Toronto, for example, there is the Access Action Council, the Black Action Defense Committee, the Coalition of Agencies Serving South Asians (CASSA), the Hispanic Council of Metropolitan Toronto, the Multicultural Coalition for Access to Family Services, the Toronto Refugee Affairs Council (TRAC), and the Urban Alliance on Race Relations. On a provincial level, the ethno-racial communities express their concerns through the Alliance for Employment Equity, the Coalition of Visible Minority Women, the Ontario Immigrant and Visible Minority Women's Organization (OIVMWO), the Ontario Immigrant Settlement Workers' Association, and the Ontario Racial Minorities Organizing Committee for Training (ORMOCT). Working on a Canada-wide basis are the Canadian Council for Refugees (CCR), the Canadian Ethnocultural Council, the Chinese Canadian National Council (CCNC), the Congress of Black Women, the National Organization of Immigrant and Visible Minority Women of Canada (NOIVMWC), and many others.[4]

THE BROADER ROLE OF IMMIGRANT SERVICE AGENCIES

Immigrant service organizations, then, contribute to the development of anti-racist social services in numerous ways. The very scope of these activities raises a broader question: What is the more general role or mandate of ISAs in the provision of human services? This question comes up more and more frequently, often in the context of common myths and serious misconceptions about the work done by ISAs.[5]

Frequently, for example, people will use the term 'ethno-specific agencies' as the counterpart to 'mainstream' institutions, which gives the impression that any particular immigrant service agency exists to serve only one distinct ethno-racial community. In this sense, the term 'ethno-specific' can be appropriately applied to most mainstream agencies that meet the needs of English-speaking members of the dominant culture.

It is of course true that some ISAs are associated with service to particular ethno-racial groups. Many OCASI member agencies, particularly the recently formed ones, have grown out of the special needs of newly arrived immigrant and refugee groups such as the Eritreans, Ethiopians, Iranians, Somalis, and Tamils. Other agencies provide services to particular groups like the Cambodians, Filipinos, Poles, Ukrainians, and Vietnamese.

On the whole, however, the notions conveyed by the term 'ethno-specific agencies' are largely false. Most OCASI member agencies serve a variety of ethno-racial groups as defined by language or country of origin, or both. Some of the bigger agencies serve literally dozens of different language groupings. In the northern parts of Ontario, the ISAs may provide assistance to all immigrant and refugee groupings in a particular city, and to Native peoples and francophones as well. Among the OCASI member agencies there are also traditional neighbourhood settlement houses, community centres, and community legal clinics that have adapted their mission to respond to the changing demographics and growing numbers of immigrants and refugees coming to them for aid. As well, there are a growing number of organizations devoted to specific *needs* within the ethno-racial communities, including refugee reception, culturally appropriate health services, family and mental health programs for particular groups like the Chinese-speaking community, cultural interpreting, health education, and skills training for immigrant women. What these agencies have in common is not so much an association with a particular ethno-racial community, but rather a broader commitment to developing and providing the services needed by a variety of immigrant and refugee communities.

In recent years immigrant service agencies have also been accused of creating a system of 'duplicate' or 'parallel' services. This viewpoint sees the growing range of activities provided by the ISAs as a threat to the 'normal' operations of the dominant system of human service delivery.

The situation is rather the reverse. The dominant institutions have failed to provide access to services for immigrants and refugees and the ISAs are both filling the service gaps and helping the 'mainstream' institutions to improve access. But this way of looking at things depends in turn on an important assumption: that access to anti-racist, culturally appropriate services is a *right* of all who live in Canada. While many people from the dominant culture may claim to agree with this principle, some have difficulties with its application. This may be because they simply take for granted that human services are available in ways they find suitable and have not thought very deeply about the extent to which these services are suitable for other cultures.

There is a slightly more sophisticated version of this fear of 'duplicate' services' that is currently popular. This viewpoint accepts the historical contributions of immigrant service agencies in the fields of settlement and integration activities, but rejects the entry of the ISAs into service fields traditionally reserved for 'mainstream' institutions. Behind this viewpoint there seems to be a belief that the ISAs are rather amateur, unprofessional organizations, providing assistance on a mainly volunteer basis. It is this outlook that lies behind the notion of 'bridging,' in which the ISAs are to be funded as referral centres funnelling their clients to the 'professional' service providers in the dominant institutions.

But 'bridging' is no solution to problems of discrimination and racism. It is based on the fundamentally erroneous belief that the privileged status of 'mainstream' institutions makes them inherently more capable of providing appropriate services. The reality is, however, quite different. The staff and management of the ISAs lack neither academic degrees nor professional competence. And although these community organizations make extensive use of volunteers from the communities they serve, they are not 'volunteer' organizations. Without training and coordination by paid, professional staff, the services of these volunteers would be of little practical use.

Most important of all, the staff and volunteer boards of directors of these immigrant service agencies, knowing the actual needs of their clientele, provide leadership in developing appropriate policies and alternative service models. If these policies differ from those in the documents produced by government bureaucracies, or if these service models depart from those developed within the dominant culture, it is because they have emerged in response to the acute and changing needs of the communities being served. It is no surprise that in general these policies and programs are not incorporated into government or mainstream policies. Immigrants and refugees are for the most part not represented in these groups.

Another way of trying to invalidate the unique contributions of immigrant service agencies is to assess and reassess their activities on the basis of 'cost-effectiveness.' ISAs are not against such evaluations – they believe that their use of both salaried staff and volunteer labour is highly efficient. At the same time, however, it is necessary to be very cautious about the assumptions behind such evaluations.

To evaluate the work of immigrant service agencies in terms of 'cost-effectiveness' requires an understanding of the wide range of benefits beyond the direct provision of services that are provided by these agencies. Because of their holistic approach and focus on prevention as well as direct intervention, ISAs provide benefits such as the creation of employment opportunities within the ethno-racial communities, the development of community leadership within the boards of directors and other volunteer activities of the agencies, and the creation of positive role models for active public participation.

Behind all of these arguments lies one basic idea – the legitimacy and recognition of multiple service models in dealing with complex and largely unrealized service needs. Immigrant service agencies are not concerned with replacing the other service providers in Canadian society, but rather with meeting needs that have been ignored and helping other service providers to transform their ways of functioning so that ethno-racial minorities have genuine access to services. In this respect, the concerns of the ISAs are not that different from those of other sectors combatting discrimination, such as people with disabilities, francophones, women's groups, and Aboriginal peoples.

CONCLUSIONS AND PERSPECTIVES ON THE FUTURE

Ontario's society has reached a critical point. The growing demographic weight of so many racial-minority, immigrant, and refugee communities within the population means that the problem of providing appropriate services to these communities will dominate the issues of human service policy for decades to come. Whatever term is chosen to describe these initiatives – multiculturalism, equity, anti-racism, or culturally appropriate services – we must face the reality of the urgent need to develop a variety of innovative models of service delivery and to validate and adequately fund existing anti-racist, culturally appropriate models.

Community-based immigrant service agencies have played, and will continue to play, an essential role in the development of these new services. The role of the ISAs includes delivering services not provided by other institutions, helping 'mainstream' organizations adapt their models of service delivery, education, and development within the various ethno-racial communities, and engaging in advocacy to change the discriminatory policies and practices of contemporary society. These contributions make the immigrant service agencies a vital link in the provision of anti-racist social services and an integral component of the network of human service providers.

Our vision of the future should not be confined to trying to imagine whether improved services will come mainly from the immigrant service organizations or from a transformation of 'mainstream' institutions. This formulation of the problem is essentially bureaucratic. From the perspective of the needs of the ethno-racial communities, it seems clear that the ISAs will have to continue to evolve in response to developing needs, and that the dominant institutions must transform their policies and practices to an even greater degree. There is every possibility of creative and equal partnership – but such an alliance depends on recognition of the nature of the problem and of the special expertise of the immigrant service agencies.

There are some encouraging signs of change, such as the relatively new initiatives of different government departments in providing improved translating and interpreting services, and the recent decisions of the Ontario Ministry of Community and Social Services to fund immigrant service agencies providing access to the welfare system. But the roots of discrimination and racism run deeply in Canadian society, and there is much that must be done to eradicate all forms of inequality. Future progress in achieving genuine equality depends not only on cooperation among the different providers of human services, but also on a unified political will to identify, combat, and eliminate all forms of discrimination.

NOTES

Valuable community input into the content of the article was provided by the following persons from OCASI member agencies: Kay Blair, Larissa Cairncross, Sudha Coomarasamy, Miranada Pinto, and Julia Tao. Significant contributions to this article were also made by Brian Conway and Howard Sinclair-Jones. OCASI is the provincial association of more than 130 community-based immigrant service organizations in Ontario.

1 From the point of view of community-based immigrant service organizations, the term 'mainstream' refers to the established social service institutions of Canadian society, which remain dominated by an Anglo-Canadian cultural outlook. In this sense the term is used as an implicit criticism of these institutions' failure to provide access to ethno-racial minorities.

2 We are not suggesting that this period represented the *birth* of the immigrant settlement agency. Many OCASI agencies have origins that predate this time. And organizations like the various Chinese benevolent associations, which were funded entirely within a particular ethnic community and could be seen as the true precursors of today's community-based immigrant organizations, have been operating in Canada for many decades. Nevertheless, we would argue that the period of the late 1970s and early 1980s, in Ontario at least, represent a turning point in the development of settlement agencies. We see this development in relation to the number of agencies that were founded, the diversity of activities they undertook, and the beginning of public (federal and provincial government) commitment to their existence.

3 There are many other forms of racial discrimination that appear in what we might call the 'public' or 'political' domain: participation of immigrants' children in the school systems, the policing of ethno-racial communities, racist barriers and stereotypes in the arts and the media, etc. These, while extremely important, are beyond the scope of this article.

4 This list is by no means complete, but is simply meant to provide some indication of the numbers of advocacy organizations in which OCASI member agencies are currently very active. It does not include the many OCASI member agencies directly involved in independent advocacy efforts. Nor does the listing contain all the numerous ethno-racial organizations working on a pan-Canadian level, many of which are very active in advocacy for immigrant and refugee rights.

5 Some of the approach in this section is stimulated by Churchill's (1990) discussion of the methodological problems in evaluating the benefits of French-language education in Ontario.

PART FOUR

Implementing Change

COMMENTS:

Equitable Access Is a Right, Not a Privilege

Kass Sunderji

Historically, Canadian social service agencies in urban centres have operated on a model that assumed a racially homogeneous clientele with a well-defined value system and knowledge of at least one official language. The significant influx of non-European immigrants in the 1970s and the 1980s challenged traditional service-delivery models. And just as cultural agencies have sometimes hidden behind legislation in order to keep non-Europeans from having a voice in the cultural life of their respective communities, welfare and family-service agencies have occasionally cited legislation to justify their inability to accommodate cultural differences.

The view that equitable access to social services is a right not a privilege has pushed many organizations to engage in a process of multicultural and anti-racism organizational change. While this type of organizational development encourages organizations to better reflect the composition of the communities in their catchment areas or target populations, only structural change that results in power sharing and equality of opportunity will be effective. Although many agencies subscribe to organizational change, they tend to shy away from the 'anti-racism' component of that change. This half-hearted stance invites criticism from racial minorities, who feel it produces cosmetic results rather than encouraging critical self-examination and fundamental change.

Many racial-minority groups also question whether human service agencies are committed to becoming more equitable and accessible. Many are only willing to commit themselves to change when funding is available, and then are prepared only to develop and put into operation an outreach plan or enhance an existing program. Rarely is the process self-initiated and self-financed and even less frequently does it involve radical recasting of organizational mission, values, structures, policies, and personnel in response to community needs.

The questions that dominate the discussion on the absence of racial minorities in the cultural fabric of Canadian society – who gets to make decisions about what issues – are also part of the 'access to services' discussion. The composition of the staff and board of a service agency is a critical factor in determining the vision and the corporate culture of an organization. If community voices are not represented and heard, then policies, procedures, structures, and modes of service delivery, based and developed on a narrow set of views, experiences, and assumptions, will meet the needs of some and automatically (and often unintentionally) exclude others.

Unless organizations take up the challenge of examining their powers and privileges and undertake institutional change that will increase the presence of racial minorities as clients, volunteers, staff, and board members, a significant number of Canadians will continue to be relegated to subordinate or second-class status, their quest for equality of opportunity, a right ostensibly guaranteed by the Canadian Constitution, not yet fulfilled.

Chapter 10

The Anti-Racist Cast of Mind

Charles Novogrodsky

Anti-racism, the work of undoing and unlearning racism, makes us advocates in the community, in our workplaces, and in our educational practice. Anti-racist actions – the nitty-gritty of what we say, how we say it, and how we regard those with whom we speak and work – are all informed by our own anti-racist outlook. This essay is a reflection based on my anti-racist practice in a variety of organizational and training settings. It discusses the challenges of anti-racist work, key ingredients of effective advocacy, and the anti-racist cast of mind.

CHALLENGES OF ANTI-RACIST WORK

Those who work to advance ethno-racial equity frequently encounter resistance. Challenging someone who makes a racist remark can provoke such resistance – the person so challenged may express resistance in body language, may offer the defence that the remark is 'just a joke,' may even threaten, or offer, violence. While there are many ways to express resistance, its source is the same: the challenge to the belief that there is social sanction for her or his behaviour, a sanction based on a defined social norm that places the ethno-racial identity of the joke-teller above that of the 'other.' This belief system justifies the subjection of that other to ridicule and discrimination.

Because resistance based on this belief is a fact in our everyday lives and our work lives, those seeking to challenge racist practice and thought can expect opposition. Today, most of this opposition focuses on policy and legal efforts, such as employment equity, which is intended to redress and prevent the effects of racism in employment.

Effective advocacy in the face of contention and resistance is not easy. The *organizational advocate* may be pushed to the margins of organizational culture and decision making. The advocate working in the fields of education and training may be accused of 'preaching.' Worse, for effective learning, *anti-racist educators* may find themselves *becoming* preachers. In the face of institutional opposition and resistance, *community advocates* may compete or turn inward, and thus lose sight of the anti-racism objective of a society of full participation, equal access, and fair outcomes for all.

The challenge for those with an anti-racist cast of mind is to be an effective advocate in the community, in education, and in the workplace.

KEY INGREDIENTS OF EFFECTIVE ADVOCACY

Effective advocates speak and act not just with like-minded people, but also with persons holding assimilationist and multicultural outlooks. Effective advocates are able to build ethno-racial equity in and into our community and social institutions while consciously rejecting blaming and the imposing of guilt. Effective advocates make friends and allies, are self-aware, respectful of others, and anchored in the realities of community and organizational life.

Those possessing an effective anti-racist cast of mind reflect on their own ideas and practice, expanding their consciousness and practice to include all social oppressions. They honour the particularity of each and include all in a common effort to build fair relations and institutions free of bigotry and discrimination.

Equity practitioners owe a big thank-you to those who, against opposition, have articulated important tenets of anti-racist thought and practice. Anti-racism thinkers have struggled against racist structures and the age-old ideas backing those structures. For over twenty years Canada has experienced ethno-racial equity practice based on multiculturalism. At present there is debate over multiculturalism's role as an ideology and policy for social change. Some have argued that it helped Canadians to accept cultural difference and cultural expression. According to them, multiculturalism has helped to mobilize ethno-racial communities in Canada to defend and advance their political and social rights.

Others have argued that anti-racism had to go beyond multiculturalism and structural analysis to examine how social systems perpetuate racism. Anti-racists holding this perspective have also questioned aspects of everyday life taken for granted by the majority – words, body language, the issue of voice in literature – which have frequently served as 'hidden' pilings supporting racist social organization. This type of analysis has given us new insight into the meaning of the term 'unlearning racism.'

The anti-racism mentality concerns itself not only with its own premises and practices, but with how others think about issues of racism. Most people's ideas on these issues come from one of three outlooks – an assimilationist outlook, a multicultural outlook, or an anti-racist outlook.

The assimilationist outlook is based on an Anglo-Canadian point of view (see chapter 1). It yearns for a Canada of Anglo-Canadian conformity. While life in an Anglo-Canadian world may well have been the dominant experience for many Canadians, we need look no further than Aboriginal Canadians to discover the limits and sad results of an Anglo-conformist practice in Canadian history (see chapters 2 and 3 and Jette's comments).

Multiculturalists have celebrated cultural difference. People of colour and those oppressed by ethnic strains of racism (Jews by anti-Semitism; immigrant people by anti-immigrant and anti-allophone sentiments) have legitimately asked multiculturalists: 'Where are you when we are discriminated against?' and 'Where were you when, after the nice-sounding words of multicultural attitude adjustment ended, the fact of discrimination remained?'

It is important for anti-racists to acknowledge that most Canadians fit into either Anglo-conformist or multicultural schools of thought. Sometimes, in seeking to build strength from anti-racist law and policy, we overlook the present state of most people's thinking. Advancing anti-racist practice and implementing anti-racist policy means taking stock of how to move people's thinking at the same time as we initiate anti-racist organizational practice.

The anti-racist advocate is therefore a person who must negotiate a series of interpersonal and institutional encounters with large numbers of assimilationist or multicultural thinkers. Over time, anti-racist advocates develop responses to frequently heard objections to equity efforts. To the client who says, 'I don't want a Black providing me service,' we learn to ask, 'Do you have a problem with Black people?' We challenge rather than entertain racism. To the community board member who says, 'It's hard to get a board which is reflective of the community because we need qualified people,' we ask, 'Why was it so easy all these years to find a board that did not reflect the racial diversity in our community?' and we ask, 'Do you believe White people are more qualified to serve on our board than Black people?' In the words of Suzanne Pharr: 'We must take a very hard look at our complicity with oppression, all of them. We must see that to give no voice, to take no action to end them is to support their existence ... One must have the courage to take the risks that may end in loss of privilege' (Pharr 1988: 52).

Ultimately, challenging racism in others requires us to challenge as well the system of control and privilege upon which racism rests. When we challenge racism, we are excluded from the favours that system bestows – the risk to which Pharr refers. To undertake such a risk, whether at work, with our students, or with our friends and family, requires us to understand our stake in eliminating racism.

Anti-racist educators have sought to deal with the way people think about the theoretical and practical deficiencies of a multicultural outlook. Those who have been uncomfortable with a sometimes angry anti-racist tone might consider the words of Adrienne Shadd, a fifth-generation Black Canadian:

Looking back I can see that things ran fairly smoothly as long as the question of race could be ignored, as long as I did not transgress the bounds of artificial 'colour blindness' under which I was constrained ... Blacks and other people 'of colour' are viewed as recent newcomers, or worse, as 'foreigners' who have no claim to a Canadian heritage except through the 'generosity' of Canadian immigration officials, who 'allow' a certain quota of us to enter each year ... When we moved to Toronto I was made to feel different, alien, even though no one specifically referred to my racial origin. It is a feeling which has never fully left me and perhaps explains why to this day I do not feel comfortable in the company of White people and when sometimes Whites think they are paying Black people a compliment by saying 'We don't think of you as Black' as my sister's friends have told her. This is not just a misplaced nicety; it is an insult. We are not seeking 'honourary' White status. (James 1995: 75)

The anti-racist cast of mind learns about the Anglo-conformist assumptions buried deep in everyday life. It enters the experience of those who have been relegated to a status of 'Less Powerful Other.' It takes responsibility for reworking language and taken-for-granted verbal formulas and exchanges so that the history and experience of the 'other' is treated respectfully.

The tone of effective advocacy may shift as we move from workplace or educational settings to the community setting. There must be tough advocacy; the community's power is a consequence of its organization and the strength of its voice. The community in a democracy *demands* accountability. The community voice is an anti-racist engine that powers change in the workplace and in educational institutions. Members of majority groups who are sympathetic to anti-racist work sometimes feel slighted at the tough tone of anti-racist advocates. Setting aside their own feelings of upset, they might pause to consider the pain felt and the threats received by minority community advocates who have had the courage to speak out, to take the heat of their tough advocacy efforts.

Workplace and education advocates limit their possibilities when they simply copy the anti-racist tactics of community advocates. By definition, anti-racist advocates in the workplace and in education straddle community and organizational life. Like their more public community counterparts, these advocates must also prepare for the long haul. While they may make hard demands at early stages of anti-racist organizational work, over time they should try to push an organization to change in ways that encourage thoroughgoing change.

In bringing anti-racist messages forward, workplace and education advocates face a deeply entrenched, often hostile, organizational practice. Those with an anti-racist cast of mind appreciate different anti-racist tactics employed by advocates in different settings. They might regard the three settings discussed thus far – the community, the workplace, and all places where we teach and learn – as three legs of an equity structure. Work and success on each leg is required for anti-racist efforts to succeed.

REFLECTING ON STORIES FROM ANTI-RACIST TRAINING

A while ago I gave a workshop on racial harassment to treatment-plant workers. One participant, a shop steward, said, 'Charlie, I really don't know why we are here. I've got sixty men in our local expecting me to do something about hazardous wastes in the water. I've got sixty-two other priorities. Frankly, racial harassment is number sixty-three.' Is this shop steward a racist? What cast of mind do I need in order to listen, really listen, to what he is saying?

In another workshop with managers from northern Ontario, where a large percentage of the population is francophone, an Anglo-Canadian expressed hostility to the Ontario government's efforts to broaden access and protect the French language. Another participant said that effort spent addressing inequities is misplaced, given shrinking provincial budgets for much-needed government services. What cast of mind is required to respond to the managers' hostility? Should we regard hostile and resistant expressions as intrusions into anti-racism work?

I believe we should not; the anti-racist cast of mind incorporates peoples' fears, beliefs, and anxieties into its work. An effective anti-racist advocate and educator understands the reality of the many contexts of racial and ethnic tensions. Starting with peoples' real and perceived experience, the anti-racist goes on to illustrate whose life has governed our perceptions and whose voice has been missing from our common efforts to address problems. The sequence is important. The anti-racist educator/advocate first respects peoples' present perceptions, and then assists them to identify which of those perceptions may be racist. Blaming and imposing guilt have no role in this method.

In the case of the shop steward we might ask: 'Is the problem of hazardous wastes in the workplace made better by continuing racial harassment in your workplace?' We can further discuss whether a union that ends racial harassment and thereby encourages participation from all workers is not a union in a stronger position to overcome safety hazards.

Our northern Ontario civil-service managers might be asked, once they have expressed their views, who pays for government services and whether francophones, whose labour built many northern Ontario communities and who are important taxpayers and consumers of government services, do not have the right to access those services in their own language and to ensure that they are fairly represented in local government workforces.

Multiculturalism does not bring us to connections between workplace safety, adequate government services, and overcoming discrimination. Effective anti-racism does. If the interpersonal racism of assimilationists can be effectively challenged, they are often open to connecting anti-racist work to other social problems. This connection fits with their view of a common society requiring a common solution. Similarly, the anti-racist cast of mind that makes broader social connections is preparing the groundwork for a meeting of assimilationist and anti-racist minds.

In another workshop, a Black woman broke down in tears at the painful memory of being streamed out of academic courses by a racist high-school counselling system. This is pain for which the anti-racist educator should be prepared. The anti-racist educator acknowledges this pain, and does not demand its expression for the sake of majority-group participants who need to 'see what it feels like.' When this pain appears, we go towards it. We support the person in pain, and we engage the group in a discussion about how people cope with racism's painful effects. Beyond that, we analyse those policies and practices that must be changed if racism is to be removed from the system.

Art, used selectively and appropriately, has a major role to play. For the expansive anti-racist cast of mind, the wisdom of our visual artists, writers, dancers, and other artists has a great deal to offer. Artists provide us with messages and images that inform our vision of an anti-racist world.

Consider this passage from the African-American writer Toni Morrison's award-winning novel *Beloved*, where a runaway slave woman discusses her freedom: 'Sethe had twenty-eight days, the travel of one whole moon, of unslaved life ... days of healing, ease, real talk. Days of company: knowing the names of forty, fifty other Negroes, their views, habits, where they had been, what they had done. Of feeling their fun and sorrow along with her own, which made it better. One taught her the alphabet, another a stitch. All taught her how it felt to wake up at dawn and decide what to do with the day ... bit by bit ... in the clearing, along with the others, she had claimed herself. Freeing yourself was one thing; claiming ownership of that freed self was another' (Morrison 1987: 95).

Anti-racist advocates, struggling against powerful ideas and systems that support racism, may lose sight of the interconnectedness of oppressions. Once this interconnection is lost, so too are the prospects diminished for solidarity to combat common oppressors. At times anti-racist advocates may fall into the trap of ranking or ordering pain. Ordering pain may mean, for example, arguing that the pain of colour oppression, of anti-Black racism, is more serious than pain based on another aspect of social identity, that it should be at the top of a hierarchy of pain. From this would follow the argument that anti-racist policy and practice must always accord top priority to issues of racism as they affect people of colour.

It is, I think, more useful to rank *opportunity structures*, in which case anti-Black racism may, at particular times, be the most pressing problem. Even so, in Canada, one must be cautious to acknowledge the special historic and on-going oppression experienced by Aboriginal–First Nations peoples.

The expanding anti-racist cast of mind welcomes explorations into opportunity structures. It forges links among different struggles for equity. It seeks out friends and allies from oppressed groups and in those others who, by their actions, show they have joined equity work. Women, persons with disabilities, people of minority religious identity, Jews, gays and lesbians, and immigrants and refugees for whom neither English nor French is a first language have, by virtue of the discrimination directed against them, unique contributions to make to the wider anti-racist effort.

Just as multiculturalism has tended to be blind to the unique ways that colour operates to perpetuate inequity, anti-racists must realize that, at various times and places, language, religion, sexual orientation, gender, nationality, and disability are the basis of discrimination and inequity. *The expanded anti-racist cast of mind accommodates the paradox of the similarity and uniqueness of each oppression. It does not require the ranking of pain to claim strategic leverage in anti-racist work.*

While some of the most oppressive manifestations of racism appear in the interpersonal realm, anti-racists must be cautious about focusing on oppressive inter-personal behaviour as the sole object of anti-racist work. While such behaviour is felt first and lends itself best to direct challenge, interpersonal racism is, in the end, a symptom of larger social ideologies and structures that perpetuate racism. Anti-racists might best keep their eyes on the larger prize, the removal of social oppression in the public sphere.

Many Anglo-Canadians have been schooled in a vocabulary of individual effort. The notion of recognizing and overcoming social oppression may be foreign to them. They would rather talk about 'pulling oneself up by one's own bootstraps.' How useful is it, ultimately, for anti-racists to engage in endless challenges to interpersonal aspects of racism? While interpersonal challenges have their place, effective anti-racist strategy must move talk and work into the *public sphere* of work, school, public services, and culture, where everyone has a stake in full participation and equity.

Human-rights legislation plays a vital role for the anti-racist educator or advocate. It offers a clear legal direction for equity, including the basis for programs such as employment equity, to redress and unearth entrenched oppressions. Used as an entry point, human-rights legislation can involve many assimilationists and multiculturalists who otherwise might not consider the wider legal basis for equity in a discussion of the social implications of racism.

THE ANTI-RACIST CAST OF MIND

In summary, what are some essential ingredients for an effective anti-racist cast of mind? First, recognize the value of thinking as a tool. Reflect on *your* ideas and those of your colleagues. Reflect on *your* practice. Second, honour other views: be creative in finding ways to expand others' thinking beyond assimilationist and multicultural outlooks. Third, locate anti-racism work in a respect for everyday perception and life – hazardous waste and racism are both poisons. Fourth, respect both the hard advocacy of the community and the survival tactics employed by anti-racist organizational practitioners. Fifth, find appropriate ways to use the wisdom of artists in anti-racist work. Sixth, avoid blame and guilt; make friends and allies. Seventh, avoid ranking pain; seek links among all forms of social oppression. Finally, find common ground in the public sphere; use public policy and human-rights legislation where appropriate.

Together, these eight principles can help us to become more effective advocates in our community, in our workplace, and in our educational practice.

Chapter 11

From Uni-versity to Poly-versity*
Organizations in Transition to Anti-Racism

Arnold Minors

Like other living creatures, organizations use energy to preserve their integrity, or uni-versity. They treat staff, volunteers, and clients who are different in much the same way biological organisms treat viruses and bacteria. Organisms use their resources to isolate or expel intruders, even when the intruders help them respond to serious threats, and, over time, very few organisms survive without adapting to the environment. Similarly, over time, very few organizations are successful without changing in response to internal and external forces. In order to survive and thrive, human service organizations must be able to change their practices. In particular, they must respond and adapt to a workforce, volunteer pool, and client base that are increasingly diverse. In short, they must move from UNI-VERSITY (a monocultural, excluding world-view) to POLY-VERSITY (a genuinely multicultural, including world-view).

In this chapter, I examine the pressures that motivate organizations to change by presenting a six-stage model of anti-racist organization development. The model is based on ideas originally put forward by Bailey Jackson and Rita Hardiman in an unpublished work in 1981 and further developed by Jackson and Evangelina Holvino in 1988. Each stage of the model is described in relation to organizational mission, structure, values, employment practices, availability of services, and ability to deal with differences. Organizations may use the model as a tool to assess the extent to which they are inclusive and as an aid to move towards more equity and access.

I know of many organizations that have carried out activities appropriate to a Stage 5 organization, for example, when their organizations

---

* The terms 'Uni-versity' and 'Poly-versity' are copyrighted by Arnold Minors.

are really located in Stage 2. The result has been frustration for employees, increased resistance to change within organizations, and, in fact, a firmer fixing of the organization in its (earlier) stage.

It is natural that people will want to put their best foot forward. It is natural, therefore, that they might want to conclude that their organization is doing better than it is. It is important, however, to face 'what is,' in order to design stage-appropriate activities that will move the organization to 'what it wants to become'; that is, to successfully make the transition to POLY-VERSITY.

FROM UNI-VERSITY TO POLY-VERSITY

Canadian organizations are struggling with the idea of POLY-VERSITY. In the past, most have drawn their clients, volunteers, and staff from predominantly white, Christian communities. But the community has changed dramatically. There are increasing numbers of people of colour in the workforce; people with disabilities are demanding equitable treatment; poor people want greater participation in the decisions that affect them; Aboriginal people are increasingly asserting their rights.

Oppression on the basis of gender, sexual orientation, class, ability, and race has traditionally excluded the voices of women, gays, lesbians, and bisexual people, poor people, people with disabilities, people of colour, and Aboriginal peoples. Racism is, in fact, pervasive in our society. It is impossible to live in Canada today without being affected by racist attitudes, actions, policies, structures, and social systems.

Not-for-profit organizations are at various stages in their struggle to become anti-racist. Organizations may show evidence of being anti-racist in one program, non-racist in another, and racist in a third. As they move towards anti-racism, changes reach deeper and deeper levels. At first, individual behaviours change, followed by interpersonal and intergroup behaviours. Gradually, organizational rules and practices, missions, norms, policies, and structures change. Finally, relationships with the community change.

These changes occur along a continuum of growth that sees organizations move from Discrimination (UNI-VERSITY) to Non-Discrimination to Anti-Discrimination (POLY-VERSITY). Discriminatory organizations are composed of Excluding (Stage 1) and Passive Club (Stage 2) members. These organizations promote the dominance of traditional power groups in society. They are monocultural and racist both in the way they are organized and the way they deliver services.

DISCRIMINATORY		NON-DISCRIMINATORY		ANTI-DISCRIMINATORY	
• monocultural • promotes dominance – within organization – within society • racist • excludes differences		• ignores dominance • non-racist • denies differences		• multicultural • promotes diversity – within organization – within society • anti-racist • includes differences	
UNI-VERSITY				POLY-VERSITY	
EXCLUDING ORGANIZATION	PASSIVE CLUB	TOKEN ACCEPTANCE	SYMBOLIC EQUITY	SUBSTANTIAL EQUITY	INCLUDING ORGANIZATION
STAGE: 1	2	3	4	5	6

Non-Discriminatory organizations are composed of Token Acceptance (Stage 3) and Symbolic Equity (Stage 4) members. These organizations have begun the work to put themselves in the path towards inclusiveness. They recognize superficial differences among groups, but believe that everyone is basically the same and therefore should be treated the same way. Although these organizations are non-racist, they base their structures, systems, and modes of service delivery on the same set of narrow assumptions that guide Stage 1 and 2 organizations.

Anti-Discriminatory Organizations are composed of Substantial Equity (Stage 5) and Including Organizations (Stage 6). Their anti-racist philosophy and practice recognize and seek to redress the power inequities among individuals and groups. They work with people inside and outside the organization to identify strategies for change at the individual, institutional, and societal levels. They are responsive to, and reflective of, their various constituencies and work actively to eliminate all forms of oppression.

Although organizations may express similar or identical behaviours at more than one stage, the reasons for the behaviour and its impact on the organization will differ. For example, a woman of colour may assume a leadership position in Stages 2, 3, 4, 5, and 6. In Stage 2, she may have been hired because she is 'white enough' or incompetent enough to pose no threat to the status quo. In Stage 4, she may have been hired because she is extremely well qualified and the organization needs a 'multicultural' person to be a token symbol for 'ethnic' clients. In Stage 6, she is hired because she brings a unique set of skills, knowledge, and experience that is recognized, valued, and supported at all levels of the organization.

In the following pages, I explain the stages of the model and the behaviours that typify them in greater detail.

STAGE 1: THE EXCLUDING ORGANIZATION

The Excluding Organization is an inflexible structure *designed* to maintain the dominance of one group over all others. Excluding Organizations only hire staff, recruit volunteers, and serve members from the dominant group. Where such practices are prohibited by law, peer pressure enforces unwritten rules and procedures. For example, senior managers may want to meet all potential employees to ensure they will 'fit in.' By tacit agreement, Aboriginal people and women and men of colour won't fit in. Consequently, they are never referred for interviews. People who try to change these rules are isolated or fired.

The Excluding Organization has similar rules for clients who don't 'fit in.' Long waits and other service inconveniences ensure that people of colour won't return. Inflexible modes of service delivery also hinder outreach. In the view of the Excluding Organization there is no such thing as ineffective counselling; only inappropriate clients. As a result, Aboriginal peoples, people of colour, and others learn either not to expect help or to seek assistance elsewhere.

The Excluding Organization is like fate – it neither changes nor learns. It attempts at all costs to preserve its integrity or 'uni-versity-ness.' The Excluding Organization believes strongly in preserving established interests and works hard to deny the existence of people with different beliefs, histories, or values.

Excluding Organizations are very difficult to change. Only external pressure – for instance, from legislation or the fear of litigation – can drag them, kicking and screaming, into the Passive Club.

WHAT YOU MIGHT HEAR AT STAGE 1

- Find some way to make that Indian woman wait. Forever, if necessary.
- Those Black people don't belong in here with us. They just don't understand what we're all about.
- It's important to preserve our Christian values; that's what the Canadian society is based on. If you bring in all those other beliefs, who knows what we'll come to?
- You have to do things our way; it's the only way.

STAGE 2: THE PASSIVE CLUB

While organizations in the Passive Club stage do not advocate explicitly on behalf of white people, their policies, procedures, and practices are designed to maintain the privilege reflected in the dominant values of society. People traditionally excluded get very little support from the system. Only a small number of racial minorities, First Nations peoples, and others are hired – and only when they have the 'correct' perspective.

Passive Club members provide services 'as they always have been provided.' They make no attempt to adapt and respond to client needs. The underlying intent of Passive Club programs is to ensure that people assimilate into 'Canadian' – that is, Western European – society. An English as a Second Language (ESL) program, for example, can be used as a device to encourage people of colour to see and value themselves only to the extent that they 'act white.'

Passive Club members make few attempts to let in 'inferior' people. When people of colour, persons with disabilities, and others with similar disadvantages are hired, they receive very little support. They are also the first to go when budgets are cut. Although they are seen as spokespersons for their entire group, they rarely participate in the decision-making process. Alternatively, the organization hires people of colour known to be incompetent. Such hiring practices draw upon and reinforce negative stereotypes and increase resistance to change.

Again, external pressure is required to move organizations in the Passive Club to Stage 3. This pressure can come in the form of additional demands from an increasingly restive client base, from the threat of litigation or imposed legislation, or from the fear of losing funding.

WHAT YOU MIGHT HEAR AT STAGE 2

- If they need our services, they'd better learn to speak English!
- You see, we knew that Indians couldn't make the grade here.
- That Paki sure is good. He's just as good as one of us.
- We have to have a white president. That's our funding base.
- What do Black people think about the Persian Gulf war?
- You know, you can't even tell he's an Indian, unless you look at him.
- Chinese social worker in 'mainstream' agency: 'Either I get all the crappy assignments or they give me only the Chinese clients.'

STAGE 3: TOKEN ACCEPTANCE

In Stage 3, organizations begin to design procedures that will provide access to all qualified people, including Aboriginal people and people of colour, at the bottom of the organization. They advertise themselves as non-discriminatory, with the implicit promise being that anybody can succeed. In practice, however, very little changes.

Organizations at the Token Acceptance stage emphasize the need to preserve the merit principle by getting 'qualified people.' Curiously, these same organizations often support mediocre or incompetent white employees. Only when people of colour are considered for volunteer or paid positions do discussions regarding merit intensify. From time to time, a 'token' person of colour is promoted into management. Those promoted, however, are usually 'team players' with substantially higher qualifications than their colleagues.

In Stage 3, top managers in larger organizations order middle managers to 'fix' the bottom levels. Usually, front-line staff resist because they know that changes in their behaviour will not be supported by the supervisors. This resistance is then used as confirmation that 'the problem is at the bottom.' As a result, managers do little to change the management practices that support and maintain institutionalized racism.

Similar superficial changes occur in service delivery. Organizations may have one or more people able to provide services in a language other than English. Some organizations hire 'multicultural' front-line workers to work with 'their communities.' These staff members, usually people of colour, are frequently marginalized. In some organizations, advertising may occasionally show visible-minority clients doing the same things in the same ways as the previously all-white advertisements. The implicit assumption is that all people are the same.

Pressures to move organizations in Token Acceptance to Stage 4 come from staff (usually senior people who have worked in other organizations), from clients, and from legislation in equity-related areas. Funders may also threaten to withdraw or reduce funding if agencies don't become more reflective of and responsive to their communities.

WHAT YOU MIGHT HEAR AT STAGE 3

- We want to hire Aboriginal people (or people of colour) just as long as they're qualified.
- We are an equal-opportunity employer. We do not discriminate on the basis of race.

- We have a very good race-relations program here. Our staff are learning how to deal with *those* people.
- We don't discriminate around here. Anyone can join this department, provided *he's* qualified.
- You have to be very good to get a promotion around here. I don't care what anybody says, if you're South Asian, you've gotta be twice as good to get half as far.
- I guess she got the assignment because she's Japanese; you know they're worth a lot of points around here.
- Boy, that was a great training program. Now I know why Black people won't look me in the eye when I'm questioning them.
- We'd like to make a change. But it takes time. And we can't move any faster than the people now here will allow us, you know.

STAGE 4: SYMBOLIC EQUITY

This stage is called Symbolic Equity because changes come in the form of symbols rather than substance. Many organizations assume that equity will be achieved if barriers in employment practices are removed. This assumption ignores the impact of organizational culture on the extent to which people of colour and Aboriginal people feel welcomed as staff, clients, board members, and service volunteers.

The organization in Stage 4 is committed to eliminating discriminatory practices by actively recruiting and promoting women and men of colour and Aboriginal people. Yet, all members of the organization are expected to continue to conform to the norms of the dominant group. The leaders of the organization may, for example, try to avoid real equity by assigning accountability for employment equity to a staff person who has no real power. In such cases, employment-equity staff are programmed to fail because they lack the authority to effect real change. By the same token, no manager is held accountable for achieving results either in employment or service equity.

In Stage 4, organizations begin to ask how they can respond to the needs of their clients. Typically, the 'response' is to reshape existing programs to fit the emerging needs of new clients. The 'problem' is described as a marketing one: given a new market, how can we best serve that market? Organizations at Stage 4 do not yet understand that, in order to make services and employment and volunteer opportunities more equitable, they must change power relations within the organization, and with the community.

Multiculturalism programs, incorporating cross-cultural or intercultural communications and race-relations training, are prevalent at Stages 3 and 4. Organizations at Stage 4 may have a 'token' president or executive-committee member of colour. Often, this individual is not seen as a credible spokesperson by the community.

The pressure for movement to Stage 5 comes from a critical mass of women and men who demand equity at staff, board, and committee levels, and from a momentum for change within the organization.

WHAT YOU MIGHT HEAR AT STAGE 4

- She got the assignment because she really knows how to act like a man.
- We pride ourselves in delivering all our counselling programs in response to cultural sensitivities. Unfortunately, our collective-bargaining agreement doesn't permit us to link our professional staff with community workers.
- If we appoint a visible-minority person to our board, we have to make sure that she isn't a single-issue person.
- Look, if you can't take a joke, you probably shouldn't be a volunteer here. We all had to put up with those kinds of jokes. I had to listen to jokes about limeys, you know. And those WASP jokes ...

STAGE 5: SUBSTANTIAL EQUITY

The organization in the Substantial Equity stage has a flexible, responsive structure. Its leaders review their policies periodically. They may even revise a previously sacred mission statement. The new structure ensures that men and women of colour, Aboriginal peoples, and others previously kept out of the decision-making process help shape and reshape the organization's mission, systems, and modes of service delivery. Some organizations in Stage 5 decide that hierarchies – with their implicit assumption of 'power over' rather than 'powerful with' – are no longer appropriate.

Stage 5 organizations may set up task groups to identify community needs and wants. They also institute monitoring processes to *ensure* that services are delivered in ways that people of colour and Aboriginal people – employees and service recipients – describe as equitable. At this stage, multiracial teams of women and men work together at all levels of the organization to develop strategies and establish short- and long-term action plans.

Based on research and consulting experience in a variety of organizations, it is my opinion that few, if any, Canadian organizations are in

Stage 5, although some may have programs or departments at that stage. Pressure to move to Stage 6 comes from the momentum of change built up in previous stages; leadership from senior management, staff, and communities served; and increasingly clear evidence that service and employment equity contribute to organizational effectiveness.

WHAT YOU MIGHT HEAR AT STAGE 5

- Did you hear about the Working Group? They're going to be working on the Community Service Project. I heard that they're bringing in new volunteers from the communities. They'll be making decisions right along with us. I wonder how it'll go.
- Allan Young just became President of XYZ agency. He's very good. Knows this agency inside out and is well connected to his community. But I'm still surprised that a Korean has become president, this year. Especially since we have so many visible-minority people on the board.
- I'm excited about the possibility of a new vision for this agency. Some of us have been talking about this for years and it seemed like nothing was ever gonna happen. It's still amazing to me that our executive director admits in public – on television, yet – that there's racism in the voluntary sector and in our agency.

STAGE 6: THE INCLUDING ORGANIZATION

The Including Organization reflects the contributions and interests of various groups in its mission and operations. Members of the larger community participate at all levels and help make decisions that shape the organization and influence its direction. Indeed, in the Including Organization boundaries between staff, volunteers, and clients may either disappear completely or shift in response to changing conditions.

The Including Organization sees itself as part of the broader community. Its members support efforts to eliminate all forms of social oppression and to enhance the worth of all. It actively seeks the views of various communities and designs and refines its structure to reflect and respond to the expressed needs.

The major difference between organizations in Stages 5 and 6 is one of effort versus results. Organizations in Stage 6 maximize the knowledge, skills, and talents of their staff, volunteers, and community members. They are equitable, responsive, and accessible at all levels. Organizations in Stage 5 are in transition. Although they have appropriate structures and systems in place, they have not yet achieved the goals of equity and participation for all.

WHAT YOU MIGHT HEAR AT STAGE 6

- We are pleased to announce that Deputy Chief [of Police] Brenda Larson has accepted an assignment as full-time president of Charity Foundation for a 2-year term. She'll be seconded there, because of her outstanding experience in our various communities. We are delighted at the support received for this secondment from government, the African-Canadian Coalition, the Chamber of Commerce, and the Charity Foundation.
- It certainly is a treat to be able to be funded to work directly in the Somali communities. We learn so much about how we need to operate. And we're able to help create an actively anti-racist municipality. I've been here – off and on – for 15 years and this is definitely a new place. Of course, the city is getting to be a new place, too.
- Our latest Task Team on sustaining services to new communities will disband. We want to thank the team members – paid and volunteer staff – for their outstanding contributions in helping us to achieve the goal.

A CASE STUDY

[The names are fictitious.] Roop Singh is a caseworker in a child-welfare agency. He is a part-time worker, hired to relieve the case load in one of the agency's branches in response to the agency's desire to 'increase its multicultural staff.'

Singh applied for one of several openings for full-time caseworkers; he did not get any of the jobs. When he asked why, he was told that his 'experience was too narrow' because his casework dealt only with South Asian clients. Roop met with his supervisor, Anne Smith, to find out what he could do to get broader experience within the agency in order to compete more favourably for full-time positions. The supervisor told him that he was doing an excellent job, and it was her perception that 'as we deal with more and more of your people, we're going to need people like you for full-time positions.' However, she also agreed to begin assigning him a few non–South Asian cases. She stressed, though, that she 'needed him for the cases in his "own community."'

Anne has been an employee of the agency for more than twenty years, and is a strong believer in the dictum that 'our clients are always right.' She sincerely believes that 'multicultural' workers cannot work with a cross-section of clients, though they may be useful working in their own communities.

Roop Singh is the only person of colour in the agency. It is not uncommon for staff to share racial and ethnic jokes and comments, sometimes directed at clients. When he objected, he was told that if he was going to live in Canada he had to learn to 'take a joke'; after all, nobody had called him a 'Paki.' Another caseworker with whom he was friendly advised him to relax and 'ride with it. Nobody means any harm. And getting aggressive about it just upsets and threatens people.'

In the meantime, Roop has met again with his supervisor, who has now told him that a couple of his new cases have complained about having to deal with a 'Paki' and want to be assigned a 'Canadian' caseworker.

Roop has written to the executive director, a white woman, complaining about a racist environment that prevents people in his situation from having equal access to job opportunities. Roop has sent a copy of his letter to Malcolm Ward, chair of the board's personnel committee, who has been pushing to make the agency 'more responsive to our clients and their needs.' Malcolm is the only person of colour on the board.

Analysis: Is the Organization in the Case Study at Stage 2?

If this organization is in Stage 2, there is a strong likelihood that Malcolm Ward was chosen by the board as its token minority member. It would be likely that he was seen as 'one of us' and would not rock the boat. His attempt to push the agency into being more responsive is, most likely, unexpected and not a stance for which he would have been known.

Anne Smith has a strong belief that people should work with 'their own kind.' Her behaviour serves to keep Roop isolated and the agency operating as it always has.

The organization could point to its hiring of a minority worker as evidence that it is not, in fact, racist, and insist that it will continue to hire more minorities. In this way, the agency could deflect attention from its hiring and promotion practices.

Similarly, the appointment of Malcolm Ward seems to demonstrate a willingness to choose people of colour for leadership positions. I would expect that there would be considerable pressure on Malcolm – perhaps through subtle offers to assist him in his business, for example – to stop rocking the boat. Alternatively, the screening process for the next board member of colour would be much more careful to exclude 'activists' with a single interest.

Analysis: Is the Organization in the Case Study at Stage 3?

The organization has hired a person of colour to work with people from 'his community' – a characteristic Stage 3 behaviour, and a very small advance over Stage 2 behaviour. Though Malcolm Ward is a person of colour who might begin to influence organizational policies, it is not likely that there will be sufficient support for his efforts. For any real change to occur, there must be a 'critical mass' of people of colour and Aboriginal people on the board.

While there has been a change in organizational policy so that a volunteer and a staff member have been selected from communities of people of colour, there has been no change in the environment that would explicitly support them to challenge behaviours they experience as racist. Indeed, Anne Smith is seen by both board and staff as an exemplary supervisor, in spite of behaviour that is, at the very least, negligent. The almost exclusively white staff does not seem able to adequately serve an increasingly varied population. Though there is no information about the demographic make-up of the volunteers, in a Stage 3 organization they are also likely to be white.

Analysis: Is the Organization in the Case Study at Stage 4?

It is unlikely that this organization is in Stage 4, although Roop Singh's branch may be. One person of colour has been hired to work in this branch of the agency and is providing competent services to members of the South Asian community.

There is no indication that data from various communities are used to make decisions about programs. Instead, there seems to be an implicit assumption that programs are delivered as they always have been, though recognition of the need for responsiveness to different communities has begun.

If this organization were in Stage 4, one would see much more active recruiting of staff and volunteers of colour. There would also be plans in place for explicit training and career development for staff and volunteers of colour. In addition, staff would be trained to respond to expressions of racism. There would also be more active support from senior management for the resolution of complaints about racism.

There would also be more active efforts made at desegregation. At the moment, Anne Smith seems to operate under the assumption that South Asians are competent to work only with other South Asians, while white staff are competent to work with anyone.

Analysis: Is the Organization in the Case Study at Stage 5?

It is extremely unlikely that this organization is in Stage 5, though it is possible that a core of board members is at that stage. This would explain the choice of Malcolm Ward as a board member; this core may be using the conditions in the external environment as a way of moving the rest of the organization towards Stage 5.

Analysis: Is the Organization in the Case Study at Stage 6?

There is no evidence to support an assertion that any part of this organization is in Stage 6.

CONCLUSION

The transition to anti-racism, though challenging, is essential. Anti-racism promotes equity in organizations and in society. A considerable and growing body of research and experience also indicates that anti-racism improves organizational effectiveness. It ensures that women and men from diverse racial groups are brought together – in equal power – to combine their considerable resources.

Successful transition to anti-racism requires organizations to
- identify behaviours, practices, or structures that need to, and can realistically, be changed;
- determine necessary sanctions and supports, including training and education;
- plan for and implement changes appropriate to each stage; and
- review, monitor, and institutionalize the changes.

Anti-racism education alone will not make organizations equitable, accessible, and responsive. The move from UNI-VERSITY to POLY-VERSITY requires deeper interventions at all organizational levels and, ultimately, requires organizational interventions in the broader community. Organizations on the path to greater equity and access have to determine accurately at what stage they currently are and chart a course for where they want to be in the future. Ultimately, the only organizations within reach of POLY-VERSITY are those committed, motivated, and prepared to change. Ironically, these organizations are also the first to realize that there is no room for complacency – that change is continuous and the work of creating an anti-racist organization, and indeed an anti-racist society, is never done.

Chapter 12

Towards an Equitable, Efficient, and Effective Human Service System[1]

Adrian Johnson

My purpose in this chapter is to highlight a framework that may provide guidance to practitioners who must facilitate anti-racism change within organizations charged with delivering accessible human services. This framework is characterized by the interaction of the practitioner with service issues at a number of levels. These are the personal level, the community level, the political level, the agency level, the funding level, and the system level. While I will discuss each separately, it is important to bear in mind that they are all interrelated factors. Hence, issues that affect one factor will necesarily affect the others.

THE PRACTITIONER

At the very outset, the practitioner should be aware that the work of anti-racism change can be very costly to those responsible for its facilitation. Practitioners can feel threatened and may themselves be subject to emotional and physical risk. At the very least they are exposed to a tremendous professional risk when, for a host of reasons, the change process fails, gets out of hand, or makes the organization dysfunctional. Individuals resistant to the change process have an array of tools at their disposal to undermine it. These include misrepresenting information to others or refusing to comply with requests.

Practitioners constantly face the prospect of being marginalized by others who are responsible for conducting the organization's 'real' business. It is incumbent on them to ensure that they have the skills to facilitate people and systems through a difficult process before they venture into the task. They need to recognize both the professional and personal support they will need, which may include counselling to deal with their own fears and anxieties. Senior staff involved in the process must be prepared to provide this support.

Early preparation within an organization should ensure that all the key change agents are given the opportunity to develop the skills they will require to move the process forward. These skills are both process- and content-oriented and include understanding the issues and concerns of a pluralistic workplace.

While it is critical that issues of organizational development be addressed in this training, in the end anti-racism organizational change is a human-development process; as such, it cannot be separated from the real-life experiences of people who will be affected by the change. Practitioners must be aware that many of these people will have experienced oppression first-hand, and this process will force them to revisit those experiences. This can be painful. This past experience can also explain their impatience when apparently obvious needs for change are resisted. Those who have never experienced oppression may feel no urgency for change and may indeed feel threatened by the possibilities of change. These two perceptions can cause tremendous tensions. This conflict, if not resolved properly, can become the focal point for a crisis all of its own, completely undermining the original intention for change.

Everyone in the organization will experience the change in different but equally valid ways. The way individuals experience this change process will depend in great part on other experiences in their lives. Acknowledging that this process is an inclusive one, that everyone will benefit from having participated in it, is important. People who have experienced forms of oppression other than racism must be supported in the knowledge that all forms of discrimination are interrelated and that a well-conceived and successful anti-racism organizational change process does not rank or exclude oppressions, but creates structures to remove them from the organization and prevent their re-emergence.

Effective communication is one of the most critical elements of anti-racism change. False expectations must be avoided by setting realistic goals and time frames, by keeping all players apprised of the issues as they emerge, and by making everyone aware of the potential gains for individuals, for organizations, and for communities. Above all, good communication maintains the integrity of the process and the parties involved. For these reasons communication must be thoughtful, honest, and ongoing. Any breakdown can stall, if not derail, the process. Opening channels should be made a priority.

Practitioners must understand communication in its broadest context. This includes the transmission of real values and intentions through symbols. The power of symbolic communication is that it is the 'walk' as opposed to the 'talk.' Every aspect of traditional communication – written, oral, electronic, or whatever – is laden with symbolic qualities. Every *action* serves as an icon for the real value system that is at play. And practitioners must be aware of the power of symbols so that day-to-day activities and decisions can be informed.

THE COMMUNITY

Practitioners must ensure that agencies are cognizant of the needs of the communities they serve or should be serving. The most effective way of determining these needs is to do so in partnership with the communities. A similar joint process would also establish whether programs and services are effectively meeting the needs identified by the community as its priorties. For example, Bedassigae-Pheasant notes in chapter 3 how ill-served First Nations people were when the federal government acted on its decision for full-scale educational integration of Native children: 'participation in decision making and tuition agreements with the provincial authorities did not include the people who would be affected most by this unilateral action.' In order for a partnership between a service-provider and the community to be effective, the respective roles of the two in the provision of service will need to be negotiated. Acknowledging that communities have a sense of their own service needs, and of the skills and abilities that reside in their communities, is critical if the partnership is to flourish. So also is the need to clarify who constitutes 'the community,' for we have numerous examples of how imposed notions of community have not benefited the community.

In addition to the establishment of needs and the assessment or evaluation of responding programs and services, the service provider must engage the community in a joint process to determine what, in fact, the most appropriate service response should be. An essential aspect of this approach is setting out the roles for both partners and determining who will be responsible for delivering which elements of the service response. In acknowledging the skills that exist within the community, this new mode represents a reversal of the 'missionary' philosophy that informs traditional social service delivery.

There are far-reaching structural implications for organizations and communities in this model, which include such aspects as decision-making processes, accountability systems, and communications with stake-holders. But as Sunderji mentions in his comments, 'only structural change that results in power sharing and equality of opportunity will be effective.'

THE AGENCY

Practitioners intent on facilitating system-wide change must resist the temptation to move directly to micro-intervention. They must take a strategic approach that includes a holistic view of the organization's world. Choices of action must fall out of a broader organizational context if they are to be effective, long-lasting, and mutually supportive.

The practitioner's first step would be to determine how ready the organization is to begin the process. It is critical to assess accurately where on the continuum of organizational development the organization is located (see Tator and Minors) so that the appropriate action can be taken to move the organization forward. Part of this assessment would be appraising the perceptions and attitudes of board member and staff to ascertain the degree of support or resistance that will be encountered in the anti-racism effort. (It is critical that agencies' board of directors demonstrate their unequivocal support for the change process.) A complete gap analysis must be conducted to document the structural changes and changes to practices that will be necessary to achieve a truly anti-racist workplace.

A thorough review of systems in both the internal and external contexts will facilitate this learning and will provide the leverage and the organizational energy with which to begin to effect movement. The internal review should examine systemic discrimination and barriers in the way people are hired, promoted, and supported, and would include the governance of the agency. The external review should establish the accessibility of the organization to all service users. This service-equity review should also consider the manner in which programs and services are provided to service users and whether they may be discriminatory, exclusionary, or biased in some way.

Complex organizational change cannot be conducted in isolation from an organization's overall purpose. Simply tacking anti-racism organizational change onto the organizational mission will result in dissonance if the change effort is not properly integrated into the organization's purpose. Redrafting the mission for relevance and integrating objectives around anti-racism early in the process is critical.

From a strategic point of view a determination must be made about how access to services will be assured for all those who require it. Partly, this question can be resolved by assessing the availability of services within the area and creating partnerships with other service providers to establish a net of services that will encompass all service users' needs. For example, as Beyene and colleagues have discussed, there is a need for dual-agency service provision (and perhaps even multi-agency service provision) where immigrant service agencies work with 'mainstream' institutions to ensure accessible service.

Practitioners must advocate for this process unerringly. In demonstrating their steadfastness, despite the complexities and difficulties they will encounter, they should provide the necessary leadership for others in the organization who are anxious or afraid or otherwise unprepared for change.

The practitioner must not just be prepared to be, but must plan to be, transparent in the organizational change process. Anti-racism organizational development needs to be an integral part of ongoing organizational existence. As such, its success must be seen as the continuing responsibility of every person in the organization. It must account for, and accommodate, the needs of each individual member of the organization and of each individual service user, including the need for accommodation based on racial, cultural, religious, or ethnic differences. When this notion stops being extraordinary, real change will take place.

Everyone within the organization is affected by this process of change, and so everyone must be given open and unfettered access to information and education about the process. This is especially true when engaging in a systems or service-equity review. The need for being honest with staff and community regarding what may be seen as the failures of the system cannot be overstated. Lack of information and trust can severely inhibit the process.

A truly anti-racist organization adapts its programs and services to ensure relevance at all times. If, as is occurring in many metropolitan areas like Toronto, the demographics are shifting dramatically, then the agency must have a fluid and dynamic process that continually assesses who the service users are, what their needs are, and how the agency should respond.

FUNDERS

Demands for change comes from all quarters and are not always in concert. Funders, for example, find themselves being subjected to mounting demands for resources at a time when their resource base is being eroded by competing political and social interests. In turn, they demand *efficiency* from service providers.

Private donors, both corporate and individual, are at once affected by economic conditions and subject to greater pressure from a myriad of agencies as private fund-raising is depended on increasingly to replace public funding. In this context, donors are becoming more selective and are demanding fiscal responsibility from service providers (and central fund-raising organizations). An even more resounding call for relevance is being heard in the face of changing demography. The ethno-racial composition of the donor base continues to shift, and with this shift comes a more strident demand for sensitivity to community in programming and service delivery.

The funding environment does not lend itself easily to inter-agency cooperation. And yet, cooperation and coordination, rather than competition, in service delivery is needed. There should be grave concern about the need for coordination between all funders. There is a perception that some of the overlaps and gaps created by funders' mandates and policies may not serve the fullest interests of the community.

However, cooperation and coordination need to be equitable in order to work. Partnerships cannot exist between agencies if the power to dictate the terms of the relationship and the resources to act are disproportionately divided. This does not mean that everyone must get the same annual grant, but it does mean that everyone must have equal access to money and decision making.

Even where organizations may want to cooperate, however, the funding structure applied to one agency might not be applicable to others. There must be evidence of proportionality – of funding based on the proportionate needs of communities. Such a notion would offer a very special challenge to organizations to rethink their purpose. The current fiscal reality is that funds are scarce. It is, therefore, exceptionally important that every available dollar be spent on direct service as opposed to administration and infrastructure. Any models of funding that are utilized must be built around this premise. This approach must not, however, be applied in a differential way. Asking ethno-racial agencies to share photocopiers and accountants, but allowing large, mainstream agencies to maintain sophisticated bureaucratic structures, does not foster cooperation and certainly isn't equitable. (The poor cannot be asked to pay for the crisis that has resulted from the excesses of the rich.)

Funding cycles are also a barrier to cooperation and to agencies remaining true to the principle of placing the client's needs in the forefront. The current practice, based on an assessment of need that might be outdated once the money is actually released, ties up money for one to three years and creates an artificial 'shortage' for emerging needs.

The practitioner must recognize the stresses that the funding universe puts on the anti-racism process. By being knowledgeable about the mechanisms involved, the practitioner will be able to facilitate the kinds of cooperative solutions that will be necessary for responding to the service users' needs for accessibility.

'MAINSTREAM' VERSUS 'ETHNO-SPECIFIC' AGENCIES

An honest analysis will reveal that social service organizations have become self-preservationist and organize themselves around principles of survival as opposed to principles of service. Funding mechanisms, as described earlier, are at least partly responsible for this reality. The current system fosters competition among agencies – for government grants, donor dollars, volunteers, and clients. This competition is at the hub of the 'mainstream' versus 'ethno-specific' agencies debate, and is even seen between ethno-specific agencies; some have more credibility than others based on numbers of constituents, length of existence, or ability to speak the social service 'lingo.' Where is client's need in this hierarchy?

In a society that is evolving, the capacity of agencies to provide service to everyone must be reviewed. In recent times the number of diverse groups in society has been accelerating. Beyene and colleagues point out that 'the growing demographic weight of so many racial-minority, immigrant, and refugee communities within the population means that the problem of providing appropriate services to these communities will dominate the issues of human service policy for decades to come.'

New volunteer groups are emerging to provide assistance to these new service users. This development is a direct result of the incapacity of the present network of service providers to accommodate the emerging needs of new communities, and it feeds the debate about, and the competition between, established 'mainstream' agencies and newer 'ethno-specific' groups. To be entirely accurate, however, one must acknowledge that 'ethno-specific' agencies have been around for a long time. They sprang up then for the same reasons they do now – service gaps. (It would also be naïve not to acknowledge the dynamics of power that contribute to the ongoing debate in this area.)

There should be no argument with the contention that there is a desperate need for culturally sensitive services. However, in the absence of more rational information on what groups are 'out there' and whom they represent or service, and the confidence that they have the wherewithal to provide services, the response of Funders is to continue to fund 'mainstream' organizations. Of course, this rational framework is difficult to establish without funders' support – a 'chicken and egg' dilemma. In fact, addressing the costs of the social-service needs of these communities will strengthen them and provide a sense of security. This is one aspect of real empowerment.

The traditional approach used to the largest extent by 'mainstream' agencies is extremely resource intensive. As long as funders continue to provide the resources to this subsector almost exclusively, the funds will continue to be spent on high-cost alternatives such as new, specialized staff (outreach workers, multicultural coordinators, and so on). One way to disempower communities is to restrict their access to organizations and to information to these single points of contact. Such alternatives are not productive.

The distinctions between 'mainstream' and 'ethno-specific' in the social-service delivery system must be removed. The human service network needs to be viewed as a 'whole body,' with the interests of the service user at the heart of it.

THE NEED FOR GENERAL SYSTEM CHANGE

So what of the future? What kind of change do we, as anti-racism organization development practitioners, need to facilitate to ensure a responsive human-service delivery system? As we move into the second half of the decade, we know that all around us the reasons for change in our political, economic, and social institutions grow more evident. While the pressures for change are well documented, it would appear from our collective actions that we, as a society and as a sector, do not yet fully understand what change requires of us.

Discussions in an earlier section covered the demands for change emanating from the funding environment. At the same time, the change in service-user demography keeps pace with general population trends towards a more racially mixed society. This fact alone has significant implications for social service delivery, which must become more sensitive to these trends. The implications are made more complex as the users and their advocates demand a realignment of power. Similarly, demands for change are being made by staff, volunteers, the general public, and other stakeholders in the human-service delivery system.

What has been the response thus far to all of these pressures? Agencies have made cosmetic alterations: adding multicultural outreach workers, cutting programs, making boards smaller, increasing volunteers, and so on. But fundamental organizational change has not yet taken place. This change, if it is to occur, is not solely the responsibility of individual agencies. It must occur in the social service system *as a whole*. This, in the final analysis, is the challenge to anti-racism practitioners.

The social-service delivery paradigm must shift. A paradigm is a philosophical or perceptual framework, a filter through which we see the world. Our paradigms help us organize information, but they also block or filter out information that is not part of that framework. The current frustrations about increased pressures to do *more* with *less* might be a result of our paradigms, whereas a perceptual shift might allow us to see the issue as how we might do *better*. For example, the current concern with anti-racist organizational change has primarily been seen as a question of how to *add* more people of colour to the ranks of clients, boards, and staff. The real task, however, might be seen more broadly – as one of *quality*: that is, how to provide a high-quality, human service system that, by definition, is efficient, effective, and equitable to *all* those who need it. If this indeed is the goal, what then are some of the changes necessary to achieve it?

First, there is the necessity to reassess what is being done and why. Social service agencies exist to address needs within the community. The first step is to establish clearly what those needs are. It is not reasonable to assume that the need for which an agency was created fifty years ago now remains the same. One of the critical questions that must be asked by funders and traditional service providers is how agencies should be expected to change as the profile of newcomers or community needs changes. Which is more reasonable to expect: that agencies constituted to service particular communities or needs can shift their orientation and cultural frames of reference to successfully service new communities or emerging needs, or that new agencies must be established to take their place?

The issue is that the services must be relevant. In a 'market-driven' social service environment the 'relevance' of an agency or its 'products' should determine its efficacy and its need for growth or retrenchment.

Agencies must recognize some truths and be prepared to confront themselves with the question of the relevance of their organizations and the services they provide. An examination must take place to determine who has need, where they are, how they cope *without* the benefit of current services, and who else is concerned with addressing this need.

Second, care must be taken to avoid the leaps of logic so often encountered in social services. People need jobs, ergo do skill training; women need protection from violence, ergo build a shelter; children are being abused, ergo do family counselling. All too often the method of service delivery becomes the focus, and becomes institutionalized; soon the agency's mission is to deliver a particular service as opposed to solving a community problem or addressing a community need.

For many, however, a most debilitating debate goes on. Who really is the client? Depending on which part of the social service system one is affiliated with, the answers can be very different. Is it the child, woman, man, or family in need of some specific assistance or service? Is it the advocacy organization speaking on their behalf? Is it the whole community (either in the micro or macro sense)? Is it the contracting agency or funder on whose behalf a service is performed? Or, in the case of private donations, is it the donor?

All the pressure to be 'organizations of excellence,' to adopt premises and principles that make for well-run, efficient businesses, distract from one obvious truth – that the entire system must be focused on the needs of the individual (or family) who requires service or assistance. If at any time an individual (or family) expresses, or is identified as having, a need for some form of service and does not receive it, then the system has failed. At such a time none of the debate will be very meaningful.

Placing the service recipient's needs at the heart of the system gives the rest of the system meaning. The establishment of the agency structure, including the type of agencies and services, must arise from the clients' needs. This structure delivers against these needs using the resources available, namely the funding sources, the volunteer networks, and so on.

The overriding principles in a social service system concerned with quality must be focusing on service users and their needs; managing the processes of change; empowering stakeholders; eliminating waste; and effecting continuous improvement. In this framework, it is not difficult to see that organizations informed with this philosophy would embrace change and look forward to the learning that comes from critical self-assessment.

Such organizations would approach community service delivery in the context of a total systems view. In other words, they would look at everything that they are as organizations: their underlying organizational values and assumptions, their structures and processes, what they do, how they do it and why. They would begin by ensuring that their boards and staff reflect the people and communities that they serve. They would challenge the way they empower service users to participate in determining the services they receive. The reassessment of needs and the methods of addressing these needs cannot be done without the active involvement of the people who have those needs. It is an involvement that must be both system-wide and agency-specific. The reassessment of needs and how they are addressed will precipitate changes in the way organizations are structured and how they conduct their business.

Effective service networks must be developed, composed of traditional service providers and new service users' community groups, to share the responsibility for service delivery. The current provision of service is scattered and does not take a strategic view of, or approach to, providing for the needs of the community in a complete and holistic way. Critical to this arrangement, and to the effective servicing of any community's needs, is the recognition that equal control of this partnership belongs in the hands of the community. In practical terms this means that the community informs the service provider of what its service needs are and the service provider honours this knowledge. The risk is that what the community perceives as its needs may not be what the service provider is equipped to deliver. The resulting choices for the service provider in such a scenario would be 'retooling' or retrenchment: that is, acquiring new skills or redirecting resources (including curtailing services).

An earlier discussion in this chapter raised the need for cooperation in the division and use of resources. It is critical to remind ourselves that cooperation in the use of resources should be viewed as a manifestation of coordination and cooperation in service delivery. Without this perspective it will be difficult to rationalize and will fall victim to traditional socialized competition.

THE POLITICAL CLIMATE

One cannot escape the reality that the delivery of human services is conceived and conducted within a political context. An anti-racism organizational change practitioner must be aware of this context and its shifting-sand nature. Traditional Canadian social policy is evolving (or some might say devolving) through a kind of schizophrenia that will present the most significant challenge to the efficacy of the human service sector, particularly at a time when political parties are gravitating to the same location on the policy continuum, despite their apparent ideological differences.

Neo-conservatism, as we are now seeing, will have a profound effect on social service delivery. The social-policy agenda is about to be driven by Bay Street (and, more importantly, Wall Street). Surprisingly (although, some may argue, understandably), the shift is being engineered by political parties that have long been closely identified with the interests of immigrant and racial-minority communities. Consider the 'head tax' now being imposed on immigrants by the Liberal government in Ottawa. This policy is going to have a disproportionate impact on newcomers from racial-minority communities. Somehow, the policy feels very much like one imposed around the turn of the century (see Matas's chapter).

Also consider the 'multi-service agency' model that was established by the recent New Democratic Party government in Ontario. Many advocates have argued that the needs of racially and culturally diverse communities would be lost in the large, bureaucratic, traditional, 'mainstream' nature of the model, the objective of which was to control costs. As the 'deficit problem' is addressed, the most vulnerable are likely to experience an increase in their already elevated risk: as the 'social service safety net' begins to tear, people slip through.

Because the conservative right is dictating the relationship the state will have with communities, practitioners will have to consider carefully their strategies when responding to the service needs of racial-minority communities. There is a very real danger that now, more than ever before, 'racialized communities' (St. Lewis) will be framed by monolithic assumptions, their diversity minimized, and their existence further marginalized.

CONCLUSION

While this chapter has argued that fundamental changes are needed in the social service system, it is important to remember that changes rarely start at the macro level. It will be the efforts of individual agencies as they embark on their organizational change that will give the impetus to the larger change. In this context, the role of the anti-racism practitioner as the local change agent will be critical. The practitioner's skills will be invaluable as individual organizations begin with their own review of needs, making sure that they include racially, ethnically, and linguistically different people in this assessment. Cooperation and coordination will be needed here as well. Needs-assessment strategies, community consultations, employment-systems reviews, staff training, and so forth can all be done in cooperation with agencies in the same geographic area or serving the same or related needs. Agencies can also form networks to share resources ranging from skilled personnel to policies and procedures.

Remember that the paradigm has not shifted if all the previous privilege, perspectives, and attitudes are still in place. It appears to be a feature of our society to refuse to relinquish any of the privileges we currently have, even in the face of the demands for change. It is as if we expect the world to change and for the problems to be solved for others on the one hand, while expecting that everything will remain the same for us on the other. In this context, everyone involved with the delivery of human services must ensure that in all their processes there are mechanisms for establishing accountability. There must be a significant onus placed on boards and senior managers to recognize the roles they must play in leading the change process and accepting responsibility for its results. The skills of the practitioner will be challenged to facilitate the 'buy-in' necessary for this to happen.

One of the shifts we will have to make is away from continuous growth models to models of higher quality that foster empowerment and self-reliance, thereby reducing the need for the service. The irony is that the original purpose of non-governmental organizations was to increase community capacity for addressing social needs and to work themselves out of existence. Pressures such as reduced funding, increased demands for service, and the need for equity all require fundamental organizational change so that the human service system can continue to be viable and valuable. The change process is challenging, but by shifting our paradigm from doer-centric to user-centric, from survival-driven to community-needs-driven, from quantity to quality, from ambivalent to anti-racist, we might just be able to meet this challenge.

NOTE

1 Excerpted and adapted from a work in progress by Adrian Johnson. The author wishes to acknowledge the invaluable contribution of Jennifer Walcott to the preparation of this chapter.

Chapter 13

Human-Rights Law: A Legal Remedy

Mark L. Berlin

What are human rights? Why do we need them? How do we protect them? What impact do they have on us, our organizations, and our society? This chapter will try to answer these and other related questions by looking at human rights from a historical and comparative perspective.

WHAT ARE HUMAN RIGHTS?

Human rights can mean different things to different people. For one person it can be the right to write a letter to the editor of a local newspaper criticizing an elected politician. For another it may be having enough food to feed hungry children. For someone else it may be free access to the public institutions of the country, including those providing health-care services, education, and job training. For some it could be the basic right to freely practise their religion. And for others, like Native Canadians, it could be the right to self-determination.

Human rights are commonly divided into four categories:

- *political rights*: consisting of freedom of speech, expression, religion and conscience, and assembly
- *legal rights*: including freedom from arbitrary arrest, unreasonable search and seizure, and arbitrary imprisonment, as well as rights to a fair trial and against self-incrimination
- *economic rights*: consisting of the freedom to hold private property and the right to enter into contracts
- *egalitarian rights*: including the right not to be discriminated against and to have equal access to education, employment, accommodation, and other social benefits

To be effective, such rights must be legally entrenched. Although laws do not automatically protect the rights of individuals or groups, they reflect the values of society against which behaviour can be measured and set minimum legal standards against which deficient conduct can be judged. The Criminal Code of Canada, for example, prohibits aggressive behaviour leading to assault, burglary, fraud, and the spreading of hate propaganda. A person alleged to have committed one of these acts may be charged and brought before a court of law and if guilty may be fined, imprisoned, or suffer other consequences.

Like the Criminal Code, human-rights law establishes a code of conduct and sets a standard of acceptable treatment. Within prescribed limits, it states that no individual, group, or body, including the government, shall infringe on the fundamental rights and freedoms of another. The justice system can investigate complaints, determine innocence or guilt, and provide relief against abusive treatment or infringement of a right or freedom. Human rights in Canada are protected in a number of ways.

INTERNATIONAL LAW

Human rights have been protected under international law for hundreds of years. In 1555, for example, the Treaty of Augsburg promoted the equality of Protestants and Catholics and enabled religious minorities in certain 'free cities' of the Holy Roman Empire to coexist peacefully with the majority. Since then, dozens of treaties have been enacted to protect our expanding definition of rights.

The atrocities committed by the Nazi regime during the Second World War and the resulting deaths of millions of people, including six million Jews, forced world leaders to recognize and protect the equality of all persons under international law. British Prime Minister Winston Churchill and U.S. President Franklin D. Roosevelt, among others, proposed the formation of a new international organization from among the world's independent nations. One of the goals of the United Nations was to achieve international cooperation in promoting respect for fundamental human rights and freedoms.

On 10 December 1948, three years after its inception, the United Nations adopted the Universal Declaration of Human Rights. This document outlines the rights and freedoms to which all persons are entitled, including the right to life, liberty, and security of the person, the right to work, the right to social security and to an adequate standard of living, freedom of thought, freedom from slavery, and other rights. In its preamble, the Universal Declaration reaffirms the faith of the peoples of the United Nations in 'fundamental human rights, in the dignity and worth of the human person and in the equal rights of men and women.' It also asserts their determination to 'promote social progress and better standards of life in larger freedom.'

The Universal Declaration of Human Rights has become a standard of international human-rights law. Today, its goals and objectives are supported by two other UN documents, the International Covenant on Economic, Social and Cultural Rights, which recognizes, among others, the right to work, the right to an adequate standard of living, the right to medical care, and the right to an education, and the International Covenant on Civil and Political Rights, which recognizes the freedoms of conscience and religion, of expression and opinion, and of assembly and association. This covenant also recognizes the right of an individual to live free of torture, cruel or degrading treatment, slavery, forced labour, and arbitrary deprivation of life. It includes an Optional Protocol, which enables individual citizens to launch complaints against a government allegedly violating an international human-rights standard, a protocol that Canada has signed.

International law is important in Canada because our international obligations are taken into account when our courts interpret domestic laws. By signing these international documents, Canada accepts the obligation to ensure that the rights and freedoms outlined are available to all Canadians.

Because Canada has accepted the rules of the Optional Protocol, individual Canadians can go to an international forum and assert that Canada has violated their rights. In the past, Native Canadians have succeeded in challenging a number of Canadian laws by bringing complaints to the International Human Rights Committee. The famous Sandra Lovelace case, for example, led to the elimination of discriminatory provisions in the Indian Act that denied rights to Native women.

DOMESTIC LAW

In Canada, human rights are protected not only by international covenants, but also by the common law (composed of the body of decisions handed down by judges in individual cases) and by numerous provincial and national statutes. These include specific human-rights laws, as well as provisions in Canada's labour, social-assistance, and health-care legislation.

The Canadian Bill of Rights

In 1960, the Government of Canada enacted the Canadian Bill of Rights. This document recognizes freedom of speech, religion, assembly, association, and the press. It also recognizes rights to liberty and the security of the person and the right to hold property, none of which may be denied without due process of law.

The Canadian Bill of Rights has not been widely used. In the first place, it has limited application – only human-rights violations alleged to have been committed by the federal government may be challenged under the Bill. Second, it has not been particularly useful in advancing the rights of individual Canadians or disadvantaged groups, because Canadian courts have shied away from expanding or broadly interpreting the rights set out in the Bill. As a result, the Bill has been largely superseded by the Canadian Charter of Rights and Freedoms.

The Canadian Charter of Rights and Freedoms

With the patriation of the Canadian Constitution in 1982, the Canadian Charter of Rights and Freedoms was proclaimed the supreme law of the nation. The Charter recognizes a variety of political, legal, economic, and egalitarian rights; it applies to all federal, provincial, and local laws, regulations, and policies and to the conduct of government authorities. It does not apply to disputes between private individuals – these are covered under provincial human-rights legislation. The Charter is the most important of all human-rights laws in Canada, and is the standard against which all other human-rights legislation is measured.

Section 15 of the Canadian Charter of Rights and Freedoms states that everyone is equal before and under the law and has equal right to the protection and benefit of the law. Section 15 lists several prohibited grounds of discrimination. It guarantees equal access to the courts and the administration of justice (procedural equality); gives the courts power to strike down any law whose content is discriminatory (substantive equality); and gives governments the power to protect the rights of historically disadvantaged groups through affirmative measures such as employment-equity legislation (equality of opportunity and equality of outcome). Finally, section 15 requires the courts to dispense penalties and benefits equally under the law.

In addition, section 15 prohibits discrimination on the basis of race, national or ethnic origin, colour, religion, sex, age, and mental or physical disability. Court decisions indicate that these grounds can be broadened; however, expansion into other grounds has not yet been fully identified. (Recently, however, the Supreme Court of Canada, in *Egan and Nesbit v. The Queen* [25 May 1995, unreported] recognized sexual orientation as an analogous ground of discrimination to be included in section 15.) In fact, the courts have said that grounds analogous to those specified will likely be protected under the Charter.

Of added importance is the Charter's express recognition of the multicultural nature of our country. Section 27 requires that the Charter be interpreted 'in a manner consistent with the preservation and enhancement of the multicultural heritage of Canadians.' This particular provision recognizes the multicultural diversity of our society and provides that all rights defined in the Charter take into account this multicultural reality.

In the recent case *Regina v. Keegstra* (1990 CR 4th 129), the hate-propaganda provisions of the Criminal Code were challenged as unduly restricting freedom of expression. In denying that challenge, the Supreme Court found a rational connection between the criminal prohibition of hate propaganda in order to protect members of specific groups and the need for 'fostering harmonious social relations in a community dedicated to equality and multiculturalism.' The Court declared, significantly, that in deciding such cases it would take into account section 27 of the Charter and 'its recognition that Canada possesses a multicultural society in which the diversity and richness of various cultural groups is a value to be protected and enhanced.'

HUMAN-RIGHTS STATUTES

In addition to the Canadian Bill of Rights and the Charter of Rights and Freedoms, human-rights statutes are in effect in every province in Canada. These legislative enactments, known as codes or acts, focus primarily on egalitarian rights. In general, they forbid discrimination on the basis of race, religion, sex, age, mental or physical disability, and national or ethnic origin.

Unlike section 15 of the Charter, provincial and federal human-rights legislation provide a *complete and exclusive category* of the prohibited grounds of discrimination. For example, the Ontario Human Rights Code prohibits discrimination on the basis of race, colour, sex, ancestry, citizenship, creed, religion, age, marital status, family status, sexual orientation, physical/mental handicap, receipt of public assistance (in accommodation only), and pardoned conviction (in employment only). The Ontario Human Rights Commission will also accept complaints against discrimination on the grounds of dependence on alcohol or drugs. Generally speaking, as the courts recognize new grounds for discrimination, human-rights legislation is amended accordingly.

Human-rights codes and acts differ significantly from the Bill of Rights and the Charter of Rights and Freedoms in other ways. Whereas the Bill of Rights and the Charter guard against discrimination by governments in their dealings with the people, provincial human-rights legislation is not only concerned with the relationship between government and individuals, but also guards against discrimination between individuals. Any conduct that discriminates against an individual on the basis of his or her gender, race, religion or ethnicity, and so on, in such areas as accommodation, provision of services, or employment is covered by provincial human-rights legislation. In Canada, approximately 90 per cent of all human-rights complaints are dealt with under such provincial legislation.

In general, Canadians rely on a complaint-based model to enforce human-rights standards. The victim of unequal treatment complains to an administrative body (usually called a commission), which then investigates and ultimately adjudicates the complaint. All jurisdictions follow a similar model. A commission administers the human-rights law. It investigates complaints and helps both parties negotiate a mutually satisfactory arrangement. Boards of enquiry hear and rule on unsettled cases. However, it should be noted that in Quebec the Human Rights Commission has no inquiry function and must seek injunctions or compensation through the ordinary courts.

Human-rights commissions have been in the vanguard in promoting the extension of human rights to include protection from harassment and from discrimination on the basis of sexual orientation (in Ontario, Quebec, Nova Scotia, Yukon, Manitoba, New Brunswick, Saskatchewan, and British Columbia) and the right to political affiliation. They have also played an important role in public education; in particular, they have made clear that human-rights protection is public policy.

In the thirty years since the commissions first published their case decisions, they have developed a solid body of jurisprudence on the meaning of equality and anti-discrimination. Individual complainants have access to free legal counsel and free investigation, and procedures used at hearings are both more informal and more flexible than those at court hearings.

Critics, however, argue that the present model is woefully inadequate and out of step with reality. Although human-rights commissions acknowledge the patterns of inequality for women, Aboriginal people, disabled persons, and visible minorities, they rely on individual members of these groups to bring forward complaints, rarely initiating complaints on their own.

Critics also argue that the system is very costly to operate, that investigations are overly time-consuming and lead to frustratingly long delays. They point out, for example, that 96 per cent of human-rights complaints currently before the Ontario Human Rights Commission do not receive a hearing.

Some critics also point out that the award ultimately offered does not eliminate discrimination or properly compensate the victim. Human-rights awards do not have as a prime objective the punishment of the offender, as does criminal law. Rather, human-rights legislation provides a 'remedy' to the aggrieved party by attempting to eradicate a hostile environment and ensure that the victim is given back a sense of dignity and has a chance to compete equally. Generally speaking, the size of the monetary awards (which are a component of the standard settlement), and such requirements as forcing an employer to undertake workplace human-rights training, do little to address the underlying causes of discrimination.

Every year the Canadian Human Rights Commission publishes a report on the progress made by groups such as women, visible minorities, Aboriginal peoples, and persons with disabilities, groups that have traditionally been the victims of both systemic and overt discrimination. In its 1991 annual report, the Commission indicated that visible minorities were greatly underrepresented in the public-sector workforce, particularly in management. The report showed that the majority of women do not reach high positions and have limited access to the decision-making process. Although women comprised 44 per cent of the public-sector workforce in 1990, they occupied less than 8 per cent of upper-management positions. The report also showed that Aboriginal peoples were largely concentrated in semi-skilled and labour-intensive jobs and comprised only 2 per cent of the federal public-service workforce. Finally, the report revealed that persons with disabilities represented only about 3 per cent of employees in federal departments, although they made up 5.5 per cent of the workforce . While these findings pertain to the federal public service, they reflect the situation in other sectors.

The Ontario government has recognized the deficiencies of the present system. In the spring of 1992, it initiated a public consultation into the weaknesses in the Ontario Human Rights Commission based on an issues paper entitled 'Getting Human Rights Enforced Effectively.' The Human Rights Code Review Task Force, which conducted the consultations, recommended the establishment of decentralized Equality Rights Centres to handle the large volume of complaints. The report also established time frames for filing complaints, carrying out investigations, and adjudicating cases. With the release of the report, the minister responsible for the Human Rights Commission struck a committee to review the task force's recommendations. As of 1995, the committee has not yet released its findings; the impact of the recommendations themselves on other jurisdictions in Canada remains uncertain.

CONCLUSION

By recognizing and affirming the fundamental rights and freedoms of all citizens, human-rights legislation establishes a code of conduct for Canadians and their institutions. Such legislation protects individuals from discrimination on the basis of religion, political affiliation, gender, age, mental or physical disability, race, colour, national or ethnic origin, and other grounds. It also enables governments and organizations to redress the inequities experienced by disadvantaged groups such as women, persons with disabilities, Aboriginal peoples, and members of ethno-racial communities.

In spite of the many weaknesses of the current legislation, Canadians enjoy many rights and freedoms denied elsewhere in the world. Human-rights commissions across Canada remain an effective, important, practical, and accessible means of protecting the rights of both individuals and disadvantaged groups. Improvements proposed in Ontario and elsewhere will go a long way towards making the system more equitable.

As our country becomes culturally more diverse and our definition of rights and freedoms expands, human-rights legislation will undoubtedly change. Legislation and its interpretation by the courts will increasingly define the way we relate to one another. Already the Canadian Charter of Rights and Freedoms is setting new standards for what behaviour is acceptable in a free and democratic society. Its impact and that of other human-rights legislation will be felt in all sectors of Canadian society – including the voluntary sector.

Traditionally, human service organizations have been at the forefront of protecting and advancing the rights of disadvantaged groups. In the future, agencies will face increasing pressures to become more accessible and equitable in the provision of programs and services. Disputes between individual employees within an agency, between the agency and its employees, or between an agency and the public come under the aegis of provincial or territorial human-rights codes, acts, and commissions. As Canadians become more sensitive to the needs and aspirations of different groups, human-rights legislation and the provincial and national bodies responsible for its enforcement will likely have a tremendous impact on organizational systems, structures, and modes of service delivery.

Proactive organizations can anticipate the challenges ahead in a number of ways. They can educate clients, volunteers, and staff about their respective rights and responsibilities. They can develop systems, structures, and services that are accessible, equitable, and non-discriminatory. They can press for improvements in the way human-rights legislation is administered and interpreted, and they can also advocate on behalf of disadvantaged groups whose rights have yet to be recognized.

Chapter 14

The Nuts and Bolts of Employment Equity: A Quick Primer for Social Service Agencies

Cynthia Stephenson

> It is not that individuals in the designated groups are inherently unable to achieve equality on their own, it is that the obstacles in their way are so formidable and self-perpetuating that they cannot be overcome without intervention. It is both intolerable and insensitive if we simply wait and hope that the barriers will disappear with time. Equality in employment will not happen unless we make it happen.
>
> *Royal Commission on Equality in Employment*

Social service agencies are out on the front line every day, working to help people from all walks of life, all backgrounds, and all parts of the country cope a little better with their problems, improve the quality of their life, and find hope and dignity. They deal with everyone from unemployed professionals to public-school drop-outs, from Canadians with roots going back generations to new immigrants, from ex-offenders to victims of family assault. Some agencies are focused on specific client groups, but the bottom line is always *people*. Staff and volunteers are committed to providing the best possible service they can, within the ever-present constraints of their resources, regardless of sex, race, colour, creed, or any of the other elements of discrimination. In this context, it almost seems superfluous to talk about employment equity: wouldn't you be preaching to the converted?

Yes and no. It's easy to forget, given the focus on burgeoning case-loads and constant cutbacks, that social service agencies are employers too. Like small private-sector companies and big government departments, they hire, promote, and lay off staff, run a payroll, and are subject to the same employment rules and regulations. In fact, as groups advocating fair treatment for their diverse client groups, social service agencies are under a singular obligation to make sure that they treat their employees as fairly as their clients. Many agencies have already done this – their staff and volunteer complements mirror the communities they serve – but others are just starting to grapple with the concept. For these employers, a little dose of 'Employment Equity 101' can't hurt.

There's a lot of discussion about employment equity these days, in boardrooms, classrooms, government offices, and on the street, and much of that discussion is, to say the least, heated. 'Employment Equity,' its sometime-synonyms 'equal opportunity,' 'equality in employment,' 'affirmative action,' and 'pay equity,' and its antonyms, such as 'racism,' 'sexism,' and plain old 'bias' and 'prejudice,' are emotion-packed terms. They reflect our deepest values, beliefs, and attitudes, and it's understandable that people react strongly when they hear them. Sometimes all the emotions can cloud the issue, and we need to step back, disconnect the automatic responses, and *think* about what employment equity really means.

JUST WHAT IS 'EMPLOYMENT EQUITY'?

In a nutshell, employment equity means ensuring that *all* job applicants and employees have a fair chance in the workplace. It means that no one is denied a job or a promotion for reasons unrelated to their qualifications and abilities.

On the surface, this sounds quite clear and straightforward, a 'motherhood' kind of issue, like 'fair play' or 'honesty is the best policy.' But in practice, employment equity involves the daunting prospect of fundamental change on all levels – personal, corporate, and societal.

The quotation heading this chapter encapsulates three of the fundamental concepts of employment equity: designated group members *have* the skills to do the job; but for a variety of systemic and other reasons, they've been prevented from doing so; and so, as individuals, as organizations, and as a society, we have to take steps to remove the barriers and level the playing field.

WHO ARE THE 'DESIGNATED GROUP MEMBERS'?

In the past, certain groups have faced unfair employment barriers,

resulting in higher unemployment rates, underemployment, disproportionate part-time and seasonal work patterns, lower-than-average pay
rates, and concentration in occupations that are lower paid and have
less chance of advancement. These groups include *women*, *Aboriginal
peoples* (status Indians, non-status Indians, Inuit, and Métis), *visible
minorities* (non-Caucasian or non-white persons, such as Blacks, Chinese, Japanese, South Asians, Southeast Asians, and Latin Americans),
and *persons with disabilities* (that is, persons with persistent physical,
mental, psychiatric, sensory, or learning impairments that affect their
employability). These groups have been 'designated' under federal and
some provincial employment-equity legislation to make them eligible
for special programs and short-term measures to address historical
inequities.

Of course, these aren't the only groups that have faced barriers in the
past. The Canadian Charter of Rights and Freedoms and the Canadian
and provincial human-rights acts prohibit discrimination on other
grounds as well, such as age, religion, and sexual orientation. Although
these groups aren't specifically mentioned in the employment-equity
legislation, there could be a spin-off effect for them if employment policies and practices were modified so that only employment-related factors were considered in hiring, promotion, and termination decisions.

WHY DO WE NEED LEGISLATION TO HELP DESIGNATED GROUPS?

The federal government sponsored a Royal Commission on Equality in
Employment in the early 1980s, chaired by Judge Rosalie Silberman
Abella. The Commission concluded that although many people recognized that there was a problem and that change was required, voluntary
change was happening so slowly that it would be decades before past
inequities were addressed. In the meantime, opportunities were being
missed and talents wasted.

The federal government agreed that a more proactive approach was
justified, and the Employment Equity Act, covering crown corporations
and federally regulated businesses (such as banks and telecommunica-
tion and transportation companies) with more than one hundred
employees, was enacted in August 1986. The Act was reviewed by a parliamentary committee in 1991 and 1992, and amendments to broaden
and strengthen it are currently being considered.

The federal government also decided to 'put its money where its
mouth was' in terms of making support for employment equity (that is,

development and implementation of a customized employment-equity plan) a prerequisite for contractors with one hundred or more employees who want to provide goods or services worth over $200,000 to the government. This is the classic 'carrot' approach, and even though it's not enacted in law, the financial incentive can be very effective: if contractors fail to follow through on their commitment, then their eligibility to bid on future federal contracts is withdrawn.

The federal government isn't alone in actively supporting employment equity. Many provincial governments already have human-rights legislation and are planning to introduce legislated employment equity. For example, Ontario's Employment Equity Act was proclaimed on 1 September 1994. This act covers all sectors (public, broader public, and private) and all but the smallest employers in the province. Some municipalities and other employers also have employment-equity programs in place.[1]

The bottom line is that designated-group members already compose more than 60 per cent of the workforce, and 70 per cent of new entrants, and those numbers are rising (for further details, see Statistics Canada's 1986 and 1991 census data). In today's global and rapidly changing economy, it makes neither business nor social sense to underutilize the skills and abilities of two-thirds of our working population. Governments are willing to take the necessary steps to pass legislation that will help speed up the process of change.

WHAT ARE THE BARRIERS FACED BY DESIGNATED GROUPS?

Designated group members face a wide range of obstacles to finding and keeping employment, some obvious and intentional, and others not. For example, in some cases:

- women job applicants are asked questions related to marital status or children that are not asked of male applicants;
- the working environment is hostile – sexual and racial slurs or jokes proliferate;
- job requirements aren't work-related – there are arbitrary height and weight requirements that tend to exclude women and some visible minorities;
- the work site isn't accessible to persons with disabilities (heavy doors, narrow corridors, no ramps, light switches and elevator buttons out of reach);

- recruitment practices (word-of-mouth, internal hiring policies) limit applications from designated group members;
- training and development aren't provided to designated group members in proportion to their participation in the workforce, and as a result they aren't prepared for promotional opportunities.

Numerous studies and reports have shown that employment policies and practices like these either prevent designated group members from getting a job in the first place or from moving up inside the organization once they *do* get a foot in the door. What's more, persons who are members of more than one of the designated groups (such as a visible-minority woman, or a Native person with a disability) experience even *more* barriers to employment.

SO WE SHOULD JUST TREAT EVERYBODY THE SAME, RIGHT?

Not quite. Sometimes employment equity *does* mean treating everybody the same, despite their differences. For example, companies make sure that *all* staff receive the training and development required to do their jobs, no matter what occupation they're in, or what level they're at, or what group they belong to. However, sometimes employment equity means accommodating differences in order to treat everybody fairly. An organization might install ramps and automatic doors to facilitate access by persons with disabilities, or it could accommodate religious holidays by introducing a flextime policy.

In some cases, the motivation behind the introduction of some measures by the employer is the wish to help designated group members, but in the end those measures are applied universally to all employees. For example, setting up a workplace day-care centre might help the employer attract and retain female employees, but male employees can take advantage of it too. Flextime policies have a similar widespread application. Measures like these are called *supportive*, because they support the philosophy behind employment equity, but they're not restricted to members of the designated groups.

Other measures, called *remedial* or *positive* measures, are temporary redress mechanisms, aimed at correcting over a specified period of time (usually short- or mid-term) employment imbalances caused by past discrimination against designated group members. Remedial measures could include targeted hiring from selected designated groups, or a special training program. Once the employment balance is established, remedial measures can be eliminated, but while in place, they're a perfect example of treating people differently in order to treat them fairly.

AREN'T SPECIAL MEASURES ILLEGAL?

Not at all. They're permitted by law in the Canadian Charter of Rights and Freedoms (section 15), in the Canadian Human Rights Act (section 15), and in the various pieces of provincial legislation (such as section 13 of the Ontario Human Rights Code).

AREN'T SPECIAL MEASURES A KIND OF REVERSE DISCRIMINATION?

No again. 'Reverse discrimination' implies that a qualified non-designated group member was denied a job or promotion, and a designated group member got it, not because the latter was qualified, but simply because he or she *was* a member of that group. Far from promoting employment equity, this kind of tokenism actually sabotages it. The designated group employee is set up for failure, past discriminatory practices are reinforced, and the myth that designated group members aren't as capable as white, able-bodied Caucasian males is perpetuated. Most members of designated groups get quite upset over statements that employment equity gives them an unfair advantage. They only ask for a fair shake, and recognition of their legitimate qualifications, skills, and abilities.

Employment equity's guiding principle is that employment decisions should be based on merit alone, and not on any outmoded, limiting, non-job-related criteria.

IF EMPLOYMENT EQUITY REALLY IS ABOUT FAIRNESS FOR ALL, HOW CAN YOU EVER JUSTIFY PREFERENTIAL HIRING OF THE DESIGNATED GROUPS?

If preferential or targeted hiring is introduced with little or no research and planning, or if it's the only measure being implemented because that's what the employer (mistakenly) thinks employment equity is all about, then it's not unreasonable for the people affected by this measure to feel frustrated and upset. It's hard to justify *any* measure taken under circumstances like that.

However, when special measures such as targeted hiring are deliberate actions taken by an employer to remedy the effects of past discrimination and to prevent future problems, as part of a well-thought-out employment-equity plan, customized to fit the needs of a particular organization, they're very easy to explain and justify. The organization can show where the problems were in the past, and demonstrate why targeted hiring over a specific period of time is a reasonable way to address those problems. In fact, in organizations where targeted hiring is practised, it's usually just one of several measures being taken to remove barriers for the designated groups and improve the workplace environment for all.

It's important to remember that the merit principle still applies in situations like these. Just because you're encouraging designated group members to apply for vacancies, or giving them special consideration during the interview and evaluation process, doesn't mean that you're hiring unqualified people. On the contrary, you're *broadening* your pool of candidates to include previously overlooked sources.

The bottom line is that each organization has to decide-based on its own situation, if targeted hiring would be an appropriate element of its employment-equity plan or not.

IN PRINCIPLE, EMPLOYMENT EQUITY SOUNDS GREAT, BUT HOW CAN ANY ORGANIZATION AFFORD TO IMPLEMENT IT DURING A PERIOD OF ECONOMIC DOWNTURN?

It's true that implementing an employment-equity program has some costs attached (for example, it takes time and effort, not to mention money, to collect and analyse data on an organization's workforce, to review employment systems, and to develop a relevant plan). But the hidden costs of *not* doing so are even greater. The Canadian birth rate is declining, the population is aging, and the proportion of designated group members in the workforce is increasing. Statistics also show that visible minorities in general have a higher level of education than non-visible-minority Canadians, and some university programs now have more women in them than men. In this kind of environment, if employers continue to use employment systems and practices that exclude designated groups from the pool of available candidates for hirings and promotions, they're limiting their choices to only 30 to 40 per cent of the labour force and increasing the chance that they *won't* hire the best-qualified individual. Such exclusionary practices are bound to affect the employer's productivity and effectiveness and, ultimately, for profit-generators, their balance sheet.

Another argument for implementing employment equity is the changing client base. The same demographic factors that are changing the make-up of the labour force are also changing the clientele. Companies and agencies are having to provide goods and services to different groups of people than in the past. Who better to understand and interpret the needs of those clients than members of the same groups? That's not to say that a non–designated group member can't, with sensitivity and imagination, respond to the situation of a designated group client. But if a company's or agency's workforce reflects the diversity of the society in which it provides service or does business, then it's already in a position to identify and respond more quickly and easily to the broader range of clients' needs.

Of course, the challenges of implementing an employment-equity program in the midst of an economic downturn are different from those experienced during a boom. In hard times, many employers either restrict new hiring or lay people off. That obviously reduces the number of opportunities to address past imbalances by means of external recruitment. But there are other steps that can be taken. An employer can review employment systems and retention strategies for their impact on designated groups, plan for normal attrition, address training needs, provide diversity training, implement supportive measures, develop a harassment policy, and implement pay equity. The precise 'how-to's' may vary from one economic cycle to the next, and even from one organization to the next, but the principles remain the same.

SO WHAT ARE THE STEPS IN IMPLEMENTING AN EMPLOYMENT-EQUITY PROGRAM?

You'll go through five stages in the development and implementation of your employment-equity plan:

1 Preparation
   - Get senior-level (CEO or equivalent) commitment to employment equity. This may be self-evident, but it's also absolutely critical: the program won't go anywhere without that commitment.
   - Develop consultation mechanisms: decide *who* should have a say in how the program will run, and *how* their opinion will be solicited. If the workplace is unionized, the union(s) should definitely be active participants. (In fact, under the Ontario legislation enacted by the

NDP, in unionized workplaces, the employer and the bargaining agent(s) are jointly responsible for developing and revising the employment-equity plan.) If you don't currently have employees from all the designated groups, then you may also want to find a way to get input from those groups that are missing; for example, you may wish to consult designated group organizations in the community, or contact former designated group employees. Many organizations decide to set up an internal employment-equity committee, with members from all divisions, levels, and designated groups, to help guide the process.

- Develop a communications strategy, and dedicate resources to the task. To kick the program off, you'll want to explain the concepts of employment equity and publicize management's commitment to the process. A company newsletter or an electronic-bulletin-board message on employment equity is a great place to start.
- Assign senior staff and resources to implement the program. Because it takes time, effort, and money to get an employment-equity program off the ground, be sure to identify someone to champion the program who is high enough up in the organization to have senior management's ear, and provide him or her with the resources to do the job.
- Do a 'where are we now?' organizational analysis. What are the organization's values and attitudes? Where are you likely to encounter support and resistance? What internal and external resources are available?

2 Analysis
- Collect current data on your workforce. What employees are in what occupations? Are designated groups present, and distributed throughout the organization, in proportion to their external availability in the labour market? What employment opportunities will be coming up in the next few years? What is the organization's business plan? What is its human resources plan? Where are the gaps?

  Usually employee data for this analysis are collected by means of a survey, in which employees are encouraged to voluntarily identify themselves as members of a designated group. Self-identification is preferable to management designation (where managers tick off which groups their employees belong to), because it's more reliable (for example, not all disabilities are obvious to another person), it fosters trust and openness between management and staff (with a good communications strategy as a basis, employees aren't worried about why their supervisor wants to know these things), and it implies greater commitment to the process. (In fact, self-identification is the only data-collection method allowed under the Ontario legislation.)

- Review the organization's employment policies, practices, and systems. Are they job-related? Are they valid, necessary, and consistently applied? Do they have an adverse impact on members of designated groups? Do they conform to the federal and provincial human-rights and employment-standards legislation?
- Identify the barriers hindering full participation by members of designated groups. Are there specific problems with job classification and descriptions? recruitment processes? training and development? performance-evaluation systems? promotions and upward mobility? levels of compensation and access to benefits? discipline procedures? termination processes? building design and access to assistance? attitudes and corporate culture? If there are multiple barriers, which ones are the most significant, and do they affect all the designated groups equally?

3 Planning
- Develop an employment-equity work plan with realistic and achievable goals and timetables. This plan will be the framework within which you'll measure your performance. The goals you establish will be numerical (quantitative) as well as non-numerical (qualitative). The former include targets for addressing under-representation or concentration of designated-group members in certain occupations or at certain levels. The latter include initiatives such as improvements in access to facilities, targeted recruitment and advertising, modification of employment policies and practices, provision of developmental training, and introduction of other supportive or remedial measures.

   For simplicity's sake, it's usually a good idea to tie your employment equity work plan into your organization's strategic or operational planning cycle. That will reinforce the message that employment equity is just a normal part of doing business.

   The key to this phase of the process is to make sure that the goals and timetables are *realistic* and *achievable* in the context of your organization's particular situation. For example, if you wanted to attract designated-group members to work as social workers, but your local labour market didn't have any people with the necessary skills, then you could set a medium-term goal (maybe four or five years away) to work with your local community college to develop an appropriate training pogram. Or, if your organization were downsizing, then your employment-equity work plan would probably focus on retention strategies for designated groups rather than on external recruitment. No one expects you to implement a plan so ambitious or costly that it would put you out of business. At the same time, however, the goals should represent a bona fide effort to correct past inequities; you can't just shrug your shoulders and say that, because of this or that external factor, there's nothing you can do. It's extremely rare that an organization can't find *something* to work on as part of an employment-equity program.

- Design new or modified human-resources policies, procedures, or systems. Depending on the results of your analysis, this task can range from a little fine-tuning to a major overhaul. You might have to do a lot of research and consultation to come up with some appropriate replacements that all parties can agree on. In some cases, you might also need to table employment-equity issues as part of the collective-bargaining process.
- Develop monitoring or accountability mechanisms. It's axiomatic to say that what gets measured, gets done. You'll need to put systems in place to review performance in implementing the employment-equity plan, analyse the results, and adjust the plan as necessary.

4 Implementation
- Assign line management responsibility/accountability for implementing the employment-equity work plan. It's the people on the front line who have to 'own' it and put it into action, not the employment-equity coordinator or the director of human resources.
- Implement the plan. All the building blocks are in place; now it's time to just do it.
- Communicate the results. Employees and managers alike deserve to know what's going on. Publishing achievements is probably one of the world's best forms of recognition, appreciation, and reinforcement. Similarly, if carefully and sensitively done, reporting shortfalls can be a great way to build trust ('No, we're not perfect, but we learn from our mistakes') and encourage creative problem solving ('We value your ideas and contributions').

5 Monitoring
- Establish feedback and problem-solving mechanisms. No plan is

static. You'll always encounter bumps and detours along the way, and will have to adjust. Make sure you have a mechanism in place to modify the employment-equity plan as you go along.

- Provide orientation and ongoing training for supervisors. As a general rule, they're the key to successful implementation, so you have to ensure that they understand why the program was introduced, how it operates, how they can provide input, and what their role is.
- Integrate the reporting of employment-equity results into the normal performance-measurement process. For example, your organization could decide to include specific employment-equity goals in the managers' regular performance targets – your director could ask you as a unit manager to hire a designated-group member when the next vacancy comes up or to provide diversity training to all your staff at some point during the next year – and then your performance on these goals would be measured in the same way it would be for any other strategic or operational goal. In addition, if your organization gave bonuses or pay increases based on performance, some portion of that bonus or increase could be tied to whether or not you met the employment-equity goals.
- Reward achievements. Celebrate successes in your internal newsletter, at staff meetings, or at volunteer-recognition dinners. Give awards for the greatest improvement in a particular area or to recognize one particular group's commitment and contribution.
- Maintain and update your database. Survey new employees as they come on staff, or re-survey all employees periodically. Don't forget to amend data on employees who are promoted or change occupational groups, and to delete data on employees who have left. In order for you to be able to measure your performance in implementing your plan, your database must remain current and accurate.
- Adjust your work plan as required. Delete goals as they're achieved, or as circumstances make them irrelevant or unachievable, and add new ones. This is a dynamic, and usually a relatively long-term, process. As we've seen, it involves some really fundamental personal and organizational changes, and it won't be completed overnight.

WHAT RESOURCES ARE AVAILABLE TO HELP ME IMPLEMENT AN EMPLOYMENT-EQUITY PROGRAM?

There are lots of tools and support mechanisms out there to help you.

Human Resources Development Canada provides a free consulting service, work tools and documentation, training, data, and microcomputer software to employers covered by the federal Employment Equity Act, to federal contractors, and to other employers interested in implementing a voluntary employment-equity program. The Canadian and provincial human-rights commissions provide interpretations of the relevant pieces of legislation, background materials, and training, as well as various redress mechanisms to handle complaints. Canada Employment Centres can provide local labour-market information, process job orders, and refer job applicants. Both the federal and provincial governments provide funding for training and job creation, with a focus on designated group members. Check the blue pages of your telephone directory for contacts and phone numbers.

In addition, many universities and community colleges offer courses on employment-equity and human-resources planning. Local libraries are treasure troves of books, articles, and videos. Many private consultants are working in the field. Designated group organizations offer information, referral, and placement services. In some localities, employment-equity practitioners' associations can provide support and advice. Other organizations in your area or sector who have already implemented an employment-equity plan may be willing to share their experiences.

Employment equity is about creating a diverse workplace where the contributions of *all* employees are valued. It's about creating a harmonious, supportive working environment, and helping your employees be the best they can be. It's about improving productivity and competitiveness, thereby enhancing your organization's chances for survival. It's about fairness and simple justice. It's an element of good human-resources planning. It's about modifications to individual policies and about significant societal change. It's all this and more.

As employers, social service agencies have an important leadership role to play in implementing and promoting employment equity in their organizations and communities. Not only they, but also their clients and communities, will benefit.

NOTE

1 This refers to Ontario's Employment Equity Act, legislated by the NDP government of Bob Rae.

COMMENTS:

On the Need for Change

Corinne Mount Pleasant-Jetté

Like cellular phones and recycling bins, organizational change is the hot product of the 1990s. Social practices, demographic patterns, and other aspects of life have evolved to such an extent that to resist change is to deny reality. Corporations, agencies, and institutions across Canada have recognized clearly that the status quo is unacceptable. Thus, they must commit themselves to better communication, to environmental awareness, and to improved delivery of human services. Those organizations that respond to these challenges of the nineties will be better prepared to provide service in the next century.

There are many reasons why established norms and practices in social service organizations must be brought into line with their primary role of providing on-going support and assistance to people in need.

Cultural diversity, which has been cited as 'a fundamental characteristic of Canadian society' in the Canadian Multiculturalism Act, July 1988 represents one of the most urgent reasons for implementing significant organizational change. This means that the principle of equity, the basic premise of anti-racism practices, must be accepted and promoted in all aspects of service provision, and whereas cultural diversity is a significant component of our society, it must remain at the core of planning for organizational change.

In this respect, the age-old traditional concept of the Circle, which bears great symbolic significance for most indigenous peoples, is an appropriate reference. It represents continuity, commonality, equality, timelessness, and, above all, harmony. This symbolism is very useful in helping us to understand that cultural diversity must be seen to encompass all of the nations represented in the circle of Canadian society.

Perhaps the greatest challenge for the future lies in creating harmony between and among all cultural groups so that all of our children and grandchildren will cherish, respect, and honour the memory of their ancestors. We can hope that, with mutual understanding and respect for different cultures, the lessons of history will be learned and notions of superiority of one group over another will become a distant memory. And while some might reflect that such a vision is merely an articulation of popular 'politically correct' thinking, there is little doubt that our ancestors possessed the capacity to dream. That capacity may well have been the reason that Native cultural traditions have somehow managed to survive.

N'ya Weh.

Afterword:
Common Issues, Common Understandings

Sabra Desai

The theoretical and practical ideas in this book provide a rich resource of information that will help us to forge new ways of understanding the process of anti-racism organizational change and development. In addition, the work also provides analyses of the historical backdrop that gives anti-racism organizational development its moral synergism. Moreover, the essays point to implications for Canadian society as we take critical action towards creating more just and accessible human services. This work represents the collective knowledge and experience of educators, civil servants, consultants, and 'grass-roots' community organizers employed in many aspects of human service delivery. As educators, they have helped others to understand the complex challenge of anti-racist organizational change. As practitioners, they have facilitated the first cautious steps of many organizations embarking on the journey. As advocates, they have provided analyses and insights, acting as standard-bearers in the struggle. As activists rooted in the 'community,' they continue to organize and facilitate grass-roots action that embodies the hopes and energy of many, fuelling the agenda for organizational change and social justice.

In the introduction it is observed that this is not an exhaustive treatment of the issues related to service delivery. In addition, the contributors, like many others involved in anti-racist work, do not share absolute consonance in their perceptions and approaches. None the less, they are challenging human service institutions and practitioners in ways that require fundamental changes in the philosophy and service models that have defined the practice since the turn of the century. In large part, these challenges derive from larger political and social-justice movements, particularly the civil-rights and feminist movements. Today, however, they include the voices of other marginalized groups representing Aboriginal/First Nations' concerns and issues of race, culture, ability, ethnicity, sexual orientation, and religion.

This multiplicity of experiences, perspectives, and analyses has created a new awareness – one that has exposed the inequities, inaccessibility, and in many cases the total inappropriateness of traditional human service practices. The claim of traditional services to universality has been discredited and refuted by this new awareness, as described by contributors like Bedassigae-Pheasant, Minors, St. Lewis, and Tator. Moreover, the essentially monocultural, exclusionary, and patriarchal core of mainstream human services are revealed as the oppressive social mechanism experienced by marginalized constituencies, especially First Nations/Aboriginal peoples (Bedassigae-Pheasant, Mount Pleasant-Jetté).

Changing organizations mired in tradition is a complex, time-consuming, and long-term undertaking. Success is elusive, difficult to define, and never assured. Success is more likely when there is a clear understanding and recognition of the inadequacies of the ailing system; in other words, the understanding and recognition of 'what is,' as Minors puts it, is essential. It is also useful to begin with an overall vision of what human services ought to be. In addition, having identifiable, achievable and agreed-upon goals, derived from the commonly held vision, is critical to the successful implementation of an action plan. According to Minors, the organization must be clear about 'what it wants to become.' Moreover, as organizations evolve through the various stages of change and growth, the roles of anti-racism change agents, practitioners, and decision makers must remain clearly defined (Minors). It is equally important to have a knowledge of (1) the ideological, systemic, and individual dimensions of institutions and how they change or resist change; (2) the social and political climate in which human service agencies operate and provide services; and (3) the relationship between these internal, or institutional, realities and external realities, and how they are likely to affect the change process.

As institutions, practitioners, and change agents attempt to move human service practice towards an anti-racism framework, it is useful to establish some common understandings. One of these is the recognition that human services were conceived and developed in a particular ethnocentric mould, that is, by people of European heritage to meet the needs and interests of their own community. By its very nature, the Eurocentric design of, and approach to, current human services exclude the concerns of the Aboriginal/First Nations, Arab, African, Asian, Latin American, Jewish, and Muslim communities, to name but a few. While this model has provided for some of their immediate needs, it did so in the familiar 'missionary' (paternalistic and patriarchal) manner of ignoring the views and opinions of its 'clients' and pretty much everything else its philosophy deemed unimportant. What its designers and practitioners saw as a benign and universal approach, that is, of 'treating everyone the same,' was experienced as oppressive and assimilative by communities outside the European 'family.' For the Aboriginal/First Nations communities, the conditions and consequences of this service were particularly severe (Bedassigae-Pheasant, Khenti, Mount-Pleasant-Jetté, Tator).

This traditional mode of delivering services without consulting with its intended recipients still shapes and informs the human services system today (St. Lewis). It is only within the last decade that the system has been critically analysed and evaluated in terms of its inclusiveness and accessibility. Tator provides an excellent overview of the results of these critical reviews and outlines, among other things, many of the barriers faced by marginalized groups in accessing services and the difficulties they encounter when 'partial' access is achieved. As a direct result of being excluded from dominant-culture-based institutions and services, an entire sector of 'ethno-specific' community agencies have emerged to try and provide more accessible and appropriate services (Tator). Although well utilized under present conditions, these agencies cannot meet current demands for their services even from within their respective communities. The situation clearly points to the transformation of the traditional delivery system as the most viable solution. That these institutions are funded by public taxes which are also paid by communities of colour and 'immigrants and refugees who have great difficulty in gaining access to these essential services' only adds weight to the argument for transformation (Beyene, Butcher, Joe, Richmond).

The urgency of this transformation to the vision embodied in Johnson's 'equitable, efficient, and effective human service system,' Tator's 'integrated, multicultural/anti-racism model,' and Minors's 'poly-versity' is already palpable, but nowhere in the system or supporting institutions is this urgency reflected sincerely or consistently. After twenty-four years of an official multicultural policy that affirmed the value of racial and cultural diversity, and with a constitution that guarantees everyone equality and access to basic human services, access and diversity conferences abound. Questions such as 'What does access really mean?' 'How do we know we are serving diverse groups appropriately?' and 'How much do we need to change our programs and services?' form the basis of lengthy and often contentious discussions. In Canada change comes slowly around race issues. The conference themes none the less indicate quite clearly that the human services status quo is being questioned and that the idea of change is definitely on the agenda.

For the human services system, responding to the call for transformation is further problematized by important influences such as the lack of political will, the willingness/unwillingness of practitioners and institutions to facilitate anti-racism change processes, and the widespread tendency to deny the reality of racism in Canada, along with a noticeable discomfort in dealing with race issues. Human services in Canada are largely not administered on a fee-for-service basis, but fall almost entirely within the non-profit sector. This means that the entire system is dependent on 'funding' in the form of government grants, subsidies, loan transfer payments, or other 'handout' arrangements. Independent fund-raising by community agencies and contributions by philanthropic organizations such as the United Way and the Trillium Foundation also provide substantial financial support to human service agencies. Agencies still rely mainly on government funding in order to continue to offer their services. Human service organizations thus find themselves in competition with other government priorities such as fighting the federal or provincial deficits, winning elections, or regulating taxation.

According to public sentiment measured by the 1995 Decima Research report to the Canadian Council of Christians and Jews, titled *Canadian Attitudes Towards Race and Ethnic Relations in Canada*, funding for multicultural, anti-racism, diversity, or access issues is not considered nearly as important as other political priorities and is therefore an easier target for government cut-backs in these times of fiscal restraint. In the face-off between the 'multicultural lobby' and the corporate agenda, all three levels of Canadian government have a track record of backing the latter. There is good reason to heed Johnson's cautionary note that 'there is a very real danger that now, more than ever before, "racialized communities" ... will be framed by monolithic assumptions, their diversity minimized, and their existence further marginalized.'

Practitioners and decision makers within dominant-culture-based institutions will also play a pivotal role in the process of transforming traditional human services. Together they determine if their organizations and institutions will respond to the call for transformation, and should funding criteria require that they do respond, policy makers and front-line service providers will decide on the pace and quality of that response (Minors). Minors doubts, however, that any Canadian organization is at the stage of 'substantial equity.' It may be argued that such fundamental changes in organizational structure and operations are best accomplished by slow, deliberate, and incremental progress rather than by sporadic spurts. However, one must examine whether the slow pace is a reflection of carefully orchestrated progress or the result of stubborn resistance by influential decision makers and like-minded employees. Both factors may be operating at the same time, but there is reason to suspect that the latter may be the greater force of the two.

Based on the data presented in a 1991 study, Tator concluded that 'systemic barriers, first identified in the early eighties, continue to operate in the delivery of family services to [ethnic and racial-minority] communities.' This conclusion takes on added meaning in light of Rees's findings of 1987, as quoted by Tator, that organizations and practitioners in the field were 'generally appalled' by the suggestion that they may 'contribute to racism.' They also found it 'difficult to believe' that their norms and practices may 'serve to disadvantage.' Perhaps there is a direct relationship between the outrage of agencies and practitioners and their failure to take action to remove systemic barriers identified over a decade ago (Tator). If we may extrapolate from Matas, 'we do not need laws to have racist discrimination practices. All we need is unlimited bureaucratic discretion ... or racists in positions of power to make apparently neutral laws racist.'

This outrage may be a reflection of a pervasive Canadian myth that racism is 'not so bad here.' As Brown and Brown point out, it is common to hear Canadians pointing to the United States, where racial inequities and tensions are more pronounced, without realizing that it is much easier to deal with overt experiences of racism than with the polite, insidious form our Canadian racism commonly assumes. These 'comparativists' also seem not to realize that if nothing is done about our racial situation, that is, if it continues to be ignored or denied, racial dynamics in Canada can become as explosive and as intractable as in the United States. There is as yet no vocal lobby in Canada espousing separatism as a solution to racism. The lobby is overwhelmingly for access and accommodation. Governments, service institutions, and individuals would do well to exploit these supportive sentiments rather than frustrate them into open hostility and exclusive non-negotiable demands for equity and access.

However, in spite of the resistance there are people within the human services sector who recognize the need for change in their organizations and are willing to enter into some form of access-related change processes. These individuals may come from various racial and ethnocultural backgrounds, including the dominant ethno-racial group, and may work at different organizational levels. They none the less have in common a motivation to change, while working within and contending with the constraints of a restrictive organizational culture. They also share the vulnerability of being isolated, ostracized, or, if conditions permit, terminated because their ideas make it difficult for them to be 'part of the team.' Tator has looked at the potential role that people of colour play in this situation. The similarities with like-minded white colleagues should also be recognized. Further, as outlined by Minors, when change agents are attempting to define the 'critical mass' so important for moving organizations from one stage of development to another, these people should also be valued and supported for their commitment and potential as valuable internal allies.

This organizational dynamic mirrors a situation in the larger Canadian society where, simultaneous with the denial of racism and with resistance to measures to alleviate or eradicate it, there is a contradictory stream of consciousness and activity among groups and individuals from within the dominant ethno-racial Canadian community. While not essentially anti-racist in motive or orientation, this loose social-justice 'movement' does include anti-racist organizations along with other access- and equity-seeking groups. Given the enormity of the resources stacked against Aboriginal/First Nations and ethno-racial access and equity issues, anti-racism change agents may do well to explore some forms of alliance with local expressions of this movement. Several contributors (Bedassigae-Pheasant; Beyene, Butcher, Joe, and Richmond; James, Khenti, Minors, Mount Pleasant-Jetté, and Tator) have mentioned it directly, but in a very real sense the entire book alludes to the importance of the larger social environment in facilitating and maintaining anti-racist organizational change. Change agents need to be as closely attuned to those external tides and resources as they are to organizational realities. And, in the often seemingly hopeless task of transforming institutionalized norms, values, ideas, and practices, they need to be vigilant and ever ready to exploit possibilities that may assist in tipping the ideological balance in favour of anti-racist organizational transformation. It is only within an anti-racism social context that anti-racist human services will no longer be resisted or merely tolerated, but valued, supported, and respected for the moral triumph that they will prove to be.

Bibliography

Abella, Irving, and Harold Troper. 1983. *None Is Too Many*. Toronto: Lester & Orpen Dennys.

Abella, Rosalie Silberman. 1984. *Equality in Employment: A Royal Commission Report*. Ottawa: Supply and Services.

Adams, Howard. 1989. *Prison of Grass: Canada from a Native Point of View*. Saskatoon: Fifth House Publishers.

Adler, Peter S. 1977. 'Beyond Cultural Identity: Reflections upon Cultural and Multicultural Man.' In R.W. Brislin, ed., *Culture Learning*, 24–41. Honolulu: East-West Center.

Agard, Ralph. 1987. 'Access to the Social Assistance Delivery System by Various Ethnocultural Groups.' Social Assistance Review Committee Report. Toronto.

Agocs, Carol, Catherine Burr, and Felicity M. Somerset. 1992. *Employment Equity: Co-operative Strategies for Organizational Change*. Toronto: Prentice-Hall Canada.

Ahmed, Sharma. 1981. 'Children in Care: The Racial Dimension in Social Work Assessment.' In J. Cheetham, W. James, et al., eds, *Social and Community Work in a Multiracial Society*, 139–45. London: Harper & Row.

Allen, Paula Gunn. 1986. *The Sacred Hoop: Recovering the Feminine American Indian Traditions*. Boston: Beacon Press.

Allport, Gordon. 1958. *The Nature of Prejudice*. New York: Doubleday Anchor.

Anderson, Alan B., and James S. Frideres. 1981. *Ethnicity in Canada: Theoretical Perspectives*. Toronto: Butterworths.

Ansley, Frances Lee. 1989. 'Stirring the Ashes: Race, Class and the Future of Civil Rights Scholarship.' *Cornell Law Review* 74: 993–1077.

Anti-Defamation League. 1989. *Confronting Anti-Semitism: Guidelines for the Christian Community*. New York: Anti-Defamation League of B'nai Brith.

ARA Consultants. 1985. *Wife Battering among Rural, Native and Immigrant Women.* Toronto: ARA Consultants.

Arnold, Rick, Bev Burke, Carl James, D'Arcy Martin, and Barb Thomas. 1991. *Educating for a Change.* Toronto: Between the Lines.

Bambrough, Janine, Winnie Bowden, and Fred Wien. 1992. 'Preliminary Results from the Survey of Graduates from the Maritime School of Social Work.' Maritime School of Social Work. Halifax: Dalhousie University.

Banton, Michael. 1992. 'The Relationship between Racism and Antisemitism.' *Patterns of Prejudice* (Institute of Jewish Affairs and the World Jewish Congress) 26 (1&2)

Barman, Jean, Yonne Hebert, and Don McCaskill, eds. 1986. *Indian Education in Canada. Vol. 1 – The Legacy.* Vancouver: University of British Columbia Press.

Barnlund, Dean C. 1958. 'Communication in a Global Village.' In L.A. Samovar and R.E. Porter, eds, *Intercultural Communication: A Reader,* 5–14. New York: Wadsworth.

Barrett, Stanley R. 1987. *Is God a Racist?* Toronto: University of Toronto Press.

Bayefsky, Anne F. 1992. *International Human Rights Law: Use in Canadian Charter of Rights and Freedoms Litigation.* Toronto: Butterworths.

Beaujot, R., K.G. Basavarajappa, and R.B.P. Verma. 1988. *Income of Immigrants in Canada: A Census Data Analysis.* Ottawa: Supply and Services Canada. (Published by Statistics Canada as part of *Current Demographic Analysis* series, J. Dumas, ed. Catalogue no. 91-527E.)

Bell, Derrick A., Jr. 1992. 'Racial Realism.' *Connecticutt Law Review* 24: 363–79.
– 1993. 'White Superiority in America: Its Legal Legacy, Its Economic Costs.' *Villanova Law Review* 33: 767–79.

Benedict, Ruth. 1983. *Race and Racism.* London: Routledge & Kegan Paul.

Benimadhu, Prem, and Ruth Wright. 1992. *Implementing Employment Equity: A Canadian Experience.* Ottawa: Conference Board of Canada.

Benton, Michael, and Jonathan Howard. 1975. *The Race Concept.* New York: Praeger.

Berger, Thomas R. 1992. *A Long and Terrible Shadow: White Values and Native Rights in the Americas 1492–1992.* Washington: Douglas & McIntyre, University of Washington Press.

Bergin, Betty. 1988. *Equality Is the Issue: A Study of Minority Ethnic Group Access to Health and Social Services in Ottawa-Carlton.* Ottawa: Social Planning Council of Ottawa-Carlton.

Berlin, M., and W. Pentney. 1987. *Human Rights and Freedoms in Canada: Cases, Notes and Materials.* Toronto: Butterworths.

Bernal, Martin. 1987. *Black Athena: The Afroasiatic Roots of Classic Civilization.* New Jersey: Rutgers University Press.

Berry, Brewton. 1958. *Race and Ethnic Relations*. Boston: Houghton Mifflin.

Bertley, Leo. 1977. *Canada and Its People of African Descent*. Pierrefond, Que.: Bilongo Publishers.

Billingsley, Brenda, and Leon Muszynki. 1985. *No Discrimination Here? Toronto Employers and the Multi-Racial Work Force*. Toronto: Urban Alliance on Race Relations and Social Planning Council of Metropolitan Toronto.

Bissoondath, Neil. 1994. *Selling Illusions: The Cult of Multiculturalism in Canada*. Toronto: Penguin.

Bodner, Bruce. 1971. 'Indian Education: Tool of Cultural Politics.' *National Elementary Principal* 50 (6): 22–30.

Bolaria, B. Singh, and Peter S. Li, eds. 1988. *Racial Oppression in Canada*. Toronto: Garamount Press.

Bourgeault, Ron. 1988. 'Race and Class under Mercantilism.' In S. Bolaria and P. Li, eds, *Racial Oppression in Canada*. Toronto: Garamond Press.

– 1991. 'Race, Class and Gender: Colonial Domination of Indian Women.' In O. McKague, ed., *Racism in Canada*, 129–50. Saskatoon: Fifth House Press.

Brand, Dionne, and Krisantha Sri Bhaggiyadetta. 1986. *Rivers Have Sources, Trees Have Roots*. Toronto: Cross Cultural Communication Centre.

Bridgeman, Gail. 1993. 'The Place of Mainstream and Ethno-Racial Agencies in the Delivery of Family Services to Ethno-Racial Canadians.' M.S.W. thesis, York University, Toronto.

British Columbia Task Force on Family Violence. 1992. *Is Anyone Listening?* Vancouver.

Burnet, Jean. 1981. 'The Social and Historical Context of Ethnic Relations.' In R.C. Gardner and R. Kalin, eds, *A Canadian Social Psychology of Ethnic Relations*, 17–35. Toronto: Methuen Publications.

Burrell, L.F., and C.P. Christensen. 1987. 'Minority Students' Perceptions of High School: Implications for the Canadian Context.' *Journal of Multicultural Counselling and Development* 15 (1): 3–15.

Cahn, Edgar S., ed. 1970. *Our Brother's Keeper: The Indian in White America*. New York: New York New Community Press.

Campfens, H. 1981. 'Issues and New Directions in Community Practice Related to Ethnicity.' Paper presented to Symposium on Community Organization in the 1980's, Kent School of Social Work, University of Louisville, Kentucky.

Canadian Association of Schools of Social Work. 1991. *Social Work Education at the Crossroads: The Challenge of Diversity*. Ottawa: Canadian Association of Schools of Social Work.

Canadian Council of Christians and Jews. 1995. *Canadian Attitudes Towards Race and Ethnic Relations*. Toronto: Decima Research.

Canadian Panel on Violence Against Women. 1993. *Changing the Landscape: End-*

ing Violence, Achieving Equity. Final Report. Ottawa: Panel on Violence Against Women.

Canadian Task Force on Mental Health Issues Affecting Immigrants and Refugees in Canada. 1988. *After the Door Has Been Opened: Mental Health Issues Affecting Immigrants and Refugees in Canada*. Ottawa: Health and Welfare Canada, Multiculturalism and Citizenship Canada.

Carniol, Ben. 1990. *Case Critical: Challenging Social Work in Canada*. Toronto: Between the Lines.

Carroll, Michael P. 1990. 'Culture.' In J.J. Teevan, ed., *Basic Sociology*, 19–47. Scarborough: Prentice-Hall Canada.

Carter, Robert T. 1991. 'Cultural Values: A Review of Empirical Research and Implications for Counselling.' *Journal of Counselling and Development* 70 (1): 164–73.

Chan, Anthony B. 1983. *Gold Mountain: The Chinese in the New World*. Vancouver: New Star Books.

Chan, Kwok. 1987. 'Ethnic Minorities and Accessibility to Services in a Two-Tiered, Social Service System: The Case of Chinese in Montreal.' *Currents: Readings in Race Relations* 4 (3): 6–7.

Cheetham, Juliet, ed. 1982. 'Social Work and Ethnicity.' *National Institute, Social Services Library* (London) 43: 27–37.

Christensen, C.P. 1995. 'Immigrant Minorities in Canada.' In J.C. Turner and F.J. Turner, eds, *Canadian Social Welfare* (3rd ed.), 179–212. Scarborough, Ont.: Allyn and Bacon.

– 1994. 'Linking Schools of Social Work to Aboriginal Students and Communities: Exploring the Issues.' Paper. Faculty of Social Work, University of British Columbia, Vancouver.

– 1990. 'Toward a Framework for Social Work Education in a Multicultural and Multiracial Canada.' Proceedings of the Settlement and Integration of New Immigrants to Canada Conference, 17–19 February 1988. Faculty of Social Work and Centre for Social and Welfare Studies, Wilfrid Laurier University, Waterloo, Ont.

– 1986. 'Cross-Cultural Social Work: Fears, and Failings.' *Intervention* 74: 6–15.

Churchill, Stacey. 1990. *Problems of Evaluation of Education in a Pluralistic Society: A Discussion Paper*. Paris: UNESCO, Division of Educational Policy and Planning.

Cohen, Tannis. 1987. *Race Relations and the Law*. Toronto: Canadian Jewish Congress.

Commission on System Racism in the Ontario Justice System. 1994. *Racism Behind Bars: The Treatment of Black and Other Minority Prisoners in Ontario Prisons*. Interim Report. Toronto: The Commission on System Racism.

Committee on Participation of Visible Minorities in Canadian Society. 1984. *Equality Now: Minutes of the Proceedings and Evidence*. Ottawa: Queen's Printer.

Cox, T., and J. Nickelsen. 1991. 'Models of Acculturation for Intraorganizational Cultural Diversity.' *Canadian Journal of Administrative Sciences* 8 (2): 90–101.

Creese, Gillian. 1991. 'Organizing Against Racism in the Workplace: Chinese Workers in Vancouver before the Second World War.' In O. McKague, ed., *Racism in Canada*, 33–44. Saskatoon: Fifth House Press.

Crenshaw, Kimberle Williams. 1988. 'Race Reform and Retrenchment: Transformation and Legitimation in Anti-Discrimination Law.' *Harvard Law Review* 101: 1331–87.

Cumming, Alister. 1991. *Identification of Current Needs and Issues Related to the Delivery of Adult ESL Instruction in B.C.* Vancouver: Province of British Columbia, Ministry of Provincial Secretary and Ministry Responsible for Multiculturalism and Immigration.

Cumming, Peter. 1989. *Access*. Report of the Task Force on Access to Professions and Trades in Ontario. Toronto: Ontario Ministry of Citizenship.

Davis, Peggy C. 1991. 'Contextual Legal Criticism: A Demonstration Exploring Hierarchy and "Feminine" Style.' *New York University Law Review* 66: 1635–81.

– 1989. 'Law as Microaggression.' *Yale Law Journal* 98: 1559–77.

Day, S. 1987. 'Impediments to Achieving Equality.' In S.L. Martin and K.E. Mahoney, eds, *Equality and Judicial Neutrality*, 402–9. Toronto: Carswell.

Delgado, Richard. 1992. 'Shadowboxing: An Essay on Power.' *Cornell Law Review* 77: 813–24.

Delgado, Richard, and Jean Stefancic. 1991. 'Norms and Narratives: Can Judges Avoid Serious Moral Error?' *Texas Law Review* 69: 1929–83.

Derman-Sparks, L., C.T. Higa, and W. Sparks. 1980. 'Children, Race and Racism: How Race Awareness Develops.' *Interracial Books for Children Bulletin* 11 (3&4): 3–9.

deSilva, Arnold. 1991. *Earnings of Immigrants: A Comparative Analysis*. Ottawa: Economic Council of Canada.

Dirks, Gerald E. 1977 *Canada's Refugee Policy: Indifference or Opportunism?* Montreal: McGill-Queen's University Press.

Dobbins, James E., and Judith H. Skillings. 1991. 'The Utility of Race Labeling in Understanding Cultural Identity: A Conceptual Tool for the Social Science Practitioner.' *Journal of Counselling and Development* 70 (1): 37–44.

Dominelli, Lena. 1989. 'An Uncaring Profession? An Examination of Racism in Social Work.' *New Community* 15 (3): 391–403.

– 1989. 'White Racism, Poor Practice.' *Social Work Today*, January: 12.

Dorris, Michael. 1987. 'Indians on the Shelf.' In C. Martin, ed., *The American Indian and the Problem of History*, 98–103. New York: Oxford University Press.

Doyle, Robert, and Livy Visano. 1987. *A Time for Action! Access to Health and Social Services for Members of Diverse Racial and Cultural Groups.* Toronto: Social Planning Council of Metropolitan Toronto, 1987.

Drake, St. Clare. 1987. *Black Folk Here and There.* Los Angeles: University of California.

Driedger, Leo. 1989. *The Ethnic Factor: Identity in Diversity.* Toronto: McGraw-Hill Ryerson.

Du Bois, W.E.B. 1985. *The World and Africa.* New York: International Publishers.

Economic Council of Canada. 1991. *New Faces in the Crowd.* Ottawa: Canada Communications Group–Publishing.

Faludi, Susan. 1991. *Backlash: The Undeclared War Against American Women.* New York: Crown Publishers.

Fine, Sean. 1992. 'Isaac in running to become first Black on Supreme Court.' *Globe and Mail,* 19 August: A1, A7.

Fisher, Eugene. 1990. 'The Church and Racism: Implications for Catholic-Jewish Dialogue.' In *Anti-Semitism Is a Sin,* 1–8. New York: Anti-Defamation League of B'nai Brith.

Foster, Cecil. 1991. *Distorted Mirror: Canada's Racist Face.* Toronto: HarperCollins Publishers.

Franklin, Raymond S. 1991. *Shadows of Race and Class.* Minneopolis: University of Minnesota Press.

Frideres, James S. (1974). *Canada's Indians: Contemporary Conflicts.* Scarborough: Prentice Hall.

– 1990. 'Policies on Indian People in Canada.' In P.S. Li, ed., *Race and Ethnic Relations in Canada,* 98–119. Don Mills, Ont.: Oxford University Press.

Gall, Gerald L. 1990. *The Canadian Legal System.* Calgary: Carswell.

Garnets, Linda, and Douglas Kimmel. 1991. *Psychological Perspectives on Human Diversity in America.* Ann Arbor: Braun-Brumfield.

Gay, Geneva. 1990. 'Teacher Preparation for Equity.' In H. Baptiste et al., eds, *Leadership, Equity and School Effectiveness.* Newbury Park, CA: Corwin Press.

Giordano, J., and G. Giordano. 1975. 'Ethnicity and Community Mental Health: A Review of the Literature.' *Community Mental Health Review* 2 (7): 59–65.

Goldberg, David Theo. 1993. *Racist Culture: Philosophy and the Politics of Meaning.* Cambridge, Eng.: Blackwell.

Government of Manitoba. 1992. *Issues, Trends and Options: Mechanisms for the Accreditation of Foreign Credentials in Manitoba (Executive Summary).* Winnipeg: Working Group on Immigrant Credentials.

Greaves, Ida. 1930. 'The Negro in Canada.' McGill University Economic Studies, no. 16. Montreal: McGill University.

Green, James. 1982. *Cultural Awareness in the Human Services*. Englewood Cliffs, NJ: Prentice-Hall.

Greene, Dwight L. 1991. 'Abusive Prosecutor: Gender, Race and Class Discretion and the Prosecution of Drug-Addicted Mothers.' *Buffalo Law Review* 39: 737–802.

Greene, Linda S. 1992. 'Multiculturalism as a Metaphor.' *DePaul Law Review* 41: 1173–84.

Harris, Angela. 1990. 'Race and Essentialism in Feminist Legal Theory.' *Stanford Law Review* 42: 581–616.

Harris, Cheryl I. 1993. 'Whiteness as Property.' *Harvard Law Review* 106 (1707): 1709–91.

Hawkins, Freda. 1989. *Critical Years in Immigration: Canada and Australia Compared*. Montreal: McGill-Queen's University Press.

– 1988. *Canada and Immigration: Public Policy and Public Concern*. 2nd edition. Montreal: McGill-Queen's University Press.

Hay, Malcolm. 1950. *The Foot of Pride*. Boston: Beacon Press.

Head, Wilson. 1977. 'Service Accessibility and the Multiracial Community.' *Canadian Welfare* 53 (1): 5–8.

– 1975. *The Black Presence in the Canadian Mosaic*. Toronto: Ontario Human Rights Commission.

Henkin, L., ed. 1981. *The International Bill of Rights: The Covenant on Civil and Political Rights*. New York: Columbia University Press.

Henry, Frances, 1978. *The Dynamics of Racism in Toronto*. Research report, York University, Toronto.

Henry, Frances, and Effie Ginzberg. 1985. *Who Gets the Work: A Test of Racial Discrimination in Employment*. Toronto: Urban Alliance on Race Relations and Social Planning Council of Metropolitan Toronto.

Henry, Frances, and Carol Tator. 1985. 'Racism in Canada: Social Myths and Strategies for Change.' In R.M. Bienvenue and J.E. Goldstein, eds, *Ethnicity and Ethnic Relations in Canada*, 321–35. Toronto: Butterworths.

Henry, Frances, Carol Tator, Winston Mattis, and T. Rees. 1994. *The Colour of Democracy: Racism in Canadian Society*. Toronto: Harcourt Brace.

Herrnstein, Richard, and Charles Murray. 1994. *The Bell Curve: Intelligence and Class Structure in American Life*. New York: Free Press (Simon & Shuster).

Ho-Lau, Anita. 1992. *The Employment Situation and Social Participation of Chinese Immigrants in Metropolitan Toronto*. Toronto: Chinese Information & Community Services.

– 1992. *A Profile of Chinese Immigrants in Metropolitan Toronto*. Toronto: Chinese Information & Community Services.

hooks, bell. 1992. *Black Looks: race and representation*. Toronto: Between the Lines.
– 1991. *Talking Back: thinking feminist, thinking black*. Boston: South End Press.
Hoopes David S. 'Intercultural Communication Concepts and the Psychology of Intercultural Experience.' In M. Pusch, ed., *Multicultural Education*, 10–36. Pittsburgh: Intercultural Press.
Hoopes, David, and Margaret D. Pusch. 1981. 'Definition of Terms.' In M. Pusch, ed., *Multicultural Education*, 2–8. Pittsburgh: Intercultural Network.
Huggins, Nathan. 1991. 'The Deforming Mirror of Truth: Slavery and the Master of Narrative of American History.' *Radical History Journal* 49 (35).
Hughes, David R., and Evelyn Kallen. 1974. *The Anatomy of Racism: Canadian Dimension*. Montreal: Harvest House.
Human Rights Legislation 1991. An Office Consolidation. Toronto: Butterworths.
Institute for Research on Public Policy. 1993. *Employment Equity / Équité en emploi* 14 (2, March): 3–39. Montreal: Policy Options Politiques.
Israel, Milton, ed. 1987. *The South Asian Diaspora in Canada: Six Essays*. Toronto: Multicultural History Society of Ontario, in cooperation with Centre for South Asian Studies.
Jackson, Anita P., and Ferguson B. Meadows. 1991. 'Getting to the Bottom to Understand the Top.' *Journal of Counselling and Development* 70 (1): 72–6.
Jackson, Bailey W., and Evangelina Holvino. 1989. 'Working with Multicultural Organizations: Matching Theory to Practice.' *Proceedings of a Workshop on Diversity: Implications for Education and Training*, 109–121.
– 1988. 'Developing Multicultural Organizations.' *Creative Change: The Journal of Religion and Applied Behavioural Sciences* 9 (2, Fall): 14–19.
James, A., W. Hay, M. Parry, and R. Ghumra. 1991. 'Court Welfare Work with Asian Families: Problems in Practice.' *New Community* 18 (2): 265–80.
James, Carl E. 1995. *Seeing Ourselves: Exploring Race, Ethnicity and Culture*. Toronto: Thompson Educational Publishing.
– 1993. 'Getting There and Staying There: Blacks' Employment Experience.' In P. Anisef and P. Axlerod, *Transitions: Schooling and Employment in Canada*, 3–20. Toronto: Thompson Educational Publishing.
– 1990. *Making It: Black Youth, Racism and Career Aspirations in a Big City*. Oakville, Ont.: Mosaic Press.
James, Carl E., and Hafeezah Muhammad. 1992. *Children in Childcare Programs: Perception of Race and Race Related Issues*. Toronto: Multicultural and Race Relations Division and Children's Services of the Municipality of Metropolitan Toronto.
Jamieson, David, and Julie O'Mara. 1991. *Managing Workforce 2000: Gaining the Diversity Advantage*. San Francisco: Jossey-Bass.
Jensen, J. Vernon. 1985. 'Perspective on Nonverbal Intercultural Communica-

tion.' In L.A. Samopvar and R. Porter, eds, *Intercultural Communication: A Reader*, 256–72. New York: Wadsworth.

Johnson, Sheri Lynn. 1988. 'Unconscious Racism and the Criminal Law.' *Cornell Law Review* 73: 1016–37.

Jones, James M. 1991. 'Psychological Models of Race: What Have They Been and What Should They Be.' In J.D. Goodchilds, ed., *Psychological Perspectives on Human Diversity in America*, 3–46. Washington: American Psychological Association.

Kaegi, Gerda. 1972. *A Comprehensive View of Indian Education*. Toronto: Canadian Association in Support of the Native Peoples.

Kagedan, Ian. 1993. *Hate Propaganda: Facts on Frauds*. Report. Ottawa: League for Human Rights, B'nai Brith Canada.

Keene, J. 1992. *Human Rights in Ontario*. 2nd edition. Toronto: Carswell.

Kinloch, Graham C. 1974. *The Dynamics of Race Relations: A Sociological Analysis*. Toronto: McGraw-Hill.

Knowles, Caroline. 1990. 'Black Families and Social Services.' In *Anti-Racist Strategies: Research and Ethnic Relations Series*, 123–41. Aldershot, Eng.: Gower.

Knudtson, Peter, and David Suzuki. 1992. *Wisdom of the Elders*. Toronto: Stoddart.

Lechy, Olga. 1992. 'Health Care System Must Adapt to Meet Needs of Multicultural Society, MDs Say.' *Canadian Medical Association Journal* 146 (12): 2210–14.

Lee, Enid. 1985. *Letters to Marcia*. Toronto: Cross-Cultural Communication Centre.

Li, Peter S. 1988. *The Chinese in Canada*. Toronto: Oxford University Press.

Li, P.S., and B.S. Bolaria, eds. 1985. *Racial Oppression in Canada*. Toronto: Garamond Press.

Louis, Chrysostom. 1992. 'Issues Affecting African-Canadian Children in Alternative Care.' *Multiculturalism* (Cross-Cultural Communication Centre) 14 (2&3): 58–60.

Lorde, Audre. 1984. *Sister Outsider*. Trumansburg, NY: The Crossing Press.

McDade, Kathryn. 1988. *Barriers to Recognition of the Credentials of Immigrants in Canada*. Studies in Social Policy. Ottawa: Institute for Research on Public Policy.

McGoldrick, D. 1991. *The Human Rights Committee: Its Role in the Development of the International Covenant on Civil and Political Rights*. Oxford: Oxford University Press.

McIntyre, Sheila. 1993. 'Backlash Against Equality: The "Tyranny" of the "Politically Correct."' *McGill Law Journal* 38: 1–63.

McNab, David. 1981. 'Herman Merwile and the Colonial Office: Indian Policy in the Mid-Nineteenth Century.' *Canadian Journal of Native Studies* 1 (2): 277–302.

Malarek, Victor. 1987. *Heaven's Gate*. Toronto: Macmillan of Canada.

Matas, David. 1989. 'Fairness in Refugee Determination.' *Manitoba Law Journal* 18 (1): 71–103.

Matas, David, and Ilana Simon. 1989. *Closing the Doors: The Failure of Refugee Protection*. Toronto: Summerhill Press.

Mawhiney, A.M. 1995. 'First Nations in Canada.' In J.C. Turner and F.W. Turner, eds, *Canadian Social Welfare* (3d edition), 213–30. Scarborough, Ont.: Allyn and Bacon.

Medeiros, John 1991. *Family Services for All: Study of Family Services for Ethnocultural and Racial Communities in Metropolitan Toronto*. Toronto: Multicultural Coalition for Access to Family Services.

Mental Health Program Services. 1992. *Improving Mental Health Supports for Diverse Ethno/Racial Communities in Metro Toronto: A Community Planning Project*. Toronto: Metropolitan Toronto District Health Council.

Mies, Maria. 1986. *Patriarchy and Accumulation on a World Scale*. London: Zed Books Ltd.

Miller, J.R. 1991a. 'Owen Glendower, Hotspur and Canadian Indian Policy.' In J.R. Miller, ed., *Sweet Promises: A Reader on Indian-White Relations in Canada*, 323–52. Toronto: University of Toronto Press.

– 1991b. 'Aboriginal Rights, Land Claims and the Struggle to Survive.' In Miller, ed., *Sweet Promises*, 405–20.

Milloy, John. 1991. 'The Early Indian Act: Developmental Strategy and Constitutional Change.' In J.R. Miller, ed., *Sweet Promises: A Reader on Indian-White Relations in Canada*, 145–54. Toronto: University of Toronto Press.

Milner, David. 1975. *Children and Race*. London: Penguin Books.

Mohawk, John. 1992. 'Looking for Columbus: Thoughts on the Past, Present and Future of Humanity.' In M.A. Jaimes, ed., *The State of Native America: Genocide, Colonialization and Resistance*, 439–44. Boston: South End Press.

Morrison, Toni. 1987. *Beloved*. Scarborough, Ont.: New American Library.

Mukherjee, Arun. 1993. *Sharing Our Experience*. Ottawa: Canadian Advisory Council on the Status of Women.

Nahanee, Teresa. 1994. 'Sexual Assault of Inuit Females: A Commentary on "Cultural Bias."' In J.V. Roberts and R. Mohr, eds, *Confronting Sexual Assault: A Decade of Legal and Social Change*, 192–204. Toronto: University of Toronto Press.

National Indian Brotherhood. 1973. *Indian Control of Indian Education*. Ottawa: National Indian Brotherhood.

Neufeld, Mark. 1992. 'Can an entire society be racist, or just individuals?' *Toronto Star*, 25 October: 137.

OCASI. 1991a. *Immigrant Services Database Research Bulletin Vol. II No. 1*. Toronto: Ontario Council of Agencies Serving Immigrants.

– 1991b. *Immigrant Settlement Counselling: A Training Guide.* (Developed by Janis Galway.) Toronto: Ontario Council of Agencies Serving Immigrants.
– 1990a. *Immigrant Services Database Research Bulletin Vol. I No. 1 (Client Demographics).* Toronto: Ontario Council of Agencies Serving Immigrants.
– 1990b. *Immigrant Services Database Research Bulletin Vol. I No. 2 (Services to Immigrant Clients).* Toronto: Ontario Council of Agencies Serving Immigrants.
Ontario, Ministry of Citizenship, Office of the Employment Equity Commissioner. 1992. *Opening Doors: A Report on the Employment Equity Consultations.* Toronto: Queen's Printer for Ontario.
Ontario Human Rights Code Review Task Force. 1992. *Getting Human Rights Enforced Effectively.* Toronto: Ontario Human Rights Commission.
Patterson, Charles. 1982. *Ancient Roots in Anti-Semitism: The Road to the Holocaust and Beyond.* New York: Walker Publishing.
Pedersen, Paul B. 1991. 'Multiculturalism as a Generic Approach to Counselling.' *Journal of Counselling and Development* 70 (1): 6–12.
Pharr, Suzanne. 1988. *Homophobia: A Weapon of Sexism.* Little Rock, AR: Chardon Press.
Philips, Marlene Nourbese. 1991. *Frontiers: Essays on Race and Culture.* Stratford, Ont.: The Mercury Press.
Pontifical Commission 'Iustitia et pax.' 1987. *The Church and Racism – Towards a More Fraternal Society.* Vatican City.
Poplin, Mary. 1992. 'Educating in Diversity.' In Peter F. Drucker, ed., *Educating for Results*, A18–24. Baltimore: National School Boards Association.
Powell, John A. 1992. 'New Property Disaggregated: A Model to Address Employment Discrimination.' *U.S.F.L. Law Review* 24: 363–83.
Ramcharan, Subhas. 1982. *Racism: Nonwhites in Canada.* Toronto: Butterworths.
Ratushny, E., and G.A. Beaudoin, eds. 1989. *The Canadian Charter of Rights and Freedoms.* 2nd edition. Toronto: Carswell.
Redway, Alan, P.C., Q.C., M.P. 1992. *A Matter of Fairness: Report of the Special Committee on the Review of the Employment Equity Act.* Ottawa: Queen's Printer for Canada.
Rees, Tim. 1987. 'Equality of Access.' *Currents: Readings in Race Relations* 4 (3): 1–2.
Response of the Government of Canada to Equality Now Report. 1984. Ottawa: Queen's Printer.
Rich, E.E. 1991. 'Trade Habits and Economic Motivations among the Indians of North America.' In J.R. Miller, ed., *Sweet Promises: A Reader on Indian-White Relations in Canada*, 157–79. Toronto: University of Toronto Press.
Richmond, Anthony H. 1988. *Immigration and Ethnic Conflict.* New York: St Martin's Press.

– 1967. *Post-War Immigration in Canada*. Toronto: University of Toronto Press.

Robbins, Rebecca L. 1992. 'Self Determination and Subordination, The Past, Present and Future of American Indian Governance.' In M.A. Jaimes, ed., *The State of Native America: Genocide, Colonialization and Resistence*. Boston: South End Press.

Ross, Thomas. 1990. 'The Rhetorical Tapestry of Race: White Innocence and Black Abstraction.' *William and Mary Law Review* 32: 1–40.

Royal Commission on the Donald Marshall Jr. Prosecution. 1989. *Report*. Halifax: The Royal Commission.

Rush, G.B. 1977. 'Occupation and Education in Canada: The Context of Political Economy.' In R.A. Carlton et al., eds, *Education, Change and Society,* 24–35. Toronto: Gage Educational Publishing.

St. Lewis, Joanne, and Sheila Galloway. 1995. 'Reform of the Defense Provocation.' Discussion paper. Toronto: The Ontario Woman's Directorate.

Sampat-Mehta, R. 1973. *International Barriers*. Ottawa: Harpell's Press.

Samuel, John T. 1992. *Visible Minorities in Canada: A Projection*. Toronto: Canadian Advertising Foundation.

Sanga, David. 1987. 'A Systematic Approach to Discrimination in the Provision of Social Services: South Vancouver.' *Currents: Readings in Race Relations* 4 (3): 8–9.

Schoeps, Hans Joachim. 1963. *The Jewish Christian Argument*. New York: Holt, Rinehart, Winston.

Serow, W.J., C.B. Nam, D.F. Sly, R.H. Weller, eds. 1990. *Handbook on International Migration*. Westport, CT: Greenwood Press.

Sirros, C. 1987. *Rapport du Comité sur l'accessibilité des services desanté et des services sociaux du réseau aux communauté culturelles*. Québec.

Sisskind, Judith. 1978. 'Cross-cultural Issues in Mental Health.' *ERIC Reports*.

Smith, Elsie J. 1991. 'Ethnic Identity Development: Toward the Development of a Theory Within the Context of Minority/Majority Status.' *Journal of Counselling and Development* 70 (1): 181–8.

Smith, Joan. 1989. *The Essential Legal Handbook*. Toronto: McClelland and Stewart.

Sodowsky, Gargi R., Edward W.M. Lai, and Barbara S. Plake. 1991. 'Moderating Effects of Sociocultural Variables on Acculturation Attitudes of Hispanic and Asian Americans.' *Journal of Counselling and Development* 70 (1): 194–203.

Special Committee on Participation of Visible Minorities in Canadian Society. 1984. *Equality Now: Minutes of the Proceedings and Evidence*. Ottawa: Queen's Printer.

Strickland, Rennard. 1986. 'Genocide-at-Law: An Historical and Contemporary View of the Native American Experience.' *Kansas Law Review* 34: 713–55.

Sue, D., and D.W. Sue. 1990. 'Issues and Concepts of Cross Cultural Counselling.' In *Counselling the Culturally Different: Theory and Practice*, 27–118. New York: John Wiley and Sons.

Task Force on Access to Professions and Trades in Ontario. 1989. *ACCESS! Task Force on Access to Professions and Trades in Ontario*. Toronto: Ministry of Citizenship (Queen's Printer).

Tator, Carol. 1990. 'Strategy for Fostering Participation and Equity in the Human Services Delivery System.' *Organization Change Toward Multiculturalism*. Toronto: Access Action Council.

Taylor, Charles. 1992. *Multiculturalism and the Politics of Recognition*. Princeton, NJ: Princeton University Press.

Thomas, Barb. 1987. *Multiculturalism at Work: A Guide to Organizational Change*. Toronto: YWCA of Metropolitan Toronto.

Thompson, Neil. 1993. *Anti-Discriminatory Practice*. Basingsoke, Eng.: Macmillan Press.

Tobias, John L. 1991. 'Protection, Civilization, Assimilation: An Outline History of Canada's Indian Policy.' In J.R. Miller, ed., *Sweet Promises: A Reader on Indian-White Relations in Canada*, 212–40. Toronto: University of Toronto Press.

Turner, J.C. 1995. 'The Historical Base.' In J.C. Turner and F.J. Turner, eds, *Canadian Social Welfare* (3d edition), 75–88. Scarborough, Ont.: Allyn and Bacon.

Ubale, B. 1982. *Working Together: Strategy for Race Relations*. Toronto: Ontario Human Rights Commission.

United Way of Greater Toronto. 1991. *Action, Access, Diversity! A Guide to Anti-Racist/Multicultural Organizational Change for Social Service Agencies*. Toronto: United Way.

Upton, L.F.S. 1973. 'The Origins of Canadian Indian Policy.' *Journal of Canadian Studies* 8(4): 51–61.

Walker, James G. 1984. *Racial Discrimination in Canada: The Black Experience*. Toronto: Canadian Historical Association.

– 1980. *History of Blacks in Canada: A Study Guide for Teachers and Students*. Ottawa: Minister of State, Multiculturalism.

Wallis, Maria. 1989. *The Effect of Canadian Immigration Policies on Racial Minorities in General and Racial Minority Women in Particular*. Toronto: Women Working with Immigrant Women.

Weatherford, Jack. 1988. *Indian Givers*. New York: Fawcett Columbine.

Weissman, Harold. 1982. 'Fantasy and Reality of Staff Involvement in Organizational Change.' *Administration of Social Work* 6 (Spring): 37–45.

West, Cornel. 1993. *Keeping Faith: Philosophy and Race*. New York: Routledge.

Whitaker, Reginald. 1987. *Double Standard: The Secret History of Canadian Immigration*. Toronto: Lester & Orpen Dennys.

Williams, Patricia J. 1987. 'Spirit-Murdering the Messenger: The Discourse of

Fingerpointing as the Law Responds to Racism.' *University of Miami Law Review* 42: 127–57.

Williams, Robert A., Jr. 1990. *The American Indian in Western Legal Thought: The Discourse of Conquest.* New York: Oxford University Press.

– 1990. 'Gendered Checks and Balances: Understanding the Legacy of White Patriarchy in an American Indian Cultural Context.' *Georgia Law Review* 24: 1019–44.

Winks, Robin. 1971. *The Blacks in Canada.* Montreal: McGill-Queen's University Press.

Working Group on Immigrant Credentials. 1992. *Issues, Trends and Options: Mechanisms for the Accreditation of Foreign Credentials in Manitoba* (Executive Summary). Winnipeg: Government of Manitoba.

Wright, Ronald. 1992. *Stolen Continents.* Toronto: Viking.

Yeboah, Samuel Kennedy. 1988. *The Ideology of Racism.* London: Hansils.

Yi, Sun-Kyung. 1993. 'An Immigrant's Split Personality.' In E.C. Karpinski and I. Lea, eds, *Pens of Many Colours: A Canadian Reader,* 406–9. Toronto: Harcourt Brace Jovanovich Canada.

Legislation

Canada. *Canadian Charter of Rights and Freedoms,* Schedule B, Part I, *Constitution Act,* 1982 (U.K.), ch. 11.

– *Indian Act,* Revised Statutes of Canada, 1985, ch. I-5, as amended.

– The Criminal Code, Revised Statutes of Canada, 1985, ch. C-46, as amended.

Case Law

Bhadauria v. Seneca College of Applied Arts and Technology (Board of Governors). (1980), 27 O.R. 141 (Ont.S.C.), 1981 124 D.L.R. (3d) 193.

Pitawanakwat v. Canada (Canadian Human Rights Commission). (1987) 9 C.H.R.R., D/4825–D/4826.

Smithers v. The Queen. (1977) 34 C.C.C. (2d) 427 (S.C.C.)